Crafting True Stories

Lucy Calkins and Marjorie Martinelli

Photography by Peter Cunningham

HEINEMANN ◆ PORTSMOUTH, NH

This book is dedicated to Ali Marron, whose upbeat spirit and tenacious commitment to beautiful writing and teaching have given wings to this book.

DEDICATED TO TEACHERS™

firsthand
An imprint of Heinemann
361 Hanover Street
Portsmouth, NH 03801–3912
www.heinemann.com

Offices and agents throughout the world

The author and publisher wish to thank those who have generously given permission to reprint borrowed material:

From *Come On, Rain* by Karen Hesse. Copyright © 1999 by Karen Hesse. Used by permission of Scholastic Inc.

Cataloging-in-Publication data is on file with the Library of Congress.

ISBN-13: 978-0-325-04732-4
ISBN-10: 0-325-04732-4

Production: Elizabeth Valway, David Stirling, and Abigail Heim
Cover and interior designs: Jenny Jensen Greenleaf
Series includes photographs by Peter Cunningham, Nadine Baldasare, and Elizabeth Dunford
Composition: Publishers' Design and Production Services, Inc.
Manufacturing: Steve Bernier

Printed in the United States of America on acid-free paper
17 16 15 14 13 ML 1 2 3 4 5

Acknowledgments

THIS UNIT RADIATES A COMMITMENT to the craft of writing. Our attention to lifting the quality of students' narrative writing is nurtured by the knowledge of our colleagues. Specifically, we are grateful for Shana Frazin's knowledge of children's literature, for Annie Taranto's knowledge of ways to scaffold learners, and for Mary Ehrenworth's knowledge of close reading. Our attentiveness to craft has also been nurtured by James Howe, author of *Bunnicula,* and Sarah Weeks, author of *So Be It,* both of whom have taught a semester-long course on writing fiction here at Teachers College, and we have benefited both from those courses and from their presence in our lives.

As the first book in the third-grade year, it was especially important to us that we get methods of teaching exactly right. This required us to think long and hard about all the ways those methods needed to change in this new Units of Study for Opinion, Information, and Narrative Writing series. We're grateful for Kelly Boland Hohne, Anna Gratz Cockerille, Janet Steinberg, and Hareem Atif Khan for help with this and for PS 59 third-grade CTT teachers, Jeannette Martimucci and Lori Talish, who allowed us to learn from their students. Ali Marron, to whom the book is dedicated, has been especially helpful, and we can't thank her enough. She not only helped along the way, but also read the entire book over in the final moments, drawing on her deep knowledge of narrative writing and of the series to help make the book all it can be.

Like all the other books in this series, this book was written in cycles and layers. First, there were the years of teaching children and teachers alike, then eventually the rough draft plan for this book, more teaching to try out the specifics of that plan, and then drafts and revision that stretched across a great many months. During that time, others helped us with the actual writing, as well as with reviewing. We are especially grateful to Julia Mooney and Kate Montgomery, writers extraordinaire, who helped us time and again to think of the apt metaphor, the perfect mentor text, the surprising detail that made the book—and the unit—sing. Kim Thompson tended to details that could have clogged up the entire process.

Meanwhile, when the book passed from our hands to the hands of editors and the production team at Heinemann, a whole new cast of characters took up the baton. Teva Blair's graceful edits helped polish our words, while our energetic production team, Abby Heim and Elizabeth Valway leading, pulled all the pieces together. Fine art photographer, Peter Cunningham, captured the heart and soul of young writers at work, and David Stirling, project manager, then tagged and sorted, cropped and placed thousands and thousands of photos in this series. Steve Bernier, manufacturing, has spearheaded the effort to change these intangible books into real, paper and glue and ink creations, and art guru Jenny Greenleaf used her design skills to make this book a pleasure to hold. It's an extraordinary team of passionate craftspeople, each rising to the occasion. We're grateful to them all.

The class described in this unit is a composite class, with children and partnerships of children gleaned from classrooms in very different contexts, then put together here. We wrote the units this way to bring you both a wide array of wonderful, quirky, various children and also to illustrate for you the predictable (and unpredictable) situations and responses this unit has created in classrooms across the nation and world.

—Lucy and Marjorie

Contents

Welcome to the Unit

THIS BOOK IS AN IMPORTANT ONE because it introduces third-graders to the upper-grade writing workshop. It channels children who are accustomed to writing a book a day to work on longer writing projects that require a much more multifaceted writing process. Meanwhile, the book also is written to exactly align with the Common Core State Standards and to benefit from all that the Teachers College Reading and Writing Project has learned during the past decade of working with an earlier iteration of this unit.

Those of you who know the original unit, *Launching the Writing Workshop,* will see both continuities and differences. Many of the differences involve our renewed commitment to helping students work with enormous productivity and increasing independence. You'll see attention to teaching in ways that increase the degrees of cognitive challenge in students' work and that support students working toward crystal clear goals with concrete and helpful feedback. You'll see a deep effort to support small-group work and differentiation and to help students set goals and self-assess.

September in a third-grade writing workshop is an exciting time. You'll establish a well-managed, productive workshop, luring children to invest in a familiar genre, and meanwhile induct these young writers into a version of the writing process that is, in fact, quite different from that which they knew during the primary grades. That is, in third grade, instead of students thinking about a piece and sketching it, then immediately writing it, we generally suggest that students invest more time in rehearsal for writing, collecting lots of quick drafts of possible stories in notebook entries, then selecting just one of these to put through the writing process, resulting in publication.

At the same time that you induct your youngsters into this more adult writing process, you will also help them continue to draw on all they have learned in previous years. Third-graders who have grown up in writing workshops will already know that it is important to focus on narrative, to write in sequential order, and to include the details that bring the episode to life.

This unit also provides you with the opportunity to teach your class the work called for by the Common Core State Standards (CCSS) for narrative writing. The emphasis on writing standards is parallel and equal to the emphasis on reading in the CCSS. These narrative writing standards support a writing process approach that emphasizes the importance of students rehearsing, drafting, revising, and editing their writing. They also describe a progression of skill development that is expected across grades in a spiral writing curriculum, one grade building upon the next. As you prepare for your entering third-graders, read the second-grade end-of-year expectations for narrative writing, noticing what is similar and what is new. You will quickly see how the CCSS raises the ante for third-grade writers. Then you will want to look ahead to the fourth-grade standards, which become more specific and nuanced, to become aware of future expectations. This also helps ensure that students always have something to aspire to—a challenge to strive toward.

For example, while both second-graders and third-graders are expected to write narratives that include details, use temporal words, and provide a sense of closure, third-graders are also expected to "establish a situation and introduce a narrator and/or characters; organize an event sequence that unfolds naturally" (W.3.3.a), and fourth-graders are expected to "orient the reader" to this situation (W.4.3.a). This is the first time the word *character* is mentioned in reference to narrative writing. When you look at the reading standards for third grade, you will see that children no longer merely "describe characters" while reading fiction, but are now asked to "explain how [characters'] actions contribute to the sequence of events" (R.3.3), then in fourth grade, also "drawing on specific details in the text." There is a certain reciprocity in this, and the standards seem to be calling third-grade writers to develop a story that is more than just plot-driven, but instead is driven by characters' experiences (and responses to those experiences). Third-grade writers are expected to "use dialogue and descriptions of actions, thoughts and feelings to develop experiences and events or show the response of characters to situations" (W.3.3.b).

In this unit, students' knowledge of language and its use is especially highlighted when the class studies mentor texts for word choice and literary language (L.3.3). You'll continue to emphasize these reading-writing connections, channeling your students to engage in close reading of complex mentor texts such as *Come On, Rain!* by Karen Hesse, to learn more about narrative craft. You will especially highlight the importance of "show, don't tell." Learning how to write effective narratives will help children engage in purposeful, deliberate revisions. These revisions will tend to feel a bit like carpentry as youngsters scissor apart their drafts to add a blank page at the heart of the story, attach flaps on sections that need elaboration, and tape new versions of leads or endings on top of existing ones.

Since editing is integrated into each bend, many more of these language standards are also addressed during this first writing unit. Children learn to use simple verb tenses and produce simple and compound sentences (L.3.1.e, i). Punctuating dialogue, using conventional spelling for high-frequency words, using spelling patterns, and using reference materials to check and correct spellings (L.3.2.c,e,f,g) are all introduced during this unit, with the understanding that children will continue to work on them until they master them by the end of third grade. Like the standards, we have high expectations for students, and our goal is to accelerate student achievement in authentic and engaging ways.

This unit also supports many of the expectations in the areas of the speaking and listening standards. Writing partners can listen to and read each other's writing, asking questions, giving each other feedback, and explaining their ideas, all the while following "agreed upon rules for discussions" (SL.3.1.b). During each share session, writers are encouraged to come prepared to discuss some aspect of writing or the writing workshop (SL.3.1) or to listen carefully to a piece of writing being read aloud and to ask and answer questions (SL.3.2, 3.3). And implicit in all of this is that children are encouraged to speak in full sentences, elaborating and clarifying as needed (SL.3.6). This unit introduces many of the skills third-graders will need to become skilled collaborators as the year progresses.

One of the hallmarks of this unit and of all units in this series is the emphasis on productivity—on sheer volume of writing. Third-graders should be able to write a page-long entry in one sitting. For children who enter third grade writing in a word-by-word fashion, taking a break after every word or two, this is a monumental challenge but an important one. To support fluency, the unit sets students up to "flash-draft" an entire story in a day several times over the course of the unit and to cycle through the writing process several times, too. Without doing this, third-graders, who are not apt to find it easy to write a sequence of entirely new drafts, might come to expect that writing a new lead and ending constitutes a day's work.

Students will cycle through the entire writing process in Bend III: generating new entries and selecting one to rehearse, draft, revise, and edit. They will then have two finished pieces from which to choose as they prepare for final publication. The ultimate goal of this first unit is for children to develop increased independence and dramatic growth in the level of their writing as they become confident, engaged members of a larger, caring community of writers.

OVERVIEW OF THE UNIT

At the start of the year, you will want to move heaven and earth to recruit your young writers to become invested in the writing workshop, so the way you launch this unit is critical. In addition to establishing the structures and routines of a third-grade writing workshop, the first bend sets children up to make discoveries about what third-grade writing looks like by examining actual examples of writer's notebooks, to share these observations with each other, and to make New Year's resolutions, imagining the kind of writing they want to make and setting goals for themselves. As children learn ways to generate personal narrative entries that they will capture in their writer's notebooks, you will invite them to reflect on what is going well, what is hard, and how they might ramp up their work a notch by looking closely at a mentor text, *Come On, Rain!* by Karen Hesse, to study storytelling moves and by using checklists and rubrics to help them self-assess. For some children this will mean increasing their volume and stamina; for others it will mean writing with more attention to conventions or to craft. This first bend, then, provides a vision for the kind of writing third-graders can do, builds upon what they could do as second-graders, and sets clear expectations, all in a celebratory, can-do way.

Bend II introduces children to what is new and different about keeping writing in a notebook versus a writing folder. Children will learn to reread all their stories, select a seed idea, and then develop that seed idea by story-telling over and over again. As they do so, they will try out different ways the story might go and sound, which includes drafting several different leads. Then it is out of the notebook and into a drafting booklet, where you will show them that writers draft by writing fast and furiously, working to relive the moment on the page. The beauty of this fast draft is that children can spend more time on revision. Specifically, they'll study a mentor author, Karen Hesse; they'll investigate how she makes her storytelling voice so good, name precisely what she does, and then try out these discoveries in their own drafts, revising as they go. This bend ends with you introducing your third-graders to paragraphing as a way of organizing and grouping related sentences. You'll show them, too, how to elaborate on their paragraphs, adding step-by-step actions, dialogue, thoughts, and feelings. Throughout this bend, children will work with partners as they wade together into these new writing waters and splash about.

The third bend emphasizes independence and initiative. You'll remind children that when writers finish one piece, they don't just sit with their hands folded and announce, "I'm done!" No way. Instead, writers finish one piece and begin the next right away. This allows students to transfer their knowledge to a new story and apply all that you've taught to higher levels of expertise and independence. Going through the writing process more than once, quickly, provides the repeated practice writers need to become more fluent. You'll set a deadline by which all children need to be done—temporarily—with their first piece of writing and move on to the second. As children revisit their writer's notebooks to collect more entries, choose a new seed idea, and write another draft, you'll encourage them to become their own job captains, drawing on all they've learned. This means referring to the charts as reminders and helpful tools, looking at the goals they set along the way, and using mentor texts to craft their writing. Much of what you teach during this time will depend on what you observe when you compare your students' writing with the narrative writing learning progression and the student-facing rubrics you have developed. Chances are you'll continue to emphasize the importance of storytelling versus summary, as well as focus and detail. Besides this revision work, you'll introduce students to the conventions of punctuating dialogue.

Once they've written this next draft, you'll encourage writers to look between their two pieces, asking, "Which is the best? Which is good enough that it deserves to be revised and edited for publication?" During this final bend, after students have selected the drafts that they will publish, you will want to rally them to tackle a whole new fast draft. They'll need to rehearse for this just as they rehearsed for the first draft, envisioning the story in a way that unfolds bit by bit across the pages. You'll also be holding students to carry forward all they've learned so far about writing process and writing craft and applying that expert knowledge to every minute of their writing. Then you'll teach children, once again, to look to professional authors to learn ways writers deliberately craft the endings of their stories. Children can then try out these techniques as a way of improving their own stories. Finally, you'll show students how to use an editing checklist to do a final edit of their drafts in preparation for the publishing celebration. You will create a special bulletin board that has a space for each child in your classroom to hang up his or her published writing, and then you will invite the public to read and admire all the efforts put forth by these blossoming third-grade writers.

ASSESSMENT

In this unit, you'll strive toward two goals—increased independence and dramatic growth in the level of your students' writing. You will want children to see that it is usual for their writing to improve in obvious, dramatic ways with each new unit of study. These two goals are utterly interrelated because essentially you need to organize a writing workshop within which students work with great investment toward clear goals and within clear structures. To hold yourself and your students to these goals, it is critically important that you start the year by devoting a day to an on-demand writing assessment that will provide you with a baseline and create a starting point for your students. Such an assessment will ensure that as the unit unfolds, your instruction is calibrated around this data and that you make sure the students' work gets progressively better.

You can make this on-demand writing feel celebratory by giving your students a chance to show off what they already know about narrative writing. You can use the prompt from the book *Writing Pathways: Performance Assessments and Learning Progressions, K–5*, which goes like this:

> "I'm really eager to understand what you can do as writers of narratives, of stories, so today, will you please write the best personal narrative, the best Small Moment story, that you can write? Make this be the story of one time in your life. You might focus on just a scene or two. You'll have only forty-five minutes to write this true story, so you'll need to plan, draft, revise, and edit in one sitting. Write in a way that allows you to show off all you know about narrative writing. In your writing, make sure you:

- "Make a beginning for your story
- Show what happened, in order
- Use details to help readers picture your story
- Make an ending for your story."

You might offer children varied paper choices if this is something they were accustomed to in second grade. During the writing time on this day, be sure you do *not* coach into what they are doing. Don't remind them to write with details or to focus. You want to see what they do in a hands-off situation, and frankly, you will want to be in a position to show great growth from this starting point. Your students come to you with competencies and histories as writers. You cannot teach well unless you take the time to learn what they already know and can do, and the data in hand that you collect by doing an on-demand writing assessment will be invaluable.

Once these on-demand writing assessments are complete, it will be helpful to sit with your grade level team to assess student work to ensure consistency across the grade. Together, using the Narrative Writing Learning Progression from the *Writing Pathways: Performance Assessments and Learning Progressions, K–5* book, you can choose a piece of student work that exemplifies the levels of writing you find in your grade (for example, one piece for level 2, one piece for level 3, one piece for level 4). The conversation that ensues during this process will help you to make sure all teachers in the grade are consistent in how they assess writing using the learning progressions. This will also make it easier for each teacher to get a quick read on his or her children, so it doesn't become an arduous process. Then decide at what level the majority of your class is, because this is where your teaching must begin. Your assessment of each student's work will help you make plans for individuals and small groups of children, informing the trajectory of work they do.

The next step will be to help students understand what is expected so they can set goals worth striving toward. In this unit, you'll give students the opportunity to study examples of what they are aiming to create by providing third-grade exemplars to study closely, annotating and noting the qualities they want to replicate, as well as engaging in close reading of mentor texts to learn more about narrative craft. Use the checklists for children that are based on the Narrative Writing Learning Progression to help students reflect on their own writing, develop their goals, and note places of growth as they move forward in the unit. This work, combined with your close listening and observing, will help you meet the needs of each and every writer in your classroom. In the end, hold yourself to the challenge of strengthening their work and plan to repeat the on-demand assessment after the unit to measure this growth.

GETTING READY

Because this unit is the first time children will be using a writer's notebook, you will want to create a certain fanfare around this very grown-up, professional writing tool. You will also want to make sure you have your own writer's notebook filled with various entries that have been sparked by thinking about memorable moments with special people or events that happened in special places. (If you don't have one, make one or borrow one or find a famous writer's notebook on the Internet!) If you plan to have your students decorate their notebooks with photos and pictures that might spark stories, then you should decorate yours also in a similar way. If you want your students to carry their notebooks with them always, then you should also, sharing stories of how you were able to jot down events right after they happened or how disappointed you were when there was a time you didn't have your notebook with you. You will probably be the first living, breathing author they know first hand, so everything you do as a writer will inspire them to do the same.

You will also want to gather examples of third-grade writing so your students have a vision of the kind of writing they will be doing at the start of the year. You can find some examples on the CD-ROM, but the best are examples that come from your own students or the students of colleagues because that way you know the inside story behind the stories, which children always find intriguing. In addition, throughout the sessions, we suggest returning to the same familiar author, Karen Hesse, and familiar text, *Come On, Rain!,* so that children can become used to reading closely like a writer. Of course, you can choose any author and book you love that has the qualities of good writing you hope to teach, but in either case, the important thing is to have an author who becomes like your co-teacher in the room, sitting on your shoulder, whispering writing advice into your ear and eventually into your students' ears.

Writing Personal Narratives with Independence

Starting the Writing Workshop
Visualizing Possibilities

IN THIS SESSION, you'll invite students to become writers and teach them that writers make New Year's resolutions; they think about the kind of writing they want to make and set goals for themselves to write in the ways they imagine.

GETTING READY

✔ Writing workshop meeting area, framed by beautiful books, carpeted and comfortable. At the head of the meeting area, place your chair and an easel containing a pad of chart paper and markers. You may also want access to a white board and a document camera.

✔ A pointer or chopstick to use as a baton to ring in the New Year

✔ Seating arrangements for students in the meeting area and writing tables

✔ Chart with heading "What Third-Grade Notebook Writers . . ." (see Teaching)

✔ A third-grader's writer's notebook to be used as an exemplar. Make enough copies so that each table has at least three different pages to study.

✔ Chart paper and markers on each table (see Active Engagement)

✔ Document camera or overhead projector to display the third-grade notebook writing

✔ Your own writer's notebook, decorated with photos and pictures and filled with ten-plus page-long personal narrative entries, some starred, some with marginal notes alongside, to be used in the Share and throughout the year

✔ Two sample New Year's resolutions on chart paper, one written by you and one written by an exemplar third-grader (see Share)

✔ Narrative Writing Checklist, Grade 2 (see Share)

✔ A writer's notebook and pen to pass out to each student (see Share)

✔ Sticky tape for children to tape exemplar writing from the third-grader's notebook in their notebook to remind them of their goals and to act as a mentor text

COMMON CORE STATE STANDARDS: W.3.5, W.3.8, W.3.10, RL.3.5, RL3.1, SL.3.1. a,b,c,d; L.3.6

THREE DECADES AGO, when the field of teaching writing was new, I began my now classic book, *The Art of Teaching Writing* (1994), with words that are more true now than ever:

> If our teaching is to be an art, we must draw on all we know, feel, and believe in order to create something beautiful. To teach well, we do not need more techniques and strategies as much as we need a vision of what is essential. It is not the number of good ideas that turns our work into art but the selection, balance, and design of those ideas.

> Artists know this. Artistry does not come from the quantity of red and yellow paint or from the amount of clay or marble but from the organizing vision that shapes the use of those materials. It comes from a sense of priority and design.

At the start of the year, when nothing is yet in place, when everything seems essential, it is helpful to stand back and to think about Stephen Covey's adage: first things first. Out of all the things that you could teach and cover and do—what feels most important? Where does one start? What's foundational to everything else?

I believe that one of the most important things we must do at the start of the year is help youngsters imagine the texts they'll be making during the upcoming unit. The words from *South Pacific* have proved true: "If you don't have a dream, how you gonna have a dream come true?" For me personally, it has always been important to know what I am aiming for, to envision what it is I am trying to make, to accomplish. If I have concrete, clear goals, then I can work to meet those goals. And I also know from John Hattie's review of 300,000 studies of achievement, that learners—whether aspiring to be Olympic divers or to be published writers—are most apt to accelerate development when working toward crystal-clear, ambitious goals.

Today, then, instead of initiating *writing*, you'll initiate *dreaming*. You will help the youngsters in your classroom begin to imagine the kind of thing they'll be making, starting tomorrow. To nurture those images of possibility, you'll read aloud examples of the sort of writing you hope your students will produce by the end of this unit. You'll also refer them to *Come On, Rain!* by Karen Hesse (1999), a book that hopefully you will have already read to them but that now becomes the mentor text for this unit. But the even more important thing will be to help children hear and study and identify with well-written narratives by other third-graders.

This unit is not just about writing wonderful personal narratives. It is also about growing into the identity of being a writer and about living writerly lives.

For your children, this unit is not just about writing wonderful personal narratives. It is also about growing into the identity of being a writer and about living writerly lives. Just as we dress aspiring soccer players up with high socks and jerseys to help them assume their new roles, it is also important to outfit youngsters with writerly tools. Today you will create a drumroll around a brand-new and very grown-up tool—the writer's notebook. This first bend in the unit will help children become keepers of notebooks. The unit, then, is more centered on teaching children the writing process—a new, more grown-up version of the writing process—than is typical for a unit of study. Because that process is especially symbolized by the writer's notebook, you'll devote a good part of today to giving children an opportunity to study writer's notebooks, doing this study collaboratively with their friends, working to generate language that captures what it is that this writer has done that they, too, could aim to accomplish.

Starting the Writing Workshop
Visualizing Possibilities

CONNECTION

Suggest that today is New Year's Day for the writing workshop and invoke a mini in-place celebration.

"Writers, I've pulled all of us together in this meeting area because today is the very first day of our new writing workshop. It is sort of like New Year's Day. Have any of you ever had a New Year's celebration? Have you celebrated by blowing horns or throwing confetti or clanging on glasses?" I demonstrated a few of these actions.

"In a minute, let's celebrate the New Year for our writing workshop. I am going to be like the conductor at the symphony. When I throw open my arms like a conductor does, baton in hand, I want each of you to blow an imaginary horn or throw imaginary confetti or clang an imaginary glass—for one minute. It will be loud enough for all the classes around us to hear our celebration and think, 'What's going on?' But then, when I bring my baton back to the center," and I demonstrated, "let's be totally silent.

"You ready to celebrate New Year? Watch me." I waited a few seconds and then made a grand sweeping gesture that signaled, 'Do it!' For a moment, the room was filled with blaring horns and clanging glasses. Then, with a decisive arm signal, everything became (almost) silent.

Point out that most people also celebrate New Year by making New Year's resolutions.

"Writers," I said, and waited for them to settle down and give me their attention. "We celebrate New Year not just with horns and confetti, but also with New Year's resolutions. People say, 'This year, I'm going to push myself to run every day,' or 'This year I'm going to save up enough money to get myself a bike.' These are resolutions."

❖ **Name the teaching point.**

"Today I want to teach you that writers, too, make New Year's resolutions. They think about—they imagine—the kind of writing they want to make, and they set goals for themselves to write in the ways they imagine. Then they work hard to reach their goals."

Notice that every minilesson begins with a section titled "Connection" that is patterned like this first one. In today's connection, I use New Year's as a vehicle to rally excitement for this session's work—which involves making resolutions and working toward them.

Every connection ends with the teacher naming precisely what it is he or she aims to teach. We call this the teaching point. Some people refer to this instead as the goal. Usually the teacher embeds this teaching point in a sentence that literally says, "Today I will teach you that. . . ." You will notice that the teaching point is reiterated often throughout a minilesson.

TEACHING

Tell students that writers benefit from having a clear picture of the kind of thing they are trying to make. They might, for example, study an exemplar writer's notebook.

"The other day, I started work on a jigsaw puzzle. Here's the thing. Before I started, I looked on the lid and saw a picture of a golden retriever puppy in a red wheelbarrow. As I set to work, putting the pieces of that puzzle together, I knew that in the end, the puzzle would look like the picture on the lid.

"I am telling you this because when writers start working on a piece of writing (like we'll start doing tomorrow), it helps to have a clear picture in mind of the sort of thing they want to make. And the first thing that we'll make this year is not a picture of a golden retriever in a wheelbarrow, or even a finished published personal narrative. The first thing we will make is a writer's notebook." I held my notebook up and leafed through some pages, doing this as if I was displaying a treasure.

"Right now, to give yourselves a goal for your writing, I'm going to give you a tour of a really great writer's notebook. It was written by Rebecca when she was a third-grader. I will read a few bits aloud to you, and as I do this, let's list all the things we notice this writer has done that we too could try." I read aloud a page and skimmed a second page, inserting comments as I progressed, such as, "Are you noticing what this writer has done that you could do as well?" Figure 1–1 shows one of the pages I read:

> Nothing. I peered into my bag. Nothing. No gym tights. No leotard. I felt tears welling up in my eyes. I thought back, yes, no, yes. I hadn't put my leotard back in the bag. I jerked down my head and pulled my T-shirt over my school tights. No, it didn't look nearly like the leotard that had been so comfortable I wore it until bed. Now my class was going to start in five minutes and I had nothing to wear. The tears came rolling. What was I to do? Hide in the closet until the class was over? No, I'd ask if I could borrow a suit. I rubbed away my tears and opened the door.

"One thing I notice is that this notebook is totally full of stories—true stories, right? And it helps to try to notice not just what the writer does, but how she does it, so let's look again at those stories. Well, it seems this story, anyhow, tells sequentially what happened first and then next and then after that. Let's put that on our list as one thing that third-grade notebook writers do. What else?"

What Third-Grade Notebook Writers . . .

Do:

- Fill their notebooks with true stories that tell what the writer did first, next, after

FIG. 1–1   Rebecca's notebook entry

If you pattern a minilesson after this one, you'll want to tell about true stories a student of yours wrote in previous years. Choose an accessible entry, so youngsters listen to it and think, "I could do that." As you read all these minilessons, remember that they are not meant to be a script for your teaching, but rather, they are meant to convey the story of my teaching, providing one example of how your teaching could go.

Often, children enter the classroom in September not believing they have anything to say. "Nothing happens in my life," they'll say. Our first job is to help children see that they do, indeed, have stories to tell. We want each child to think that, as Faulkner puts it, "my own little postage stamp of native soil [is] worth writing about and that I [will] never live long enough to exhaust it" (Cowley 1958, p. 141).

ACTIVE ENGAGEMENT

Set children up to talk in small clusters about what third-grade notebook writers do and don't do, and then convene to collect observations.

"What are you noticing? Let me reread just a bit of that one entry. Listen again, and in a second, I'm going to give you and the people next to you time to talk. You can talk about what third-grade writers do," I gestured to one hand, "and," I gestured to the other hand, "what third-grade writers don't do too," and I added a second column to our chart.

After a hubbub of conversation, I called on a few children to share their observations with the class, adding to our chart.

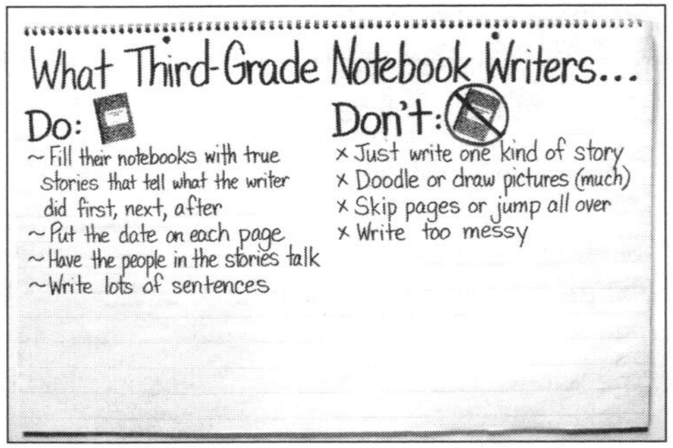

LINK

Channel students to continue this work in groups, studying an exemplar notebook and charting observations.

"I've put a few pages of some third-graders' writer's notebooks at each of your tables, along with a big piece of chart paper and some marker pens. Today, instead of getting started on your writing, let's make charts that capture what a writer's notebook is like. That way, we can make ourselves some New Year's resolutions. If you know the technical language—the fancy words—for what narrative writers do—words like *focus* or *leads*—include those words! Some of you may want to imagine what a less-than-great writer's notebook might look like and include a column for that on your chart as well. These charts will help us know what we aim to make.

"And writers, the work you are doing—clarifying goals for a unit of study—is work that *teachers*, not *kids*, usually do, so please help each other. Work with the kids at your table, studying the writer's notebook carefully so you notice a ton of things. I'll be coming around to admire the work you are doing."

FIG. 1–2 Children's observations added to a chart

Some of the charts you make will be one- (or two-) day charts, such as this one. These charts serve as quick reminders of habits we hope children learn on the spot and can be "retired" once they have been used. This particular chart will resurface again, so you'll want to keep it on hand (just not hanging on the wall).

On many days my link will send students off to write independently, drawing on a repertoire of strategies with autonomy and initiative. Today's workshop is a bit different. I've postponed the process of writing, and am asking children to spend time studying mentor texts.

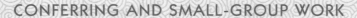

Moving Quickly among Writers, Learning Their History and Hopes

TODAY IS A BREATHER. Whereas tomorrow, each of your children will be writing first entries in their writer's notebooks—requiring you to put on roller skates so you can rush from one writer to another, making sure that everyone breaks through inertia and finds a story worth telling—today your children will be engaged in a collaborative. In this session, third-graders will work with a cluster of friends to read and talk over the writing that another third-grader has done, and they will work together to chart their observations. Today, then, offers you a crucially important opportunity to make real, I-thou, connections with individual writers.

Think about times when you have been a student in a class, in a large group, led by someone powerful, whom you respect and fear, too. Think about how absolutely important it has been for you to come to know that you are seen, recognized, and wanted. During the first days, especially, the smallest gestures can make a world of difference.

As you move among your children, then, aim first to establish contact, to convey, "Welcome. I see you. I'm so glad you are part of our writing workshop." Try to not just reach each child, but to reach the writerly parts of each child. "I love the way you read that first sentence of Evan's entry. You put so much feeling into it!" "I can tell you appreciate that detail in his story. You and I are just alike. We're both lovers of details!" "Oh my goodness, you've gotten started on your chart already. You don't waste a second, do you!" "I just noticed that you wrote down the exact words that your classmate said. That's a respectful note-taker." "Wow—you have all the writing lingo down, don't you? I can tell you know tons of stuff about good writing."

If one of your goals is to help each child in your classroom feel seen and appreciated, another goal will be to make the activity that you have organized for the day be a productive one. You'll always want to approach any day thinking about why the work you have asked students to do matters so much to you. That is, just as children need to know their goals for keeping a writer's notebook, you need to know your goals for what you will be asking students to do. And today you have asked them to read over

---

MID-WORKSHOP TEACHING   Make a Museum and Compile a Sense of What Notebook Writers Do

As soon as it seemed children were scraping the bottom of the task I'd given them, I intervened. "Writers, establishing goals is really important work. Remember the song that goes, 'If you don't have a dream, how you gonna have a dream, come true?' What you are doing now is you are making dreams for your writing.

"It is great that you are learning from people at your table, but let's also learn from others in the class. Let's make a museum of our charts. You can have five more minutes to finish yours so it is ready for the museum. Then the rest of the class can gather around your table, noticing what your group put on its chart and getting ideas for the writing they'll do starting tomorrow. Then the class can gather beside another exhibit. (I'll time you for three minutes, and then it will be time for the museum.)"

Three minutes later, I said, "Writers, clean up your work area so it looks like a museum, and then let's all gather beside this table, for starters. And writers, this is going to be an absolutely silent museum. If you see something the other group did that you like, point at it, signal silently to the rest of us."

After the museum, writers returned to their own tables and talked about their plans for their writing.

---

and talk about a writer's notebook. If you know what you are really after, you can angle your conversations to make those hopes a reality.

My sense is that one reason you are hoping to immerse children in an example of story writing is that you want them to absorb all they can from examples of good practice. Hopefully your children will note the layout of the pages, for example, seeing that there is a record of the date and the place (home/school) where the writing is occurring. Hopefully they'll notice the length of an entry. (Within the year, you should be able to expect that almost all of your third-graders will produce a page of writing in a single sitting.) You hope writers notice that they usually leave the backs of the left-hand side of their pages blank, sometimes coming back to jot notes on these pages. Writers who are working on personal narrative writing may include a few lists of story ideas scattered among their entries. The narratives are written sequentially and include dialogue and details. Although you may want to channel children to notice these and other things about the exemplar notebook, the most important thing for them to notice is the spirit in which all of this is done. For example, as children talk about the work that another child has written, you will want to coach them to approach that writing with great respect, looking past errors to what the writer has tried to say, reading the words as if they are gold. Your absolute respect for the words written by an anonymous child will signal to your children that their writing, too, will be regarded as a gift.

Although it is important for children to notice details about writer's notebooks and personal narratives, your other hope is that this low-key work will provide you and your students (and your students and each other) with opportunities to talk. Whenever I want the chance to hold especially important conversations with one of my sons, I arrange for us to do something together: a walk in the woods, some low-key chores, a long drive. In a similar way, you can use the context of today's shared activities as a backdrop for the conversations that will actually be the main event for you. Learn all you can about each child's writing history and hopes—and record what you learn, or it will easily slip out of your mind. If a child sees a quality of writing in another child's notebook—say, focus—you will want to learn what the child means when mentioning that quality. Ask, "What do you mean by that?" and learn if the youngster was taught that quality in previous years and whether she aims to do that same thing when she writes. You will, presumably, have your own meaning for any term the child might use, but your goal is to understand your children's understandings. As you chat with children about another child's writer's notebook, help them think about the topics they'll draw upon in their own notebooks—the stories they'll tell. When you look at Rebecca's notebook, say things like, "This is giving me tons of ideas for stories I can write! What ideas are you coming up with?" You'll mention your children's stories when you start your next minilesson.

Capturing Resolve through New Year's Resolutions

Review the "What Third-Grade Notebook Writers . . ." chart.

"Writers, can I have your eyes and your attention?" After the room silenced, I continued, "Please bring the notebook pages you have been studying and a pen with you to the meeting area."

After the children had convened, I said, "As you were admiring each other's lists, I gathered many of the things you'd listed and added them to our class list, which is up here. Tomorrow you'll start writing your own entries in your own writer's notebook, and pretty soon we'll be able to study your writing like we have just studied Rebecca's writing."

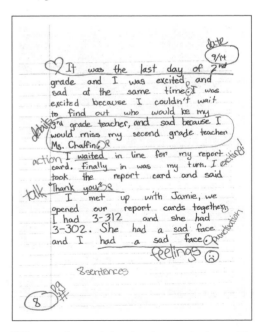

FIG. 1–3

What Third-Grade Notebook Writers . . .

Do:

- Fill their notebooks with true stories that tell what the writer did first, next, after
- Put the date on each page
- Have the people in the stories talk
- Write lots of sentences
- Tell if writing in home/school
- Write about one page each day
- Use lots of punctuation

Don't:

- Just write one kind of story
- Doodle or draw pictures (much)
- Skip pages or jump all over
- Write too messy
- Erase too much
- Trash the notebook

"I'm wondering, as you look over the chart, whether you think," and I pointed to bullet one, "'Check, I can do that.'" Then I pointed to bullet two. "'Check, I can do that.' Some parts of this might be hard to do, and you'll need to remember that writers set goals and then work hard to be able to meet those goals."

FIG. 1–4   One notebook entry marked up with students' observations

Ask students to recall goals for narrative writing that they learned last year.

"I'd like to remind you of the qualities of strong narrative writing you worked on in second grade. As I read the list to you, give a thumbs up if it is something you already do well. If so, that's great! You can be our expert on that quality of good narrative writing. Some of the items on the list, though, may be things you've forgotten or know you can improve on. When you get a chance to do some writing tomorrow, you'll want to work on those items."

I read the items on the Grade 2 Narrative Writing Checklist, one by one, asking children to look between the items and one of the entries in the notebook they'd been studying. (This checklist is available on the CD-ROM.)

Ask writers to capture their resolve, as writers, in New Year's resolutions.

"Let me ask you a question that I want you to think about silently. Here it is. What will *you* need to work hard to do for your writing to be the best that it can be? What will be your New Year's resolutions?

"I'm going to give you your very own writer's notebook, and when you get it, on the first page, write the New Year's resolutions you make for yourself—keeping in mind both what third-graders do and don't do *and* the second grade Narrative Writing Checklist." After I handed out the notebooks and gave children a minute to list their resolutions, I read mine aloud. "Listen to the New Year's resolution I wrote in my notebook:"

- I want to spend less time fiddling over every word in my writing, and more time writing strong and long so that I actually write at least a page or two each time I sit down to write.
- I want to make sure I choose words that help readers picture my story.

"I'm also fast-passing some sticky tape around: if any of the writing that you read today could be a goal for you, a mentor text for you, you can tape that piece of writing into your notebook if you want. Some of you might put stars or other decorations near parts of the writing, the places you love."

Narrative Writing Checklist

	Grade 2	NOT YET	STARTING TO	YES!
	Structure			
Overall	I wrote about *one time* when I did something.	☐	☐	☐
Lead	I thought about how to write a good beginning and chose a way to start my story. I chose the action, talk, or setting that would make a good beginning.	☐	☐	☐
Transitions	I told the story in order by using words such as *when, then,* and *after.*	☐	☐	☐
Ending	I chose the action, talk, or feeling that would make a good ending.	☐	☐	☐
Organization	I wrote a lot of lines on a page and wrote across a lot of pages.	☐	☐	☐
	Development			
Elaboration	I tried to bring my characters to life with details, talk, and actions.	☐	☐	☐
Craft	I chose strong words that would help readers picture my story.	☐	☐	☐
	Language Conventions			
Spelling	To spell a word, I used what I knew about spelling patterns (*tion, er, ly,* etc.). I spelled all of the word wall words correctly and used the word wall to help me figure out how to spell other words.	☐	☐	☐
Punctuation	I used quotation marks to show what characters said. When I used words such as *can't* and *don't,* I used the apostrophe.	☐	☐	☐

End by asking students to decorate their notebooks and collect ideas for the next session's writing at home.

"Tonight, at home, would you decorate the cover of your writer's notebook? If you decide to paste a collage of pictures onto the cover like Rebecca did and want to bring in pictures tomorrow so you can borrow our rubber cement and contact paper, I'll have those materials ready for you. One way or another, personalize your notebook. Make it special, because it will hold your writing, it will hold your stories, and it will hold your life.

"And as you decorate your notebook at home, keep in mind that tomorrow you will have a chance to write. So tonight, when you are home with your family, be on the lookout for stories. Listen for stories. When things happen at home, let them jog your mind so memories surface. When you feed your cat, maybe you'll remember the day you picked her out from a litter of kittens. When you take out the garbage, maybe you'll remember the time you saw a big raccoon on top of the garbage can. Tomorrow, come to the writing workshop already remembering some stories you could write.

"Today is New Year's day for our writing workshop. Let's celebrate again. You have your horn, your confetti, your glass ready?" With my imaginary baton in hand, I signaled for the imaginary horns to blare, the imaginary glasses to clink—and then signaled for silence.

Finding Ideas and Writing Up a Storm

IN THIS SESSION, you'll teach students that one strategy for generating ideas for true stories is to think of a person who matters, then to brainstorm small moments spent with that person.

GETTING READY

✔ Students' newly decorated writer's notebooks and a pen or pencil, to be brought to the meeting area. (The minilesson begins by celebrating the way students decorated their writer's notebooks, based on the share in Session 1.)

✔ Your own writer's notebook, to be brought to the meeting area

✔ "Finding Ideas for True Stories" chart, with the heading and first bullet pre-written (see Teaching Point)

✔ The name of a person who matters to you, or thoughts about a person who matters to you, and several memories of small moments with that person, to demonstrate choosing a topic and telling a quick, first-draft story (see Teaching)

✔ Blank notebook page enlarged or put on a document camera, to come up with a list of moments

✔ "What Third-Grade Notebook Writers . . ." chart from Session 1 (see Share)

✔ Arrow-shaped tabs or sticky notes (or some other kinds of stickers) for children to mark places in their notebooks worthy of compliment and celebration (see Share)

COMMON CORE STATE STANDARDS: W.3.3.a,b; W.3.4, W.3.5, W.3.10, RL.3.5, SL.3.1.a,b,c,d; L.3.6, L.3.1

T HE EARLY MINILESSONS in this unit of study serve a dual purpose: they teach writers strategies for generating ideas and they give writers a glimpse into the sort of writing they'll be doing.

This means that although the minilesson spotlights one particular step-by-step procedure for coming up with topics, you will also want to let writers get a feel for the actual writing that results. In this lesson, you'll start writing an exemplar piece of writing, which will then thread through many minilessons across the entire unit, giving you a place to demonstrate next steps to students. You can adapt my piece and pretend it is yours, but you'll teach with a special level of engagement if you write your own. Make sure the piece you write today is underdeveloped, as mine is, because you'll be working to improve it for the next few weeks. Look ahead to see how your writing (and mine) will change over time.

Meanwhile, your minilessons can also help students learn the norms of a typical writing workshop. Throughout today's session, tuck in comments that socialize children into the culture of your workshop. For example, you might say, "Come quickly to the meeting area! We have some important work to get done." Insist that children give you their full attention during your minilesson. You might say, "Writers, can I have your eyes and minds?" Pay special attention to transitions.

Even today, be willing to ramp up the level of students' work, including their behavior. "Table 1, that's not the most efficient way writers come to the meeting area. Let's rewind and try that again. This time, please come quickly. When you get to the meeting area, show me you are ready to listen." All of this management can be done with an aura of urgency and frequent reminders that "You don't want to waste one precious moment of our writing time." Behind your reminders and nudges is the message that writers are disciplined, aware that the only way something gets written is when, as Donald Murray says, our butt is in the chair.

Finding Ideas and Writing Up a Storm

CONNECTION

Revel over the fact that yesterday many children already began generating story ideas. Channel children to tell their stories quickly to nearby students.

"Writers, can I have your eyes and attention? As we're gathering today, I noticed how some of you have personalized your most important writing tool—your writer's notebook. Let's take some time with your partners to look at and share your notebooks. If you've got pictures of people or places that matter, tell each other stories related to them." The room broke out, buzzing over the excitement of their writer's notebooks. After some time sharing, I signaled for quiet.

"Yesterday while you were looking at other kids' notebooks, some of you came up with stories of your own that you might write today. Give me a thumbs up if you *already* have an idea for a story you might write in your notebook today!" They signaled. "Holy moly—that's great. Right now, if you have a story in your mind that you think you might write, turn and tell that story to some kids sitting near you. Go!" The room filled with a hubbub as six or seven children told their stories to others.

As I crouched alongside different clusters of children, I heard stories about getting stuck in the tire swing, poop in the pool, losing a baby sister while playing tag, pulling a loose tooth out, and discovering a hidden fort.

"We have been together for only one day, one hour, and twenty minutes, but I'm already realizing you have amazing true stories!"

By creating a space for children to storytell to each other, you continue the work of helping children know their lives brim with stories worth telling. The children who do have stories to tell will spark ideas in those who feel empty handed.

Orient students by reviewing the structure of each day in a writing workshop: a meeting in which they mostly listen, at least half an hour to write, and then time to share.

"Give me a thumbs up if you were a writer in a writing workshop last year or the year before." The children signaled if they had been.

"That's a lot of you! Think back to how your workshop went. Did it start with everyone gathering together to listen and learn something about what good writers do? Usually workshops of all sorts, including pottery workshops and sculpture workshops, begin that way, with the artists—they might be writers, they might be painters—gathering to learn a new way to do something. The teacher says, 'Let me show you a technique that has been important to my work,' and then

You'll notice that I explicitly teach children how the writing workshop generally goes. During the next few days, I plan to teach children specifics. If I see a child waiting for a personalized nudge to get started, for example, I'll say, "In a workshop, whether it's a painting workshop or a writing workshop, after the short lesson, the people go back to their workplaces and figure out what their painting needs next or their writing needs next, and they just get started on their own."

demonstrates that technique. And in your writing workshop, after a ten-minute meeting, did everyone go off to work on his or her own project? That'd be working on making a painting in an artist's workshop, but in your writing workshop, it would have been making a story, an essay, or a newspaper article. In our writing workshop, you'll have at least half an hour to write every day so you'll be able to write a page each day.

"While you write, I'll circulate and coach. Then—what happens after you write?" I gestured for children to call out, and when they mentioned partners or share time, I nodded. "You are right. We share. We meet with partners or, for now, with the whole class, to share."

❖ **Name the teaching point.**

"I want to teach you a strategy you can use whenever you are having trouble coming up with an idea for a true story. Here it is." I pointed to a bullet on the chart. "You can think of *a person* who matters to you, then list small moments you've had with that person, and then write (or tell) the story of one of those small moments."

Every unit has one or two anchor charts, such as this one, that teachers display prominently on the wall. Anchor charts address the big work of the unit and often include strategies for writing in a particular genre. Teachers add to these charts throughout the duration of the unit and encourage students to reference them periodically as needed.

Finding Ideas for True Stories

- Think of a person who matters to you, list small moments, choose one, and write the whole story.

TEACHING

First teach your children the contexts in which a writer might use the strategy you are about to teach, and gesture to the chart on which the strategy is written.

"So let's say it's writing time, and I've got my writer's notebook in front of me, open to the first blank page. I *might* pick up my pen and think, 'I know a great true story I can write,' in which case I'd just get started, putting that story onto the page.

"But, on the other hand, I *might* pick up my pen and think, 'Hmm, what am I going to write about?' When I don't know what to write, I sometimes reach for a strategy—a step-by-step procedure—that can help me come up with an idea. It helps to list possible strategies on a chart, and then I can always look up at the chart, grab a strategy—and go."

Demonstrate the step-by-step process of using a strategy to generate ideas for true stories. Think of a person, list small moments related to the person, choose one, and then write it in the air.

I gestured to the chart. "Let's each of us try today's strategy. That way we'll each have a true story we can write." I read from the chart, "Think of a person who matters to you." Then I turned to the children. "Hmm . . . Are you thinking of

Intonation is important. I use my voice to suggest that if I think, "I already know what I want to write about," then today's strategy wouldn't be relevant or necessary. On the other hand, if I'm stuck over what to write, then today's strategy will be useful indeed. A strategy is only a strategy if it helps you past a challenge, if you are using the strategy to achieve a goal. When something that could have been a strategy is assigned, and done for no purpose except because it is assigned, then it is no longer a strategy, but merely an activity. You'll notice that often, before I demonstrate how I use a strategy, I set up the context in which the strategy will be useful.

someone? Let's not think of any ol' person, like 'the man at the checkout counter at the deli.' Let's think of someone important to us. Hmm . . .

"I've got a person in my mind. Do you? Watch now, and you'll see what I do after I think of a person. See if you can do the same thing with whoever is in your mind, and later you can tell each other what you are thinking.

"I'm thinking I could write about my mom because she matters a whole lot to me, and I have a zillion tiny stories about stuff we've done. Now I have to think about," and I referenced the chart, "small moments that we spent together." I scrawled "Mum" on an enlarged notebook page and put one empty bullet under the name. "Hmm . . .

"Well, one thing I am remembering is the time she was in the hospital." I started to write that, then paused. "Wait— that was a bunch of days. It wasn't a small moment, it wasn't one time. Let me think. I know! I could write about when Dad and I brought Mum home from the hospital. I remember that well. We got on the elevator, pushed the 8 button. Then we got out and there was a nurse's station there. I can picture the whole story." I wrote that on my list.

Mum

The time when Dad and I brought Mum home from the hospital

"What else? Oh, I know! I remember when my mom surprised me with a new bike, and it wasn't even my birthday!"

Mum

The time when Dad and I brought Mum home from the hospital

The time Mum gave me a new bike (and it wasn't my birthday)

"There's another time I remember. I was your age, and my mother caught me doing something really bad. It's so bad I don't want to tell you the details, but oh, man, I sure remember it." I added a third bullet.

Mum

The time when Dad and I brought Mum home from the hospital

The time Mum surprised me with a new bike (and it wasn't my birthday)

When Mum caught me buying candy at the deli during school.

"How many of you have been thinking about small moments you've spent with your person? Let me give you a second to think of your own stories, listing them across your fingers."

The room was silent for a very long moment as writers counted stories across their fingers.

You'll notice that when we want to teach children how to use a strategy, we often teach by demonstrating. We role-play that we are a writer, and then we use the strategy in front of children. Your role-play is meant to function as a how-to or procedural guide, so act out the sequence of steps you hope children will undertake. Make them feel like part of the process by saying things like, "Let's try this . . ." or, "Think along with me . . ." But really, you are showing them how to proceed when using the strategy. In your role-play, show children the replicable steps to take whenever using the strategy.

Here I am teaching kids a strategy for coming up with a topic in a way that directs them toward writing personal narratives. The strategy will yield personal narratives only if each item in the list represents a small moment or an episode the writer experienced with the special person. If I had abbreviated my description of the strategy so that children simply wrote about a special person, they'd be apt to produce informational, not narrative, texts.

Notice that my list is comprised of common, small episodes that could easily be written chronologically. They are small and focused, the sort of stories that children could conceivably write about.

It is important to teach children that listing topics involves a few minutes, not a few days, and to show them how to shift from gathering to selecting and writing.

"I've got more moments I could add, but I still have to write today's story. So let me choose from my list. While I do, you'll want to choose from the list in your mind, too." Looking at my list, I thought aloud. "Hmm . . ." I turned my eyes, as if asking for input, and the children, not surprisingly, all clearly voted for the scandalous topic. With feigned trepidation I agreed.

Switching into the role of writer, and speaking in a musing sort of way, I said, "So where do I begin? I did this bad thing more than one time, but I want this to be a story of just one time. I need to remember the story of one time, making a movie in my mind of how it went." I looked up at the ceiling, as if pulling the memory from my memory bank. Then I dictated a bare-bones version of the story aloud, writing in the air, my hand all the while pointing to where I would be writing this, had I been writing.

> I remember one day at recess when I broke all the rules and left the school yard to buy candy at Gates' store. (I know, I know, that was very bad.) I was waiting in line with whole armloads of candy when all of a sudden my mom came walking into the store. I nearly fainted.

"I'll stop there, but if this was writing workshop time for real, I wouldn't be *saying* the story, I'd be *writing* it, and I wouldn't stop. I'd write and write and write, fast and furious, 'til I filled up the page with the story."

ACTIVE ENGAGEMENT

Help students imagine themselves in the situation that calls for the strategy. Then lead them through the steps you've demonstrated.

"Class, let's practice this strategy. Pretend it's writing time and you open *your* notebook," I opened an imaginary notebook, "and you pick up *your* pen to write and think, 'Hmm, what should I write?' If you already have a story idea, you'll think, 'Is this a good one?' And if it is, you'll just get started writing. But if you aren't sure what to write, you'll reach for a strategy—and soon our chart will hold a bunch of possible strategies. For now, let's try out the strategy we've been learning." I pointed to the only bullet on the chart.

Finding Ideas for True Stories

- Think of a person who matters to you, list small moments, choose one, and write the whole story.

"I know you have already thought, 'Who is someone that matters to me?' and you have started trying to think of small moments you and that person had together. List those across your fingers." I was silent as I did this myself in front of the class. After a minute, I coached, "You'll be remembering things you have done together, probably things that involve an hour or so." Again I was quiet, doing the work I hoped children were doing.

Who was it who said, "I don't write about my marriage because I have a happy one."

Be sure to retell the first thing (and then the second thing) that happened in the story so that the children will feel the chronological structure of this genre. If you are using your own story rather than mine, you may want to echo-write, staying close to what I've done, but putting it into your own life.

Notice the rhythm of a minilesson. First I tell children what I'll teach, then I teach it, and then I give children the chance to practice the strategy with my support. You'll see this in all of our minilessons. This active engagement portion of the minilesson provides children with scaffolding as they try a new strategy. You'll notice that I don't just assign the work; instead I guide kids step-by-step through the process of using this strategy. In a few minutes, they will try the strategy again in their writing places, this time without scaffolding.

The most important part of this may be the moments of silence. Don't skip past this! Give children a chance to think . . . watch their brains work.

"Now choose *one* of those times, and think back to that event. What happened at the start of that event? Who said what or did what?

"Thumbs up if you have thought of how your zoomed-in story begins." After children put their thumbs up, I said, "Now turn and tell the person sitting next to you what happened. If you want, tell what happened first and next, across your fingers."

As the children talked, I circulated among them, listening to a story or two, and as I did, I called out coaching tips. "Remember to picture exactly what happened and to tell the tiniest details!"

Debrief. Share the good work one child has done in a way that provides yet another model for writers to emulate.

After two or three minutes, I said, "Writers, can I have your eyes and your attention please?" I waited until there was absolute silence.

"I heard amazing stories, just as I knew I would. And they didn't just start and end in a minute. Most of the events lasted ten minutes or an hour, and the stories are long because you included exactly what you did, step by step. I'm going to ask Olivia to tell you her story."

Olivia said, "I was riding my bike through my neighborhood the other day by myself. Then this kid who lives near me said, "Can I ride with you?" and he got on his bike and joined me. We rode side by side through town. Then a bunch of little kids from across the street got on their bikes and the group kept growing until there were about ten of us riding our bikes together!"

I renamed what Olivia had done and provided a nonexample for contrast. "I love the way Olivia told what happened first and then next and then next. She didn't just jump to the end, saying, 'The other day a whole bunch of us rode bikes together.' Instead, she told how the story started and then what happened next."

LINK

Remind writers that whenever they want help thinking of a true story, they can use this strategy. After each writer gets started, writing fast and furiously, send them off.

"So, writers (with stories like these, I need to call you *writers*), every day, for the rest of your lives, always remember that if you are not sure what story to tell, you can use a strategy to get you started. One strategy," I gestured to the chart, "is to jot down a person and list small moments, choose one, and then think, 'Where did my story begin?' And start writing it.

Notice that you haven't yet put children into partnerships. As you get to know the class, think about the partnerships you'll soon arrange.

Notice the example I highlight is a sequential story of a single brief episode—one that retells a rather ordinary, everyday occurrence. The writing that I make a fuss about will tend to be the sort of writing I hope kids will produce at this point in the year. For now, I am steering kids toward sequential, detailed personal narratives.

During the link, I articulate again what I have taught, reminding children that this is a strategy they can use for the rest of their lives. You will see my closing words "As you work today, and every day for the rest of your lives," end many minilessons.

"Give me a thumbs up if you have in mind the story you will write first in your notebook." They signaled. "Great. Now remember, you need to think 'How did it start? What was I doing or saying at the start?'" The room was silent as children thought. "If you can't remember exactly what you were doing or saying at the start, that's okay. Just make it up. Think, 'How did it *probably* start? What might I have done or said?'"

Whispering, I said, "Okay, let's get started," and I opened my notebook, gesturing with my hands to suggest each writer do the same, and then I dove into my own notebook, writing fast and furiously, intent on the page, forcing myself to refrain from eyeballing the class. As my pen moved down the page, I sensed more children had started to write. After a few minutes in which one could hear the scratch of pens, I began moving among the group, tapping one engaged writer then another, on the shoulder, sending them to their desks to keep writing. Soon all but those needing help had dispersed, and I gave quick help to the remaining few.

During this first week of writing workshop, you'll want to establish a serious working tone by pointing out behaviors you want to reinforce: "Let's admire how quickly that group got to their seats to write!" or "I love the way you have gotten straight to work. It feels like your minds are on fire!"

> My Rabbit
>
> ✓ The time I got my rabbit
> ♡ The time my rabbit bit me
> ✓ The time my rabbit almost jumped in the lake

FIG. 2–1 "Think of a person who matters to you . . ." can be altered to "Think of a person or pet who matters to you . . ."

Moving Quickly among Students, Channeling Them to Keep Writing

THE WRITING PROCESS APPROACH to teaching writing is also known as the conference approach because one-to-one writing conferences are central to this method of teaching. In the end, the content that fills many of your minilessons, mid-workshop teaching, and share sessions will spring from ideas you and children invent together as you sit side by side, trying to reach for ways to tackle problems and to improve writing. One-to-one conferences, then, are important not just as especially assessment-based and potent instruction but also as a seedbed for content you will teach throughout the writing workshop.

Although conferring is essential to teaching writing, talking for five minutes with one individual writer is a luxury you probably can't indulge in just yet. Chances are good that your writers will not yet be able to carry on with enough independence for you to be able to draw a chair alongside one writer and listen closely to that child's perception of his or her work. The last thing you want to do is sit for five minutes with one writer while the whole room unravels. One of your first goals, then, will be to help your writers learn to carry on with enough independence that you can do the crucially important work of conferring.

Today, then, your interactions will help all students keep themselves going as writers. You'll be like the circus man who needs to get all his plates spinning in the air at once, racing about the room, catching one plate and then another that is wobbling, getting all those plates going again. You'll interact with writers in ways that not only keep them working, but that also support their future independence. To move swiftly about, you'll need to be willing to accept approximation—on your part and theirs. No one's work will be perfect just now. Don't worry about whether the sentences are punctuated or the pieces detailed. You can get to that teaching in another day or two. For now, your goal is for kids to work hard, writing fast and furiously. And you will want to teach writers how to sustain themselves by becoming resourceful problem solvers.

As soon as children disperse from the meeting area, move among them, using mostly nonverbal signals to help them get settled. To one child, give a decisive thumbs-up

---

MID-WORKSHOP TEACHING   Building Stamina for Writing

"Writers, can I have your eyes and your attention?" I did a 360-degree turn, eyeballing the classroom as I waited for everyone to stop working and look at me. "You know how athletes push themselves to get stronger muscles? Joggers push themselves to run farther and farther, faster and faster, and wrestlers push themselves to lift more and more weights so they get stronger and stronger muscles. Well, writers push themselves too. They push themselves to write, fast and furiously. Some of you are writing a sentence," and I acted out a lazy, lackadaisical writer, "and then taking a break, looking around." Shifting out of my brief role-play, I continued. "What I want to tell you is that to get strong writing muscles, you need to push yourselves in writing, just like joggers and wrestlers push themselves.

"So right now, get ready! In a second, we're going to start writing, and we are all going to write and write and write. We'll write so much that our hands will hurt. If you finish writing one of your stories, go up to your list and grab another and keep going. You'll absolutely get to the bottom of the page and turn to the next one. You ready?" I paused for effect. "Go!"

As children wrote, I walked among them, calling out voiceovers as I admired their efforts. "Oh my goodness, your hands are flying! Some of you are almost at the bottom of a page! Holy moly." Then, a minute later, "I hear pages turning. That is so cool. When you get to the bottom of the page, slap that page over. "I demonstrated a loud slap. "Then we can all hear it and think, 'Good for you!'" After another minute, "If you find you are repeating yourself, move to the next story. Grab another story and keep writing." "Just five more minutes. If your hand is tired, shake it out, quickly, and keep it moving."

sign, whispering "Love that you have three lines done already!" Look askance at the child who hasn't even opened his notebook, making a "What gives?" gesture. Your gestures can make a difference if you imbue them with a sense of power. You can effect change with a decisive tap on one writer's page, a star in the margin of another writer's page, a note—folded over twice—that says, "Writers write" or "See me later."

When you find yourself wanting to say the same thing to five or six writers, don't hesitate to ask for every child's attention. During these early days of the writing workshop, you'll probably lead four or five brief mid-workshop teaching points. Stand in a prominent spot and say loudly, "Writers, eyes up here, please," and then wait for the class's full attention before you quietly teach or preach. Perhaps you'll want to say that writers need to work with their full attention on their writing, otherwise it is impossible to lose oneself in a story, reliving the true details of another time and place. Perhaps you'll want to remind writers that when they finish one piece, they start another.

Leading small groups will provide you with an efficient way to reach lots of your writers. For example, you are sure to have half a dozen kids who sit over an empty page, saying, "I don't know what to write about." Don't hover over each of these children individually, pitching one story idea after another. "What about . . . ? What about . . . ? What about . . . ?" If you cater to your resistant writers in such a fashion, soon all your children will decide that acting needy is the way to get your attention. So instead of working one to one with these resistant writers, pull them together and help them each come up with an idea, even if you need to do so by practically assigning topics. Perhaps you'll remind them that *anything* can become a good story idea. "You can write about the birthday party we had in class yesterday or about coming into this classroom the first time or about the trip to school this morning. Anything can make a great story idea!" After giving a few minutes of forceful, no-nonsense support to a small group, move on, perhaps leaving these writers sitting together on the floor where you gathered them. Perhaps another bunch of kids needs to be reminded that third-graders are expected to write a whole page in one period. The students who may be worrying too much about neatness, almost carving each letter out as if in marble, may need you to promote writing faster.

In addition to leading small groups, you'll also want to give what we call "table compliments." This sort of interaction is described in the Conferring section in Session 4.

Admiring One's Writing

Cheer on your writers; extol their work, asking them to compliment themselves and to use stickers to mark the best parts.

"Writers, can I have your eyes and your attention? Nice work today. Let's meet so we can talk about how today's workshop went for you."

Once children were in the meeting area, I said, "Can you hold your writing up so I can see and admire how much you wrote? Hold those notebooks high!

"Wow, writers, you wrote a *ton!!* And how many of you wrote what happened first and then next and then next? Thumbs up. Totally cool.

"You know how yesterday you admired Rebecca's notebook and listed all the good things she did? Right now, give yourself a compliment. Say, 'It's great the way I. . . .'

"Writers, write your compliment to yourself on top of your page. And then if you find parts of your writing that are especially good, mark those in the margin."

As children worked, I said, "I'm going to pass out some really cool stickers. They are shaped like arrows so you can use them to point to Wow! parts of your own writing. Find something that *you* did in your notebook that you think deserves a sticker, and then put that sticker where it goes."

Channel some children to read their writing aloud to clusters of others, and help listeners listen well and generate compliments.

"Okay, those of you who are wearing blue, will you read your writing to someone near you? And listeners, you get ready to give really, really great compliments. If you don't know what else to admire, you can remember the things we admired in Rebecca's writing," I pointed to the "What Third-Grade Notebook Writers . . ." chart from yesterday, "and if your writer did any of those same things, that would be totally terrific. Go!"

Share sessions often involve children convening in the meeting area, but when you want to expedite things, you can simply stand in the middle of the room and call for children's attention. For now, however, your children's stamina for writing probably isn't especially strong, and you will want to create a sense of solidarity among writers. So for the next few days, you'll probably convene children in the meeting area for all your share sessions.

FIG. 2–2   Emily has given herself a compliment and used stickers to point out Wow! parts in her writing.

Drawing on a Repertoire of Strategies

Writing with Independence

IN THIS SESSION, you'll teach students that writers sometimes think of a place, list small moments that happened in that place, and then write about one of these moments.

GETTING READY

✔ Students' writer's notebooks and pens or pencils, to be brought to the meeting area

✔ Assign table monitors to take out and put away the community writing tools each day.

✔ "Finding Ideas for True Stories" chart from Session 2, with second bullet prewritten. Fold up chart to cover the bullet until ready to reveal the strategy during the minilesson.

✔ A place that is important to you, to demonstrate how to quickly draw a map of the place, with stars and labels showing moments you remember (see Teaching)

✔ A developed story from your map, to show children how to quickly start writing a notebook entry

✔ "The Hard Parts of Writing" chart, written based on observed challenges during independent writing time (see Share)

✔ Chart paper and markers

COMMON CORE STATE STANDARDS: W.3.3.a,b,c,d; W.3.4, W.3.5, W.3.10, RL.3.5, SL.3.1, L.3.6

T ODAY YOU WILL TEACH STUDENTS a second strategy for finding ideas for personal narratives, and in doing so, you will also teach them that writers carry a toolkit of strategies, choosing the one that makes best sense for them. That is, the most important part of this minilesson may be the ending of it, when you send children off and remind them that they can draw upon *either* this session or the previous session's strategy—or they can invent yet another strategy. In our professional development work with teachers, my colleagues and I often point out that one of the ways workshop instruction is different than traditional instruction is that in workshops, writers have intentions and make choices based on those intentions. Explicit instruction equips writers with a repertoire of strategies to draw upon and with a knowledge of goals—of qualities of good writing—but whenever possible, students are encouraged to pursue goals as writers, to make plans and decisions, and to do so by drawing on the growing repertoire of strategies that are explicitly taught to them. Minilessons rarely channel all students to do whatever the subject of the minilesson has been. Instead, minilessons are more apt to add to students' repertoire of possible strategies and conclude, "Use this strategy when. . . ." In this instance, for example, the strategy that is being taught is only useful if the writer struggles to come up with ideas for a story, and even then, there is no reason why today's strategy is better than yesterday's—or than strategies children may have learned in previous years.

In the previous session, you taught writers that they can think of a person who matters to them, list small moments spent with that person, choose one, and write the story of that small moment. Today you teach writers that they can start not with *a person* but with *a place*, collect small moments spent in that place, choose one, and write the story of that one time. However, instead of suggesting students *list* the small moments they recall spending in a place, you suggest they can map those small moments into a quick sketch of their place.

For me, this particular idea for generating stories is a really terrific one. My life is filled with places that brim with memories. What a treat to be able to recall all the stories that are attached with the nooks and crannies of my childhood home! Of course, it will be important to rein myself in, spending more time listening to children's stories than sharing my own. But I do want to bring the lump in my throat with me to this session and let children know that these aren't just "kid" strategies. Instead, they are ones that will work for any of us.

Students are encouraged to pursue goals as writers, to make plans and decisions, and to do so by drawing on the growing repertoire of strategies that are explicitly taught to them.

It is helpful to keep in mind that any strategy—today's, yesterday's, or a strategy youngsters have brought with them from previous years—can be used in more or less sophisticated ways. For example, a more mature writer will weigh whether a story idea feels like a good one (or not) before adding it to the list, and the more mature writer will also have criteria for assessing a story idea. "Do I have strong feelings about that story? Is it somehow, in some way, important to me?" "Is that a time I remember with crystal-clear clarity?"

Early in the session, writers will need to decide whether they want to find story ideas in the people or in the places of their lives. Later, toward the end of the session, you will help writers know that they have even bigger responsibilities. The problems they encounter during writing time are ones that require problem solving. You'll help youngsters know that they can not only choose strategies from a growing repertoire of options, but they also invent their own solutions to problems rather than waiting for someone else to do this.

Drawing on a Repertoire of Strategies
Writing with Independence

CONNECTION

Establish the systems you will use every day to convene the writing workshop, and then channel children to share their writing and their plans for writing with increasing volume.

Before the children convened, I said, "Please remember to check the section of the board that says 'Writing Workshop,' because every day it will tell you what you need to bring to the meeting area. That way we won't waste one precious minute on logistics. Today it tells you to bring your notebook with a pen tucked inside to the meeting area."

Once children had convened, I said, "Writers, can I have your eyes and your attention?" I waited for them. "Yesterday was a big day, wasn't it? For most of you, you started writing in your first writer's notebook! I wonder if writers like James Howe and Beverly Cleary can remember back to the day they began keeping *their* writer's notebooks. I bet so. Will you show the person sitting beside you what you wrote yesterday? Show that person your resolutions, too, and talk about whether you worked hard to meet them.

"Writers, you are telling each other about your story ideas, and that is wise. But will you also look at how many lines you wrote? You might even count them. Remember, yesterday we talked about writers being like athletes. They have goals and push themselves to meet those goals. Tell people near you whether you think that today, you might be able to write an even longer story. Talk about tricks you might use to push yourself to write more." The children talked for a minute about this.

Minilessons generally begin by contextualizing the lesson by referring to the previous day's lesson, to children's related work, or to the prior instruction upon which the minilesson builds. You'll also find that I often get kids engaged from the get-go by asking them to quickly turn and talk or share a bit of their work with a partner.

Remind children that writers draw on a repertoire of strategies for generating writing.

"Although we did great work in writing workshop yesterday, it was also hard work. At the start of writing time, some of you sat with the blank page in front of you and thought, 'Nothing happens to me. I don't have anything to write.'

"This happens to *every* writer. So today I want to teach you that writers do not have just *one* strategy for coming up with ideas. They have a whole bunch of strategies for finding ideas." I gestured toward the chart we had started the preceding day.

It is important to teach the kids that first a person has a need for a strategy, then that person reaches for the strategy. Help kids recall times when they have been stuck, unsure of what to write about, and then introduce the idea that writers profit from having a repertoire of strategies for generating personal narratives (or any other kind of writing).

❖ **Name the teaching point.**

"Today I want to teach you that writers sometimes think not of a *person* but of a *place* that matters to them and list story ideas that go with that place, choosing one story to write. Sometimes, instead of *listing* stories that happened in a place, they *map* them, and then they write, write, write." I revealed the next bullet on our chart.

> ### Finding Ideas for True Stories
>
> - Think of a person who matters to you, list small moments, choose one, and write the whole story.
> - Think of a place that matters, map small moments, choose one, write it.

TEACHING

Name the context that might lead a writer to use today's strategy and demonstrate reaching for the strategy.

"I'll show you what I mean when I say writers sometimes map story ideas, and then later today some of you might use this strategy to get yourself going on your writing. Others might choose to go back to yesterday's strategy.

"Remember, too, that if an idea for a great story pops into your head right away, you don't need to use this chart ('Finding Ideas') at all. No way. A writer can just start writing. But *if* you are stuck, if you are thinking, 'I just don't know what to write,' then you can look up at this chart and take any strategy from it." I gestured to and read the second bullet.

> - Think of a place that matters, map small moments, choose one, write it.

Demonstrate the strategy in a step-by-step fashion, tucking in some tips.

"So first, we need to think of a place. It should be one we know well, because writing is always better if the writer is an expert on the topic. Are you all thinking of a place you know? Hmm, I know. I'll take the backyard at my old house." I started quickly sketching and labeling the place. Soon my map showed a hill. "That's Guts-Smasher Sledding Hill," I said. "One time, when I was sledding there, I got going really fast and smashed into a tree. I'm going to jot a note here on my map reminding me I could write about that time when I was sledding. At the bottom of Guts-Smasher Hill, there is a swamp. I could also write about the day I found frog eggs there."

When you write your own teaching point, be wary of the tendency to merely name the topic you'll be illuminating. A teaching point that says, "Today I'll teach you another strategy for generating stories" doesn't actually teach at all. I urge you to spell out the essence of the mini-lesson. "Out with it," I say. This means that by the end of the connection, kids have a good grasp of what they will be learning. When we have already named the strategy in the teaching point before entering the teaching component of a minilesson, this reminds us that naming the strategy is not teaching it.

Outside of writing time, try to read texts to children that resemble those you hope they will write. It is important to immerse students in the language and sound of texts similar to those they will write. Gasp over writers who put the truth of their lives onto the page. Say things like, "She writes with exact, honest words, just like so many of you did today!"

As I teach particular strategies for finding a topic, I am also conveying some very basic expectations for narrative writing, showing children their stories will probably celebrate everyday life moments.

Debrief. Name exactly what you did and explain that writers often find true stories hiding in places that matter.

"Did you see that I first needed to think of a place, one I know well, and I started quickly mapping the place. Then I jotted notes on my map about the stories that I can locate on the map. Now I have even more small moments I can write about in my notebook."

ACTIVE ENGAGEMENT

Set children up to try the strategy you've just taught. Scaffold them through the first step, teaching them to sketch a map and label it with small moments.

"So let's try this together. Pretend you are stuck, not sure what to write about. You look up at our list of strategies," I gestured toward the chart, "and decide to think of *a place* that matters. Right now, think of a place that matters to you." I was quiet, giving students time to think. "Give me a thumbs up when you have thought of one.

"Okay, writers, you saw how quickly I sketched my map. (It took about one minute.) In your notebook, quick, quick, make yourself a map, too, and then jot story ideas onto your map." As children worked, I said, "It will be like a treasure map, only instead of mapping hidden treasures, map hidden stories." I moved among the children.

"Writers, can I have your eyes and your attention?" I waited for silence. "What treasures you are digging up in these places! Abraham sketched his parents' jewelry shop. Danielle sketched her grandmother's house. These are places that hold not only lots of powerful stories but also lots of powerful feelings. You are bringing such heart to this work, it gives me goose bumps!"

Remind writers that listing or mapping story ideas is merely a way to warm up for the important part—the actual writing of one of those ideas.

"Writers, do you think it would make sense to spend a whole writing workshop mapping stories? No? You are exactly right! Listing or mapping story ideas takes five minutes and is a way to warm yourself up for the stories you are going to write. Then comes the important part: writing, writing, writing. Right now, mark the story idea you'll write today." They did. "Now, remember what you do to start writing a story? You think, 'Where was I at the start of this?' Do that now." I left students in a pool of silence to sit beside a partnership, coaching them to think, "What did I say or do at the very start of this? Now, writers, start your entry. Write what you are remembering you did or said." I turned and started my own story on chart paper as they began scribbling away in their notebooks.

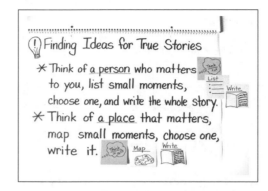

FIG. 3–1   Finding Ideas for true stories with steps added on Post-its for emphasis

When you shift from the demonstration to debriefing, students should feel the different moves you are making just by the way your intonation and posture changes. After most demonstrations, there will be a time for you to debrief, and that's a time when you are no longer acting like a writer. You are the teacher who has been watching the demonstration and now turns to talk, eye to eye with kids, asking if they noticed this or that during the previous portion of the minilesson.

In the active engagement, I could have suggested each member of the class think of a place that matters to him or her and jot that down. Then I could have prompted each child to list a couple of small moments connected to that topic. I could even have asked children to star the one Small Moment story that they particularly care about and tell this story to a classmate. That active engagement would have started each child on that day's writing. Try this if many children are staring at blank pages during writing time, or if you are teaching a class full of struggling and reluctant writers.

Notice the predictability of workshop instruction. Day after day, we use the same attention-getting device to ask for children's attention.

Sometimes when children list small moments, they try to use a single word to represent an episode, writing "soccer" instead of "the day my dad embarassed me at the soccer game."

"Look out below!" I called as I jumped belly-down onto the sled. In an instant, I was careening
down the hill, my face inches above the snow, my hands gripping the toboggan's sideboards, I . . .

I paused and looked back over the class to observe who was writing, who was thinking, and who appeared stuck, making a mental note of who might need more support.

LINK

Restate today's teaching point, setting it alongside the previous session's teaching.

"Writers, from this day forward and for the rest of your lives, remember that whenever you are sitting in front of an empty page, feeling stuck over what to write about, you can use either strategy that is on our list, or you can use a whole different strategy. Today, how many of you don't need these strategies because you already have a story to tell?"

Remind children that whenever they want help thinking of a true story, they can draw from their growing repertoire of strategies. Send them off to write.

"Let's watch how quickly and quietly the writers in the back row get started writing," I said, and gestured for those writers to move to their seats and get started.

In a stage whisper, so the entire class heard me, I said, "Oh, look, Joe is rereading what he wrote yesterday. That's smart. . . . Look, Danielle is writing—fast and furious. . . . Do you think the rest of you can zoom to your places and write up a storm? Remember, you're going to be writing fast and furiously, more than yesterday! Go!"

Notice that I start the story with dialogue and run with a very precise action. If you channel children to do likewise you may prevent them from starting a story with summary statements such as, "I remember one time when I crashed into a tree when sledding. It was scary."

A fiction writer once said, "The hardest thing about writing fiction is getting a character from here to there." The same could be said for teaching. It is very important that, at the start of the year, we purposefully teach kids how to use every minute of the writing workshop productively. This sendoff is one way to do so. Even with very young children, transitions do not need to be full of dillydallying!

Listen in Ways that Help Writers Know They Have Stories to Tell

TODAY, YOU WILL NO DOUBT WANT TO START by doing all that I discussed in the previous conferring and small-group write-up. Move about the room, settling the children into their writing. Then use quickly fashioned, urgent small groups (and table compliments, see Session 4) to address the biggest challenges you see.

But meanwhile, you will also want to begin making time for the deep listening that is absolutely essential in any writing workshop.

Donald Murray, the Pulitzer Prize–winning author who is regarded as the father of the writing process, describes teaching writing this way:

> I am tired but it is a good tired, for my students have generated energy as well as absorbed it. I've learned something of what it is to be a childhood diabetic, to raise oxen, to work across from your father at 115 degrees in a steel drum factory, to be a welfare mother with three children, to build a bluebird trail . . . to bring your father home to die of cancer. I have been instructed in other lives, heard the voices of my students they had not heard before, shared their satisfaction in solving the problems of writing with clarity and grace.

> I feel guilty when I do nothing but listen. I confess my fear that I'm too easy, that I have too low standards, to a colleague, Don Graves. He assures me I am a demanding teacher, for I see more in my students than they do—to their surprise, not mine.

> I hear voices from my students they have never heard from themselves. I find they are authorities on subjects they think ordinary. . . . Teaching writing is a matter of faith, faith that my students have something to say and a language in which to say it. (Learning by Teaching, 1982)

I was one of Murray's students, and I can still recall the great hope that welled up in me when he leaned toward me, listening with spellbound attention to my stories of growing up on a farm, struggling to find my place among the brood of nine Calkins children. Could it really be that I had stories to tell and lessons to teach that might

---

MID-WORKSHOP TEACHING
When You're Done, You've Just Begun

"Writers, can I have your eyes and your attention? Some of you are telling me that you are done. Writers have a saying: 'When you're done, you've just begun.' That means that when you think you are done, there is a lot more to do. One thing writers do when they're done is think, 'What's another true story that I've experienced—another story that happened in the same place, or in a different place, or with the same person, or with a different person?'

"They think, 'How did it start? What happened first?' and they write another story.

"How many of you think you are done, or almost done, with today's entry? Thumbs up. Okay. If you are done—today or any day—remember the saying, 'When I'm done, I've just begun.' Right now, tell the person sitting near you what you are going to write next. Don't just tell the topic, but actually write the story in the air. Dictate how it is going to go." As the writers told their stories to each other, I coached the listeners to listen with absorption, showing, by the way they listened, that the details matter.

I regathered students to leave them with a final thing to think about.

"Writers, when we listen to our partners with rapt attention, we also are doing some work for ourselves. That is to say, when writers get together, they are often inspired and reminded of their own stories by listening to what others say. Let's always listen in a way that helps our partners but also uncovers our own stories as well."

---

matter to someone? If you can give your children just one thing right now, it must be this: your unconditional faith that each one has a story to tell, a lesson to teach, and your rapt attention to what it is that your children know.

Because the one-to-one conference is at the heart of teaching writing and because listening is at the heart of those conferences, you may want to begin now to protect some time during the hurry of your workshop to really, truly listen. To do this, start by noticing ways even your body language can convey that you are listening. Sit alongside the writer, eye-level, and insist that the writer literally maintain control of the paper. The writer, not the teacher, holds the text. This is easier said than done.

It helps to listen first to where the student is in his or her writing process, to how the student is feeling about an entry, to what help the student feels he or she needs. I am apt to begin a conference with research, setting the writer up to tell me about his or her work. I might, for example, start a conference by saying, "I want to help you with your writing. Can you give me a tour of your writer's notebook and fill me in on what you have been trying to do as a writer, on how it's going, and on the sorts of help you are needing?" Listening to each writer's intentions and self-assessments and plans will be important. Charlotte Danielson reminds us that we can collect data that helps us reflect on our own teaching. You might then note how much of the talking you do, and how much the child does in a conference. Aim to be the kind of listener who leads the youngster to elaborate, to say more. To grasp the importance of this, imagine your principal coming to observe your teaching, and think about the preconversations you hope will occur. You probably hope that before the observation, your principal will ask, 'What have you been trying to do in your teaching? What have the hard parts been? What do you want help with?" You probably hope your principal listens with such attentiveness that you find yourself saying more, thinking more, than you'd expected.

As this unit and this year unfold, I'll help you begin your conferences by researching what the writer has already been doing and what he or she is trying to do. You'll learn to tailor your teaching in response to what you learn. But this week, as you try to recruit your children to love writing and to feel safe enough to put their stories onto the page, I want to stress the importance of simply listening. Listen deeply and responsively to the stories your children tell, and to their reports on their writing goals and plans.

FIG. 3–2   One student starred her favorite true story ideas.

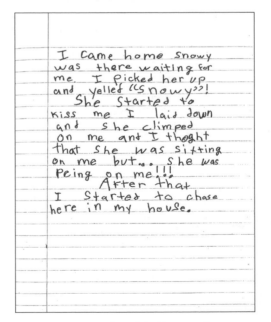

FIG. 3–3   This student filled his Small Moment story with details.

Supporting Problem Solving

Brainstorm problems and organize clusters of kids to meet in corners of the carpet to problem solve those writing problems.

"Writers, can I have your eyes and your attention?" I said, waiting an extra-long time and sweeping the room with my eyes to convene children. "Writers, I need us to gather now in the meeting area because we need to have a serious conversation." Once children had gathered, I said, "Lately you've been restless and distracted. I'm wondering if I could ask you to shift from being writers, for a minute, to being writing teachers. I think that underneath your restlessness, there are a bunch of problems—challenges—that many of you are running into in your writing. I have been trying to rush from one of you to another, helping you solve those problems, but I don't always know how to solve them. I am wondering if maybe you would be willing to try coming to some solutions. Let me list for you a few of the problems that I've been seeing and then see if some of you would be willing to think about how to solve each of those problems."

I revealed this list:

The Hard Parts of Writing!

☺ Sometimes we get tired, like we run out of steam, and we just want to quit writing.

☺ Sometimes we can't think of much to say, so we just sit there.

☺ Sometimes we are writing an entry and it turns out to be awful, and we know if we keep writing, it just gets worse and worse.

☺ Sometimes our writing feels boring.

FIG. 3–4 "The Hard Parts of Writing" chart is based on teacher observations of students during writing workshops.

At the start of the year, you need to induct children into the norms and mores of a writing community. Unless your children are accustomed to a writing workshop, you'll find they want to do a bit of writing, then stop for the day. You need to explicitly teach them to keep going. It is crucial for them to learn that when they finish one entry, they start the next one, which removes any incentive to finish entries quickly by writing in a cursory fashion. When you push for volume, you push for making the workshop a place for productive work, and this helps with classroom management.

Pointing to each of these problems, I asked, "How many of you feel like your main problem is that you kind of run out of gas halfway through writing time? How many of you think your main problem is that you can't think of more stuff to say in a story?" And so forth.

"How about if we form problem-solving think tanks?" I divided the carpet into quarters and convened a small group in each quarter. I assigned facilitators and distributed clipboards to each group so they could record their solutions. The children talked, problem solving, and I charted what I heard. "You have chart paper and markers in front of you, and you'll have just five quick minutes to come up with some suggestions, which we'll then share with each other."

Reconvene the children, sharing a chart you made of solutions one group generated and suggesting similar charts be made showing other groups' ideas.

"Let's meet as a group," I said. "While you were talking, I listened in, and these are solutions I heard to the first problem, the fact that you sometimes run out of gas. Later today, I'll help a member of each of the other groups make a similar solution chart."

When I Run Out of Gas as a Writer, I Can . . .

- Draw a quick sketch to help get my mind going.
- Reread good writing that others have written to warm myself up.
- Set a goal for myself, like writing to the end of the page without stopping.
- Look at the charts in the room and see if they give me an idea.

Name the bigger principle: Children can be problem solvers, not relying on the teacher to help at every turn.

"Writers, the bigger lesson I hope you learn is that you can solve your own problems. Like let's say your pencil broke, and you feel totally stuck. What could you do?"

Children chimed in: "Sharpen it!" "Get another!" "Get a pen!"

"And what if you want my help and I am busy? What could you do?"

Again, children chimed in some answers. I nodded. "And the bigger point is—this is *your* writing workshop. When you run into problems, you can solve them."

We continued this work for the other "Hard Parts of Writing" categories, adding to our chart.

When I Run Out of Gas as a Writer,
I can . . .
☺ Draw a quick sketch to help get my mind going.
☺ Reread good writing that others have written to warm myself up.
☺ Set a goal for myself, like writing to the end of the page without stopping.
☺ Look at the charts in the room and see if they give me an idea.

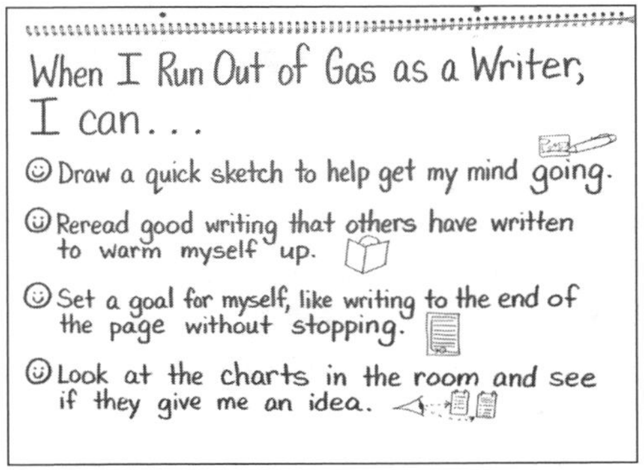

FIG. 3–5   The suggestions generated by one of the focus groups

Be sure that children date each day's writing, and that one entry follows the next, gradually filling the notebook. If they jump hither and yon, you'll have a hard time keeping track of their progress and their volume. (Perhaps they are onto this and this explains their propensity to jump around!)

"If . . . Then . . ."

This page will help you diagnose and address underlying problems of your writing workshop. Based on your assessment of how things are going, use this chart to help differentiate your instruction or make revisions to your unit as needed.

If . . .	Then . . .
IF your room is too noisy during writing workshop . . .	THEN try to get at the root of the problem. The noise is probably a symptom of another issue.
IF your students need more strategies for coming up with ideas to write about . . .	THEN perhaps being given five minutes for everyone to talk to someone, coming up with story ideas together, would channel the need to talk into the accepted time, while also helping kids get past resistance to writing.
IF the noise comes after twenty minutes of writing time, and the issue is that your children don't have stamina as writers yet or the expectation that they'll produce much . . .	THEN perhaps for a while your students need a shorter writing workshop until you can build their stamina gradually, or perhaps instituting a regular ritual of a turn-and-talk partner share, maybe embedded into the mid-workshop teaching, would give kids a chance to refuel.
IF the congestion seems to revolve around a small number of students, and you decide the issue is that those students aren't clear about how to get themselves started working with independence . . .	THEN you might regularly ask a cluster of children to stay behind at the end of the minilesson so you can help those youngsters get themselves started on their work before you release them from the meeting area. With these children, resist the temptation to deliver each child his or her own personalized pep talk and instead help the group of children think of a strategy or two for getting started, and then voice over to the group while they do that.
IF the writing workshop has just started, and within a few minutes it is like popcorn with children springing up to say, 'I'm done!' . . .	THEN teach students that during the writing workshop, there is no such thing as finishing early and then doing something else—drawing, reading, or just waiting. When a writer finishes one entry or one draft, he or she starts the next. Of course, it is also possible for a writer to shift from writing to revising, but it is easier for students to write several underdeveloped stories than to write one good one, and for now, the important thing is for children to work productively, putting their lives onto paper.
IF you notice your students growing careless with their writer's notebooks . . .	THEN you might spend a minilesson or a share session teaching your students how you expect them to take care of their writer's notebooks. "Writers, yesterday at lunch time I was reading through your writer's notebooks. I can't think of a better way to spend my lunch hour than reading your stories. But you know what? Some of them are beginning to look messy. There were pages with missing dates, some pages were skipped, some notebooks even had pages that were ripped out or crumpled up! I was so surprised, because a writer's notebook is this amazing tool for writers. So today, I want to teach you that we treat a writer's notebook like we treat a book from the library."

If . . .	Then . . .
IF your students are having trouble thinking of stories from their lives . . .	THEN you may decide to weave storytelling into your days so that each child is simply bursting with stories. Perhaps you'll want to begin or end each school day (at least for a while) by suggesting children story-tell to a partner. You might start storytelling time by simply letting the children know that you are dying to hear their stories. "Let's tell stories from times in our lives that for some reason are very clear in our memories," you could say, and then choose your own story to tell.
IF you find that a cluster of children writes incredibly slowly, producing only half a page or so in a day . . .	THEN gather these youngsters together and tell them you're going to help them double the amount of writing they can do in a day. First, these writers need to be clear about what they intend to write. Make sure each child has a story to tell and is proceeding chronologically through that story. Don't worry about the quality of writing just now. To focus on fluency and speed, these children need permission to lower their standards (temporarily). Now help children dictate a full sentence to themselves and write that whole sentence without pausing. These children are apt to pause at the ends of words or phrases. That won't do! Then help children dictate the next sentence to themselves and write it quickly, too, without rereading in the midst of writing.

Writers Use a Storyteller's Voice. They Tell Stories, Not Summaries.

IN THIS SESSION, you'll teach students that one way writers draw readers in is by telling their stories in scenes rather than summaries.

GETTING READY

✔ Students' writer's notebooks and pens or pencils, to be brought to the meeting area

✔ A shared class story written two ways, as a story and as report writing (see Connection). Display the examples on a document camera or on chart paper.

✔ Mentor text: *Come On, Rain!* (1999) by Karen Hesse or another much-loved mentor text. Mark places where the author uses descriptive details, dialogue, and actions.

✔ Your story from Session 2, to demonstrate writing in a reporter's voice instead of a storytelling voice (see Teaching)

✔ A shared class event to have students practice storytelling (see Active Engagement)

✔ "To Write a True Story" chart, (see Teaching and Active Engagement)

✔ Introduce formal partnerships. Write two names on each piece of paper, giving them a number 1 and 2, then spread the papers out in the meeting area prior to the share.

✔ "What Third-Grade Notebook Writers . . ." chart (see Share)

COMMON CORE STATE STANDARDS: W.3.3.a,b,c; W.3.4, W.3.8, W.3.5, W.4.9.a, W.4.3.d, RL.3.5, RL.3.2, RL.3.1, RFS.3.4, RL.4.2, SL.3.1, L.3.3.a,b; L3.6, L.3.1, L.4.3.a

O NE OF THE MOST IMPORTANT QUALITIES of good writing is something that people refer to as "voice." Donald Graves suggests that voice involves the imprint of the author, the sense that a real person is behind the words.

Ironically, this is the hardest quality to teach. Our strongest writers already have it; we can almost hear them talking off the page. But even children who dazzle us with a vibrant and rich *oral* expression can produce depressingly faceless, voiceless prose. Their stories are the dull summaries that writing teachers have come to dread: "My dad took me to the mall. It was fun. We ate popcorn. I got a new game for my DS. On the way back, we stopped to get gas for the car. We were so hungry. My dad let me place a pizza order myself." If you're nodding wearily from having read tons of such "stories" in your career, know that you're not alone.

For kindergartners and first-graders, an account such as that would have been an accomplishment. The goal then was for the children to narrate, bit by chronological bit, an event that transpired across a time frame. But third-grade writers need to graduate beyond this level of writing! They need to do more than recount a sequence of events. To reach the levels outlined by the Common Core State Standards, third-graders need to introduce a narrator, use dialogue to develop events and characters' responses to those events, and add detailed descriptions of the action (CCSS 2010, 20). Over the coming weeks, you'll teach each of the skills highlighted in the Common Core State Standards.

In the upcoming session, however, you'll clear the way for that teaching by letting children know that a mere account of an event is not enough. You'll teach children to *recognize bland, faceless narrative writing,* explaining that the art of storytelling *isn't* this. Your aim is for writers to wince at their own first drafts of such writing. Your aim is to inspire and cajole the dramatic storyteller within your children to make an appearance on paper. Once your children can make the crucial distinction between summarizing and reporting versus actual storytelling, *they'll* be the ones seeing a need for the sensory detail and dialogue, images and significance that you'll soon teach. And that so-hard-to-teach ethereal feature of good writing—voice—will follow. Voice will bubble forth into their pieces, once children see themselves as tellers of stories rather than writers of bland diary entries.

It is no small accomplishment for you to help children grasp the idea of "voice," this vital difference between a report and a story. It is no less than putting a writer's voice within the grasp of his or her pen.

It helps to keep in mind what the journalist Roy Peter Clark once declared: "The purpose of a story is not to convey information, but to convey experience. A report tells me how many gallons of oil are polluting the Gulf. A story transports me to a boat where old fishermen are working to save the shoreline. Whatever media platform you work from, you are not creating a story unless you are helping the reader or viewer or listener feel what it is like to be 'there.'" It is no small accomplishment for you to help children grasp this vital difference between a report and a story. It is no less than putting a writer's *voice* within the grasp of his or her *pen*.

SESSION 4: WRITERS USE A STORYTELLER'S VOICE. THEY TELL STORIES, NOT SUMMARIES.

35

Writers Use a Storyteller's Voice. They Tell Stories, Not Summaries

CONNECTION

Celebrate that your children are telling true stories from their lives. Point out that sometimes the voice they use to tell their stories is that of a storyteller, while other times it is the voice of a news reporter.

"Writers, can I have your eyes and your attention? I can see that you're filling pages of your notebooks with entries, picking small stories about people and places in your lives to write about, doing the work that real writers do. I want to congratulate you.

"You know, when I read some of your writing, I'm not just looking at the words on the page. I'm actually hearing your voices. It's like you're putting your own special voice on the paper—a special writerly voice that is as much yours as your own fingerprints or your own signature. When I read your writing, it's like I hear you talk.

"Here's the really interesting thing. A writer can have different voices. Sometimes, when I read the writing you guys do—or any other kind of writing by authors outside this room—I hear a storyteller's voice. A storyteller's voice pulls me into the story, so I actually forget where I am and start imagining that I am in that story!

"But at other times, I hear a news reporter's voice—like the writer isn't trying to pull me into a story, but is just telling me information on something that happened. The two sound so different! Let's see if you can pick out the difference. I'm going to read two different pieces aloud. Both voices belong to authors who are writing about the same day we all experienced. But one of these sounds kind of like a news reporter, while the other sounds like a real storyteller. Listen carefully to figure out which is which.

"Here's Voice A."

Yesterday we couldn't go outside so we stayed inside and listened to a read aloud instead. But we didn't hear much and were distracted with dragonflies flying around the room. We continued to listen to the read aloud.

◆ COACHING

Notice that I've not only reminded writers of the previous teaching points, I've also tried to consolidate the strategies I've taught to make them easier to remember. We hope our teaching gives students ready access to a handful of tools.

It is typical that a unit of study will begin with the teacher equipping children with a small repertoire of strategies for generating that particular kind of writing. The strategies will be a bit different depending on the genre or structure of writing under consideration, and embedded in the strategies will be some information about the genre or structure. I think it is important to limit the number of days you spend introducing strategies so that by the third or fourth day of a unit, you encourage children to draw from their repertoire of strategies, self-selecting one, while you shine a spotlight on raising the quality of their writing.

"Now listen to Voice B."

> "Listen up," our teacher said, as she opened <u>Because of Winn Dixie</u> and began to read. We were so quiet we could probably have heard ants crawling along the floor. Then our teacher lowered the book. We were about to say, "No! Read it!" But she was looking at a blur of wings that flew between us. What was that? Sam called, "Dragonflies!" And soon enough, we saw them. Now three dragonflies hovered over our heads.

"Turn to your partner and decide which voice felt more like a storyteller's voice," I said, displaying the chart of Versions A and B so children could contrast them.

"Writers, I hear many of you agreeing that the piece beginning '"Listen up," our teacher said…' sounds more like a storytelling voice. Now tell your partner what makes the storyteller's voice different from the one that sounds more like a news report.

"Writers, I heard so many smart things! One of you said the storyteller let you feel what it was actually like to be *there*, to be sitting in the classroom with that blur of wings going by you. Absolutely! One of you said the storyteller gave details of how it all happened, details, which helped you hear and see everything clearly. True!

"Here's the thing. Each one of you can talk and write in these two very different voices—your storyteller voice and your reporter voice. Writers choose which of these voices they are going to write in. If they're writing a report for the school newspaper, for example, they won't use a storytelling voice. But if they're writing a true story, a personal narrative—the kind of writing we're doing these days—they'll make *sure* to use a storytelling voice, so their reader can experience what actually happened."

❖ **Name the teaching point.**

"Today I want to teach you that to make your storytelling voices stronger, you try to make a mental movie of what happened and tell it in small detail, bit by bit, so that your reader can almost see, hear, and feel everything."

TEACHING

Highlight the way a published author has done this work.

"Let's look at how Karen Hesse has done this. She is one of the world's most famous storytellers. Hundreds of thousands of people have read *Come On, Rain!*, which is, in a way, a story about a very ordinary small moment in one girl's life. Let's listen really, really closely to see if Hesse has written in a way that lets us make a movie in our minds. Maybe we can figure out what Hesse did that we could try as well. I showed the picture of Tessie looking up, hand raised, standing straight and tall."

> *"Come on, rain!" I say, squinting into the endless heat.*
>
> *Mamma lifts a listless vine and sighs.*
>
> *"Three weeks and not a drop," she says, sagging over her parched plants.*

SESSION 4: WRITERS USE A STORYTELLER'S VOICE. THEY TELL STORIES, NOT SUMMARIES.

37

When I am trying to help students understand a concept, I often use comparisons. I'm hoping to accentuate the difference between storytelling and reporting or chronicling.

FIG. 4–1   Today's teaching point, added to the chart

"Can you picture what's going on? I can. So I'm wondering what Karen Hesse did that helps us almost *be* Tessie as we read the story." I reread it. "Hmm . . . "I'm thinking that Karen Hesse didn't start by talking *about* the story, did she? She didn't write:

> One day it was really hot. There was no rain. Plants were dying. I stood outside and felt hot.

"She didn't just give us information about what was happening, did she? Instead, Hesse seems to have gone back in her mind to that time and thought, 'What exactly was happening?' She probably asked, 'What did Tessie do or say first?' In the movie in her mind, she probably saw Tessie squinting, looking up, putting her hand across her eyes to shelter them from the sun." I cupped my own eyes, as if sheltering them from the blinding rays. "Then she wrote the *exact* actions that the people in the story did and the *exact* words they said."

> Uneasy, Mamma looks over to me.
>
> "Is that thunder, Tessie?" she asks.
>
> I climb up the steps for a better look.
>
> "It's just a truck, Mamma," I say.

As I model, I think aloud in a way that unpacks this strategy for students. I mull over Hesse's writing, imagining the questions she might have asked herself as she brought this scene to life: "What exactly was happening? What did Tessie do or say first?" These are questions I hope the children will ask as they write, too.

Set children up to research how you rehearse a story to write it in a bit-by-bit way. Deliberately model making a mistake while doing this and then fixing it.

"In my writing, I want readers to be able to see and hear what happens just the way Karen Hesse lets her readers see and hear what happened. Be researchers and watch the way I go about writing my story. Later you can try writing an entry in this same way.

"Let me think back to my story and remember how it started. I know I could start with any one of the different times. Hmm, I think I'll begin when I'm still on the playground, before I race off to the candy store." I paused to recall the picture in my mind. "What did I do or see or hear first?

"Okay, I see myself. I'm standing in the middle of the playground, with the kids all standing in front of me." I spread my arms wide to show all of the kids standing there. "Now, I'm going to make a movie in my mind of what happened first, then next, and next.

I am deliberately making some of the same mistakes students are apt to make their first time through, showing them how to catch themselves. In this instance, I first summarize and then rewind, retry, and, this time, storytell.

"So let's see," I said, trying to focus my mind on that experience. Then I started dictating the story into the air. "I explained that I was going to the store, and the kids gave me money, and then I went.

"No." I shook my head and sat up straighter. "Wait. I didn't *show* myself taking the kids' candy orders and checking for teachers before sneaking off to the store. You can't see it happening or hear it. Let me try it again. I'll play it like a movie in my mind and story-tell it step by step, bit by bit so you can see and hear what happened."

Starting again, I dictated into the air, "All of the kids were crowded around me. Some of them started pushing money into my hands. Phil told me he wanted Mars Bars, as many as I could get. Amy Jo told me she wanted some red licorice. I was so scared. I knew I would be in big trouble if I got caught. I stuffed the money into my pocket really quickly. I looked around me to see if any teachers were watching. When it seemed like the coast was clear, I headed off in the direction of Gates' Deli."

Debrief by reminding writers to make a movie in their minds, showing, not telling.

"Writers, do you see the way I'm recalling what happened like it is a movie in my mind, and then I am storytelling it, using small actions and small details? I'm not just *telling* what happened. I'm *showing* it. I bet you can picture me standing there, collecting all of the money while my classmates shouted candy orders. I can picture it, so usually that means readers can too. I have started a chart to help us remember some of these storytelling moves we are learning from Karen Hesse." I revealed a chart that captured a few pointers.

> ### To Write a True Story
>
> - Find story ideas that are focused and important to you and write lots of entries.
> - Make a mental movie of what happened, telling it in small detail, bit by bit.

ACTIVE ENGAGEMENT

Set children up to practice what you've demonstrated, using a whole-class topic.

"So let's try it together. Remember yesterday when we had a fire drill? We *could* just tell what happened saying, 'We had a hard time at the fire drill. The first-graders slowed us down. Also, it rained and we had to stand far from the building.' But we are writing stories that will draw our readers in and let them see what happened in a bit-by-bit way. To tell the story of the fire drill, we need to recall what happened first. Scroll back in your minds and think, 'What happened first?' Start playing the memory in your mind like a movie and see what happened next, then next. Thumbs up if you can see what happened in a bit-by-bit way." I waited until I saw enough thumbs to indicate that this was the case. "Okay, let's try storytelling using dialogue and describing sounds. I'll start you off, and then you can try storytelling the rest with a neighbor.

"Time for math," our teacher started to say. "Put your papers away."

"Do you have the movie playing in your minds?"

At that second I heard . . .

"Writers, keep going. What did you hear? Story-tell to your neighbor what happened then, step by step. Story-tell the movie you see in your mind. If you want, story-tell it across your fingers."

SESSION 4: WRITERS USE A STORYTELLER'S VOICE. THEY TELL STORIES, NOT SUMMARIES.

39

Debrief. Highlight what students just did that you hope they will use another time with another text.

"Writers, can I have your eyes and your attention? I was able to see the fire drill happening as I listened because you didn't just say, 'Yesterday we had a fire drill. The bell rang before math and we all left the room and we got in trouble because we followed the first-graders down the stairs and they were so slow they made us late.' No.

"Robbie story-told the memory with his partner. Listen to how his story started; Robbie said,

> I heard the fire alarm go "Wooooooo." Everyone stopped putting papers away and looked around. I counted each dong: one, two, three. Then the alarm began again even louder: "Wooooooo" making me jump up. I headed toward the door because I was the line leader. We hurried down the stairs. . . .

"Did you see how Robbie took a tiny event that happened to him (to all of us) and how he thought about that time as a movie? He thought, 'What happened first? Did I hear something? Did I feel something? Were there actions?' He made the movie in his mind, and he told the story, step by step. He did just what Karen Hesse did. He drew us into his story and let us live in it. I could hear the alarm and feel the urgency he was describing. Let's add those to our storytelling chart."

> - Make a mental movie of what happened, telling it in small detail, bit by bit.
>   - Detail the actions.
>   - Include the dialogue.

LINK

Tell the children that you expect all of them to write their stories in a storyteller's voice from now on.

"From now on, whenever you are writing a story, don't just 'talk all about' what happened; instead say exactly what happened first, then next, and next, adding descriptive details and dialogue. Use your storytelling voices just like Robbie and Karen Hesse did in a step-by-step, bit-by-bit fashion. This strategy will help you anytime you want to write stories. Let's start today by rereading our stories from yesterday and making sure we have shown what is happening in step-by-step detail to our readers. You are sure to find lots of places where a story might start out as storytelling and then—whoops!—it shifts to summarizing, to reporting. It would be so cool if some of you could begin to spot those places!

"Then you could take the part of the story that is summarizing, not storytelling, and you could tape a flap of paper over that section and rewrite it, this time making a movie of the event and writing it in a way that others can imagine what you said, and then did, and then what the other person said. Some of you won't be rewriting old entries but will instead start new ones—and they'll be so, so much better than your earlier ones."

A Storyteller's Voice Shows, Not Tells. It. . .

. . . describes actions that took place.

. . . uses dialogue.

. . . describes what we saw, smelled, tasted, or felt.

. . . describes images around the storyteller.

FIG. 4–2   After listening to children's fire drill stories, you could make this chart.

Remember, your primary goal for this first unit is for kids to be engaged with writing for an increasing length of time, to adopt the role of storyteller, and for kids to work with some independence. If a child initially writes all about a vacation and then checks herself, zooming in to write all about one brimful day, note to yourself that the child will need further coaching. But for now, celebrate that the child independently drew on a concept she'd learned. Each month you will have more time to strengthen the lessons on good writing you have taught in your minilessons.

Using Table Compliments to Keep Writers on a Good Trajectory

As YOU SEND CHILDREN OFF TO WORK and begin to survey the room, you may start to feel concerned about how to balance supporting the work of the minilesson with the many other needs of the individual writers. While some writers may benefit from working to story-tell, not summarize, other writers will need help coming up with something—anything—to write about, and still others will need help choosing more focused moments or writing within a narrative rather than an all-about frame. In general, plan that approximately half of your conferences will support the minilesson and the other half will aim to keep everything else going.

To help maintain this balancing act, you can do some strategic, quick table compliments in which you aim to remind writers to draw on previous teaching. Although most conferences include the components of research, compliments, and teaching, in a table compliment you isolate just the compliment section of a conference. For example, imagine that at one table, you spot a child who seems to have begun by writing about his trip to the Dominican Republic, then realized the topic was too large and shifted to writing about when he first saw his dad. You might say to the table full of writers, "Writers, all eyes up here." Be sure to wait until you do actually have the attention of every writer at the table, and then speak with great energy and enthusiasm. "I need to tell you about the totally powerful thing that Ray just did. He started out writing about this great big huge topic—his *whole trip* to the DR—and then he thought, 'Wait, wait. That's too big a topic. That's not a small moment!' And *now look* what Ray is writing!" And, of course, you read the new, more focused lead. This kind of teaching is called a *table compliment* because the goal is to lift the level of work for all writers at the table, so you will need to shift from extolling what one child has done to rallying others at the table to follow suit. "I'm wondering if some of the rest of you might want to try Ray's technique of pausing after you write just a little to ask, 'Is this a big huge topic or a small moment?' And maybe some of you, like Ray, will end up realizing that your topic is a huge one and get started revising your writing. Ray crossed out his first lead all on his own and then zoomed in on something smaller, which is a totally professional thing to do." That instruction will be enough to give writers who didn't have much direction a wonderful sense of possibility, so you could leave the table at that point, promising

MID-WORKSHOP TEACHING **Writing Stories Bit by Bit**

"Writers, can I have your eyes and your attention?" I paused until the room grew absolutely silent. "I want to teach you a smart thing Brooke did. One of Brooke's resolutions for herself was to write Small Moment stories, not whole-day stories. She began writing an entry that went like this." (See Figure 4–3.)

My family and friend

Jamie is one of my best friends! I knew her for almost all my life.

My mom is thirty years old, and has brownish gold hair. And works.

"Then she paused and said to herself, 'Wait a minute! I'm writing 'all about' people (my mom and my friend). I'm not even writing a story!' So she stopped right smack in the middle of writing her entry and wrote a list of small moments that she and her mom have together that went like this."

Kissing me good bye before school
Putting green ribbons in my hair

> My Family and Frend
>
> Jamie is one of my Bestl frends. I new her for almost all my live.
> My mom is thirty years old, and has brownish gold hair. and works

FIG. 4–3 Brooke's initial unfocused entry

(continues)

SESSION 4: WRITERS USE A STORYTELLER'S VOICE. THEY TELL STORIES, NOT SUMMARIES.

41

"Brooke picked the good-bye moment. She tried to remember it—not the whole before-school time, but just the things that happened right before and after her mom kissed her good-bye. This time, she made a movie in her mind of exactly what happened and wrote what she remembered. Listen." (See Figure 4–4.)

"So remember, if your writing feels like it's about a lot of things, you can stop, start again like Brooke did, and zoom in on one small moment and then write that moment bit by bit! Okay, back to writing!"

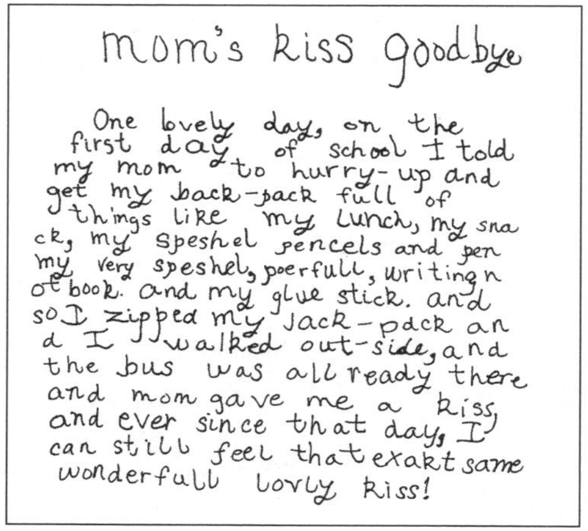

mom's kiss goodbye

One lovely day, on the first day of school I told my mom to hurry-up and get my back-pack full of things like my lunch, my snack, my speshel pencels and pen my very speshel, poerfull, writing notebook. and my glue stick. and so I zipped my jack-pack and I walked out-side, and the bus was all ready there and mom gave me a kiss, and ever since that day, I can still feel that exakt same wonderfull lovly kiss!

FIG. 4–4   Brooke's later, more focused entry

to return soon. "I'm going to check in on some other kids, and then I'll be back, and it would be so great if someone else at this table had tried Ray's technique."

Then travel to another table to observe from afar for a moment, looking for something to compliment that would help all children at the table. Say you notice a child taking a quick sideways glance toward the storyteller's voice chart you created during the minilesson. Stop the table immediately and say, "Writers, can I stop you for a moment? I have to tell you something I just noticed Takeshi doing that is such a smart strategy. His pen hovered over his notebook and then . . . he paused! He looked at the chart over there, the one that gives tips for writing a true story. He took a moment to read it over, and then when he turned back to his notebook, I bet he remembered to story-tell, not report. You can also look up at one of our charts just before you write. Right now, find one writing chart that might be helpful for your writing and reread it before you resume writing."

Instead of going straight to the children who are not on task, look for and pockets of possibility. Table compliments are a great way to name positive behaviors, and remind children of ways they can help themselves. By naming what children are doing, you confirm their sense of agency and reinforce their self-reliance.

Planning for Effective Writing Partnerships and Sharing Goals

Establish the seating arrangements and systems that underlie partnership conversations.

Once children had found their seats and their partners, I continued. "Writers, can I have your eyes and your attention? (I love the way most of you stopped what you were doing as soon as you heard me say that! Thank you.) Let's gather in the meeting area because I need to talk with you today.

"When you go to the meeting area, you'll see a paper that has two names on it—your name and another child's name—and a number, 1 or 2, next to each name. Sit where I've put the paper containing your name and your number. You and your partner will sit beside each other, facing me, each holding two corners of the paper.

"Writers, these papers are really important because they signify that the two people whose names are listed will work together as writing partners for our first unit of study. As you know if you had a writing partner last year, you won't write the same stories, but you'll sit alongside each other in this designated place every time we gather, and you'll help each other write really great stories. The numbers 1 and 2 help me let you know who will share first. If you are Partner 1, give me a thumbs up. If you are Partner 2, give me a thumbs up. Terrific."

Set children up so they name some qualities of effective writing partners and then plan with their partner how they can assume this role for each other.

"As partners, you'll help each other work toward your writing goals. In my life, I've had a few people who have helped me as a writer tremendously. Would you each think of a person who has helped you in your writing life? Maybe it was one of your writing partners from second grade or maybe someone from home. Partner 2, tell Partner 1 what that person did that helped you."

After the children talked for a while, I added, "Now would you and your partner make some plans for how you can be good writing partners for each other? Think about how previous partners have helped you or what you have done to help another writer. Again, talk together about how you two can be really helpful to each other." The partners talked together for a few more minutes, making plans.

"Writers, we started our year by studying what third-grade notebook writers do and don't do in their writer's notebooks. We studied and charted what makes a productive and useful writer's notebook. We also made resolutions for what we

You may wonder when to call an end to workshop time. Frankly, at the beginning of the year, one important factor to consider is the children's ability to keep working. Although eventually you'll want the actual workshop section of your workshop to last at least forty minutes, at the beginning of the year children's stamina for writing may not be strong enough for them to persevere this long. When the students get restless, end the writing portion of your workshop by asking them to put their work in its storage place. (You'll probably have a box to hold notebooks for each table.) Then convene writers for a longer-than-usual share session.

What Third-Grade Notebook Writers…

Do: 📓
~ Fill their notebooks with true stories that tell what the writer did first, next, after
~ Put the date on each page
~ Have the people in the stories talk
~ Write lots of sentences
~ Tell if writing in home/school
~ Write about one page each day
~ Use lots of punctuation

Don't: 🚫
× Just write one kind of story
× Doodle or draw pictures (much)
× Skip pages or jump all over
× Write too messy
× Erase too much
× Trash the notebook

FIG. 4–5

SESSION 4: WRITERS USE A STORYTELLER'S VOICE. THEY TELL STORIES, NOT SUMMARIES.

43

wanted to accomplish as writers this year. Here is the chart we created together." I pulled out the chart from Session 1 and hung it up on the easel.

Ask writers to show their partner ways they are growing as writers and how they are working toward their goals.

"Writing partners share their writing goals and plans. Then they listen very carefully to each other's goals and they promise to do everything in their power to help their partner reach his or her goals. Right now, will you share some of the resolutions you made for yourself and talk about what you've already done to meet those resolutions.

"Partner 1, would you start? You're going to take your partner on a little tour of your notebook. Start by showing your partner some of your writing resolutions from the very first day. Then show him or her specific parts where you were working toward one of your resolutions. Show the part and then name what you did to make your writing better."

As partners talked, I prompted them to show specific parts from their notebooks and to name what they had done. After a few minutes, I voiced over, "Partner 2, would you now show Partner 1 that he or she has your support? Repeat back your partner's goals to him or her, and say a little bit about how you will help support those goals. You might say something like, 'I will check in with you every few days to see if you are writing a whole page every day,' or 'I will help you remember to use lots of punctuation.'"

After a few moments, I prompted Partner 2s to share their resolutions and their work with Partner 1s. After they had finished, I convened the class and said, "Writers, this is a big day for us. Now, in addition to having a writer's notebook, a set of writing resolutions, and a few strategies for generating narrative writing, you also have a writing partner. Let's vow to help each other in the ways we promised as we continue to work on our stories."

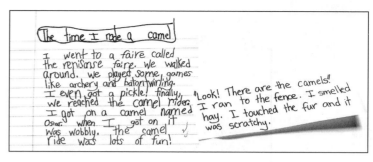

> **The time I rode a camel**
>
> I went to a faire called the renisanse faire. We walked around. we played some games like archery and baton twirling. I even got a pickle! finally, we reached the camel rides. I got on a camel named Oscar. when I got on it was wobbly. the camel ride was lots of fun!
>
> "Look! There are the camels!" I ran to the fence. I smelled hay. I touched the fur and it was scratchy.

FIG. 4–6   Emily showed her partner that she'd been working on new things, like using flaps to make her writing have more of a storytelling voice.

Taking Stock

Pausing to Ask, "How Am I Doing?"

A T THIS POINT IN THE UNIT, I strongly urge you to look at your children's writing to see if and how your instruction has influenced it. As you do this, you are, of course, learning as much about your own teaching as you are learning about your children's work. Ask yourself:

- "How many of my children have learned to write about small moments, about events that begin and end within a short span of time?"

- "How many of my children write a sequence of events, telling one after another?" If some need more help, you may want to teach time-lining or planning across pages.

- "How many of my children are gesturing toward showing, not telling, writing in ways that re-create the writer's experience of an episode in time? Do these children use direct-address dialogue to show what people said and thought? Which children start pieces this way and then shift into summary-like reporting?"

I encourage you to not only make lists of names for each of these categories, but to also, more urgently, make a pile of notebooks that don't contain much evidence that any of your instruction has made a big dent. The authors of those notebooks need more of your attention.

When you look at the pile of notebooks that represent children who have not learned much yet, you'll want to regard this as evidence that *you* have some hard work to do. Of course, those children have some work to do as well, but something magical happens if you respond to problems (and breakthroughs) in your students' progress by regarding this as a reflection of the effectiveness of your teaching. Try to assume that the problem is not the students' or the basic methods', but the specifics of your teaching. What we have found repeatedly is that if teachers are utterly convinced that it is entirely within students' reach for them to produce amazing work and that the important thing is for us to figure out how to teach with more clarity, power, and responsiveness—or with whatever it will take—the results of that mind-set are transformational.

IN THIS SESSION, you'll teach students that writers sometimes pause to consider what's going well in their writing and what they might try next to take their writing up a level.

GETTING READY

✔ Students' writer's notebooks and pens or pencils, to be brought to the meeting area. Students should sit with their partners.

✔ Prepare a metaphor that rings true for you to illustrate the point that we don't just practice something, we expect to get better at it in the process (see Connection).

✔ Student-facing checklist titled, Narrative Writing Checklist, Grades 3 and 4 (see Teaching) with individual copies for students to use and keep in their writer's notebooks

✔ A student's writing sample to assess against the student-facing checklist

✔ Marker pens, one per student, to be used when self-assessing and goal setting (see Active Engagement)

✔ "To Write a True Story" chart (see Link)

COMMON CORE STATE STANDARDS: W.3.3.a,b,c; W.3.4, W.3.5, RL.3.1, RL.3.3, RL.3.4, SL.3.1, SL.3.6, L.3.1. i, L.3.3.a,b; L.3.6

So we recommend you set out with great resolve, planning to do more to connect with the children who don't seem to be grasping what you are trying to teach. Let these children become your teachers, teaching you how to make a more significant difference in their lives. Study their written work starting with Day One of the year. Observe them during class time. Give each of these children your best attention and gather data that can inform you. Realize that you may need to recruit a colleague to join you in puzzling through the mysteries of these children.

Let the children become your teachers, teaching you how to make a more significant difference in their lives.

As you study these strugglers, consider whether your teaching has perhaps asked them to take a step that was too giant, all at once. If these children seem to you to be struggling because you or they have taken on a challenge that is too demanding for them at this time, then be sure to consider which of your goals really matter right now and which can wait for later. Consider, also, whether there are scaffolds that some second-grade teachers use that you might adapt. For example, could it be that a few of your children would profit from writing in booklets, with each page containing a two-inch square for drawing? Once you establish a workable goal and a plan, be vigilant in watching for signs of progress so that you can help the child see himself or herself as someone who is progressing forward and on an upward trajectory. Success is a pattern, not an episode, and so, too, is failure. You want to restart writers who are mired in a failing trajectory so that this time, they are following a pathway that yields success (even if the success involves fairly small steps forward). Keep in mind that a child may still be doing lots of things that are less than ideal, yet if you see palpable progress toward a goal, this merits a celebration.

Meanwhile, think also about the whole class. The written texts are windows to your students' growth. You've taught stamina; look to see if their notebooks suggest your children have developed more stamina, and if not, then address this. Look at the on-demand pieces they wrote at the start of the unit and at the work they produce during any one day now, and notice whether their writing has become more fluent and developed. In the same way, look at each of the goals you have taught and note whether writers demonstrate that your teaching has had traction. If it hasn't, reteach!

The important thing is for you to pause to look at children's work and for you to see what children *are* doing as grounds for your next steps.

Taking Stock

Pausing to Ask, "How Am I Doing?"

CONNECTION

Explain to children that when people want to get better at something—anything—they check on their progress and set goals for next steps.

"I have a good friend who's a runner. Every day she pulls on her running clothes and her trusty sneakers and hits the road. And she runs. And she runs. And she runs. But here's the thing." I leaned in close to the children, as if I was about to share a big secret. "Every day she expects herself *to get better* at running. Just the other day she was telling me how much better her stride is because she is landing on the pads of her feet. The next thing she wants to work on is her breathing. Sometimes she breathes too fast and gets tired too quickly.

"I'm telling you this because this year we won't just write every day. Every day we will work *to get better* at writing. And to do that we, like my friend who is the runner, need to notice what we are doing that is making our writing better, then think about the next thing to work on, and finally we need to set clear goals for ourselves."

❖ **Name the teaching point.**

"Today I want to teach you that when a person wants to get better at something—at anything—it helps to look back and think, 'How have I grown?' And it helps to look forward and to ask, 'What can I do in the future to get better?' Then we can work hard toward getting better."

TEACHING

Set writers up for the work ahead by reviewing the Narrative Writing Checklist, introducing new third-grade goals.

"People who want to get better at doing something have ways of keeping track of their progress. My friend the runner uses a fancy watch to help her keep track of how her stride is improving and how her time is improving. Your doctor or your parents might keep track of how tall you are by using a measuring stick. Today I'll show you another kind of a tool—one that is made for writers to keep track of ways our writing is getting better.

It's a good sign when your children have enough momentum and direction as writers that they don't rely on the daily minilesson as their source of direction. If children know how to carry on as writers and have a small repertoire of strategies to draw from, then our teaching can focus on the finer points of their work, as this minilesson does. Minilessons aren't designed to set children up for what they'll do on any one day; instead, they are always designed to lift the level of what children are doing in general.

"Remember when we looked at a little checklist a few days ago, one that reminded us of what we learned as second-grade writers? Well, today I'm going to introduce you to a new checklist for third-grade narrative writers. There is a checklist for fourth-grade writers here as well because I bet some of you will want to work toward these goals in a few weeks. For now, look at third grade. These are goals that hundreds of adults have decided *third*-graders should be able to do by the end of the year. So, you won't be doing all of these things just yet. But, you are probably already starting to do some of these things in your entries. And with practice—and goal-setting—I know they are things that all of you will be doing by the end of the year.

"Let's take a look at the list." The Narrative Writing Checklist, Grades 3 and 4 is also available on the CD-ROM.

Establish the reason for today's lesson: writers need the chance to practice using new tools together.

"Writers, today we are not going to have a typical minilesson where I teach you something, you try it, and then you go off to work independently. Instead, I want to give you a feeling for how to use this checklist to assess your writing. So we're going to do some shared assessing of a piece, working together to name what the writer is doing well and what he or she might do next, and then I'll send you off to try some of this work independently."

If you want children to become reflective, resourceful writers, you need to equip them with the tools to do so. "If you don't have a dream, how are you going to have a dream come true?

Teach through guided practice: take children through the process of assessing a piece of writing, channeling them to move between partner and whole-class conversation as they do.

Show children a piece of writing and read through it once, asking them to begin using the checklist to notice the qualities (or lack thereof) of good narrative writing.

"Writers, let's look again at Rebecca's writing, and practice using the checklist to help us name what she did and what she could do next. Let's start with 'Overall.'"

We read "I told the story bit by bit," and I explained that this first item on the checklist was meant to describe the whole piece. Had Rebecca done that? The class agreed that yes, she'd mastered that, and we checked that item off.

"The next item on the checklist says, 'I wrote a beginning in which I helped readers know who the characters were and what the setting was in my story.' Turn and talk. Has she done this?"

Narrative Writing Checklist

	Grade 3	NOT YET	STARTING TO	YES!	Grade 4	NOT YET	STARTING TO	YES!
	Structure				**Structure**			
Overall	I told the story bit by bit.	☐	☐	☐	I wrote the important part of an event bit by bit and took out unimportant parts.	☐	☐	☐
Lead	I wrote a beginning in which I helped readers know who the characters were and what the setting was in my story.	☐	☐	☐	I wrote a beginning in which I showed what was happening and where, getting readers into the world of the story.	☐	☐	☐
Transitions	I told my story in order by using phrases such as *a little later* and *after that*.	☐	☐	☐	I showed how much time went by with words and phrases that mark time such as *just then* and *suddenly* (to show when things happened quickly) or *after a while* and *a little later* (to show when a little time passed).	☐	☐	☐
Ending	I chose the action, talk, or feeling that would make a good ending and worked to write it well.	☐	☐	☐	I wrote an ending that connected to the beginning or the middle of the story. I used action, dialogue, or feeling to bring my story to a close.	☐	☐	☐
Organization	I used paragraphs and skipped lines to separate what happened first from what happened later (and finally) in my story.	☐	☐	☐	I used paragraphs to separate the different parts or times of the story or to show when a new character was speaking.	☐	☐	☐
	Development				**Development**			
Elaboration	I worked to show what happened to (and in) my characters.	☐	☐	☐	I added more to the heart of my story, including not only actions and dialogue but also thought and feelings.	☐	☐	☐

The class agreed that although they knew this was Rebecca's story and she's the narrator, she had not helped readers imagine the setting. Was she in the locker room at the gym? At dance class? They imagined possible leads ("I sat on the bench outside the gym and peered into my bag"). This item was rated "Not Yet." In the same fashion, the class proceeded along the checklist. Whenever the decision was questionable, I encouraged them to hold to high standards, explaining that Rebecca could work on the items that need work.

ACTIVE ENGAGEMENT

This time usher students to assess their own writing, celebrating growth and noting future goals.

"Writers, we've spent some time assessing other people's writing today. As I mentioned earlier, it's sometimes easier to learn to do this kind of work with someone else's writing. But the true purpose of this work is to make *us* better writers, to see the places where we've grown and also to set new goals for ourselves."

Ask children to open their notebooks and look across the work of the past few days, this time assessing their own writing using the checklist.

"Would you all open your notebooks and look back at the last entry you've written—because your writing is getting better day by day, it should be your best. If it's not, choose your best entry (but let's also talk about why your best isn't your last). Then will you read over the first item on the checklist, and if you've begun to do that work, note where. If you've mastered that work, it means you're amazing at it and you do this all the time. If you've mastered a few items, mark that. I'm going to distribute marker pens. If you find something important that you haven't yet mastered, but could, then decide if that will be a goal for you, and if so, that's *huge*. Make stars or fireworks beside that item. That's the reason to do this work, to set goals." As children set to work, I moved among them.

Show children how to self-select a goal or two for future writing.

"As I moved about the meeting area just now, I noticed that many of you were finding great strengths in your writing—things you've been doing as a writer that you may not have even known you were doing! Almost all of you also noticed things you weren't yet doing, and this is exactly what self-assessment is about. When we look at our writing critically, when we *really* look to see what we're doing as writers, we find places for new work. So right now, take a moment to name a whole bunch of goals that you'll set for yourself going forward." Again, I moved about the rug, encouraging children to name and then jot down their new writing goals in their writer's notebooks.

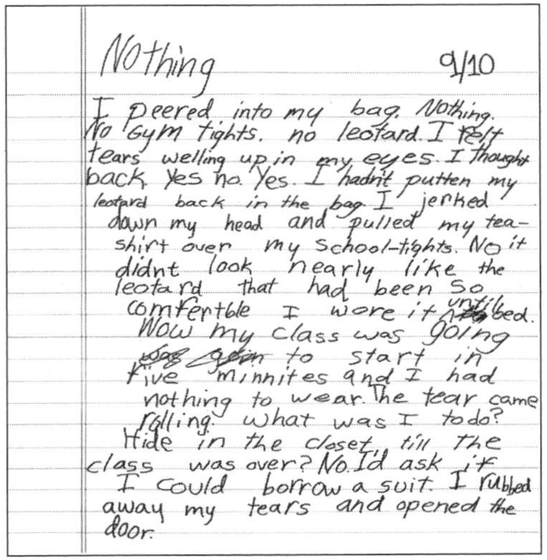

> Nothing   9/10
>
> I peered into my bag. Nothing. No gym tights. no leotard. I felt tears welling up in my eyes. I thought back Yes no Yes. I hadn't putten my leotard back in the bag I jerked down my head and pulled my tea-shirt over my school-tights. No it didnt look nearly like the leotard that had been so comfertble I wore it untibed. Now my class was going to start in five minnites and I had nothing to wear. The tear came rolling. What was I todo? Hide in the closet, till The class was over? No. Id ask if I could borrow a suit. I rubbed away my tears and opened the door.

FIG. 5–1

Do not be disappointed if children do not master the art of self-reflection in one sitting. Instead, try to see today as one step in a much bigger journey—one that will leave children with the ability to note their strengths, recognize their limitations, and set goals to exceed their own best writing. For today, be happy that kids are familiarizing themselves with the checklist and studying their own work against it!

LINK

Close the lesson and remind children that once we set goals we work feverishly to achieve them.

"Writers, we've done a lot today. We've learned to assess and set goals. This is exactly what writers do—and really, all people who want to become better at something. Then after a bit, they look back and ask, 'How have I grown?'" Going forward you are going to want to think about what you can do to meet your goals." I drew the students attention to the newest item on our chart.

To Write a True Story

- Find story ideas that are focused and important to you and write lots of entries.
- Make a mental movie of what happened, telling it in small detail, bit by bit.
  - Detail the actions.
  - Include the dialogue.
- Remember your self-assessments of your narrative writing and your goals.

Studying a Writer's Growth

JOHN HATTIE, A WORLD-RENOWNED RESEARCHER AND PROFESSOR who has dedicated his life's work to studying and compiling research on effective teaching, sets forth a synthesis of his research in *Visible Learning: A Synthesis of Over 800 Meta-Analyses Relating to Achievement* (2008). Hattie emphasizes the importance of direct instruction, independent practice, and feedback, noting that the most powerful teaching comes in the form of crystal-clear feedback: showing students what they are doing that is working and showing them what they can do next to make their writing better. Nothing a teacher can do has a greater effect than this combination: giving students clear goals, opportunities for engaged work, and feedback that includes concrete next steps.

While it is, of course, important for children to set goals for themselves, to learn to be reflective about their own writing and development, Hattie reminds us that it is equally important for us to set goals for each child and to steer them toward the goals we know will yield a big payoff in their writing. Because the next lesson marks the end of collecting entries and the start of developing one entry, this is a good time to look over your children's writing and notice ways they've changed as writers. What seems to be getting better? What hasn't changed? Use the third-grade teaching rubric (and the second and fourth, if helpful) to notice areas of strength as well as areas the writer is well positioned to grow into.

This conferring section includes a small collection of one child's work. Simeon goes to a public school in Harlem, and the work you see comes from his first year—in fact, his first few weeks—in a writing workshop. Try reading this work, looking for his strengths, assessing his growth, and thinking about future instruction for him. (See Figure 5–2.)

(continues)

MID-WORKSHOP TEACHING   **Writers Help Themselves Solve Problems**

"Writers, can I have your eyes and attention?" As always, I waited until all pencils were down and all eyes up. "I am noticing that some of you are slowing down a bit, some are fidgeting, some are talking, and some are even walking around. This reminds me of the other day when we shared a list of problems we were facing as writers, 'The Hard Parts of Writing.'"

I quickly scavenged through the chart tablet on the easel and triumphantly pulled out the list.

"Remember how we got together and came up with lots of great solutions to these writing problems? For example, 'When I Run Out of Gas as a Writer, I Can....'" I dramatically unveiled this chart sweeping across the several strategies the children had come up with.

"Take a minute right now and choose one strategy that might help you keep going as a writer. Turn and tell the person next to you what you are going to do to keep yourself writing for the rest of our writing workshop time."

I listened in as the children turned and talked about how they would keep themselves writing without stopping for the rest of the writing workshop.

"So, writers, anytime you feel yourself slowing down or unsure of what to do next, you can look at this chart and try one of the strategies you and your classmates came up with. You might also come up with new ideas, and when we come back to share, let's add to our 'Hard Parts of Writing' chart."

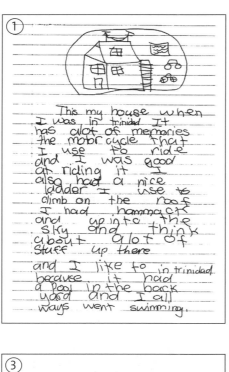

① This my house when I was in trinidad It has alot of memories the motorcycle that I use to ride and I was good at riding it I also had a nice ladder I use to climb on the roof I had hammack and up into the sky and think about alot of stuff up there

and I like to in trinidad because it had a pool in the back yard and I allways went swimming.

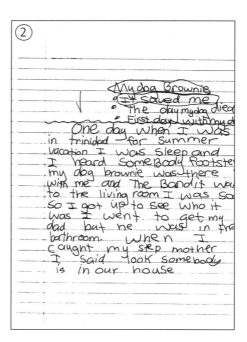

② My dog Brownie
It saved me
The day my dog died
First day with my dog

One day when I was in trinidad for summer vacation I was sleep and I heard somebody footstep my dog brownie was there with me and the Bandit was to the living room I was so So I got up to see who it was I went to get my dad but he was in the bathroom. When I caught my step mother I said look somebody is in our house

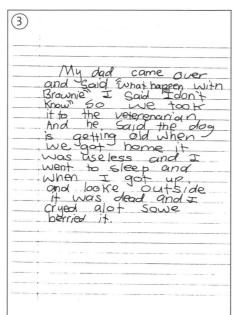

③ My dad came over and said "what happen with Brownie" I said I don't know" so we took it to the veterenarian And he said the dog is getting old when we got home it was useless and I went to sleep and when I got up and looked outside it was dead and I cryed alot sowe berried it.

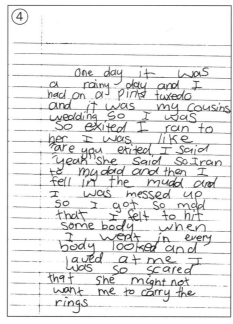

④ One day it was a rainy day and I had on a pink tuxedo and it was my cousins wedding so I was so exited I ran to her I was like are you exited I said "yeah" she said So I ran to my dad and then I fell in the mudd and I was messed up so I got so mad that I felt to hit some body when I went in every body looked and laued at me I was so scared that she might not want me to carry the rings

FIG. 5–2   Simeon's entries provide a glimpse of his strengths, interests, and needs as a writer.

The first thing I notice is that this boy has the soul of a writer. He's a dreamer; I love the image of this child, living among the huge buildings in Harlem, thinking about how he'd climb to the rooftop in Trinidad, lie in a hammock under the stars, looking up into the sky and thinking about a lot of stuff. My heart went out to him when I read in the fourth entry about him wearing a pink tuxedo because he was to be the ring bearer in his cousin's wedding, then falling in the mud and feeling so messed up that, as he put it, "I felt to hit somebody."

Next I notice the dazzling, dramatic growth toward understanding the genre of narrative writing. In the fourth entry, Simeon is writing with setting and dialogue. His story focuses on a dramatic event and is even structured like a traditional story with a problem, rising action, and solution. These are all specific things I can name for Simeon that are working for him and that show progress. After all, success is a pattern, a trajectory.

I see next steps, too. One relates to his staccato, simple sentences. While Simeon does attempt to use connecting words (*and*, *so*) to link the parts of his story together, his syntax suggests he hasn't done a lot of writing. His sentences are composed of a long chain of very simple, short, independent clauses (they could be short sentences linked together).

> <u>So</u> we took it to the veterinarian <u>And</u> he said the dog is getting old When we got home it was useless <u>and</u> I went to sleep <u>and</u> when I got up <u>and</u> looked outside it was dead <u>and</u> I cried a lot <u>so</u> we buried it.

I'm going to encourage him to write in a storytelling voice, telling his stories so that readers can experience them alongside him. I know if I help him make movies in his mind and tell the story with detail, he'll be apt to write more complex sentences. I'll encourage his teacher to share several mentor texts with him in which the writer writes with great detail, including dialogue and action.

Simeon is also ready to tackle conventions. I'll encourage him to write with end punctuation, trusting that readers will read on to the next sentence without the overuse of connectors. I may want to say, "Think one thought, write that thought, and then put a period. Think your next thought, write it out, and then put the next period." Once he is writing sentences that do not run on, he can be taught how to include subordinate clauses. Another possibility is to teach him to use alternative connector words so that instead of relying exclusively on *and* or *so* he begins to also use connectors such as *because* or *while*.

Simeon will profit from thinking about his readers, giving lots of information to them. I might teach him to read, thinking about the questions his readers will have. I want him to anticipate what a reader of his second entry will ask or what he meant by the word *it*. Simeon will probably answer, "That's my dog, Brownie. He died and we had to bury him." That needs to be the entry.

By explicitly teaching Simeon something about sentence complexity and alternative connectors, this crystal-clear feedback will help his writing become more cohesive and elaborate. But meanwhile, if Simeon continues to write and read a lot, if he is encouraged to use end punctuation, to convey feelings, and to include more detail and dialogue, all of this work will lead him toward more mature syntax.

Making Plans for Meeting Goals

Ask writers to reflect on their goals and make a plan for how to live their writing lives differently so that they don't forget these goals.

"Writers, today you've set goals for yourselves. What I know from my life is that it is all too easy to set goals and then forget about them. Like I might decide that one of my goals is to teach my dog, Milo, to stop barking at people who come to our house because he scares them. I *mean* to train him, and I even know how. I know I can get friends to stop by and ring the doorbell, and I can be ready, with Milo on a leash so that if he goes crazy I can rebuke him. But guess what? I forget to do this. Days go by and I forget my goals. Has that ever happened to you?

"Writers, I don't want the same thing to happen with your writing goals. So I was thinking that it would be good to make plans for how you can live differently so you don't forget your goals. For example, if your goal is to write more, or to punctuate or paragraph, or to write with details— or all of those things—you could write those goals on the top of each page of your writers notebook, as a reminder. You could decide to start each day's writing time by scoring yesterday's writing, based on your goals. You could ask your partner to remind you of your goals. You could make little signs for your desk that remind you. Right now, will you think to yourself of your goals, and your plans for meeting these goals?"

After a minute of silence, I asked them to turn and talk about their plans.

FIG. 5–3

Editing as We Go
Making Sure Others Can Read Our Writing

USUALLY THE MINILESSON and the share in a session bookend each other, with the one setting up some work and the other concluding it. In this session, the minilesson addresses one concern—the fact that conventions of all sorts and especially spelling need to be part of a writer's consciousness always—and the share launches an entirely different bit of work, work that sets up the week ahead.

To lead a session on conventions and, in general, to teach writing well, it is important for you and your grade-level colleagues to spend some time reflecting on what you notice about your children's control of writing conventions. I suggest you especially devise an approach to spelling—an approach you can share with parents, because research has shown that spelling is the first and biggest concern for many parents. Because it is important for your students' success that their parents trust you and because spelling can be a source of mistrust, I suggest you go so far as to send a letter home letting parents know that you have an organized plan for how you can help their children become more conventional spellers. Partly in jest, I go so far as to recommend that you tell parents that you'll have a spelling quiz every Friday, if that's what parents seem to *really* want to hear. And after all, a spelling quiz on Fridays isn't such a bad idea.

Dear Parents,

As we start this year together, I want to take a moment to convey to you some of my plans for helping your children grow in their abilities to spell conventionally. I have been assessing your children's spelling during these first few days of school, and I've come to believe that some children in the class are choosing only "easy" words to write because they are worried about whether they can spell the more advanced words correctly. My first goal, then, will be to make sure that every child is a fearless and inventive writer and that every child is willing to write *enormous* rather than sticking with *big* even if that child cannot spell *enormous* conventionally. You will see that I do not expect perfect spelling in children's first-draft writing.

The second thing I have noticed is that many children in this class haven't yet learned to spell some of the most important high-frequency words—words like *because, said,*

IN THIS SESSION, you'll teach students that writers don't wait to edit; they take a minute as they write to make sure their writing is as clear as possible for their readers.

GETTING READY

✔ Word chart with high-frequency words, word cards, and other tools your writers use for spelling

✔ Your own writer's notebook

✔ A couple sentences prepared that you can use to demonstrate writing in phrases versus writing in complete sentences (see Mid-Workshop Teaching)

✔ White board or a piece of chart paper (see Mid-Workshop Teaching)

✔ Paper clips (or some other tool) for students to mark the entry they have chosen to be their seed idea that will grow into a published book

✔ Some tools students can choose to help them with their writing

✔ Sample letter to parents explaining spelling in third grade

COMMON CORE STATE STANDARDS: W. 3.3.a,b,c; W.3.4, W.3.5, RFS.3.3, SL.3.1, L.3.2.e,f,g; L.3.1i, L.3.6

although—correctly. So, each week, I will directly and explicitly teach children a list of high-frequency words. Children will bring that list home on Mondays, they will be quizzed on those words on Fridays, and more important, they will be expected to incorporate those spellings into their writing whenever they write. I'll help them do this!

Meanwhile, there are a few children who will need extra help with spelling. We all know that there are great thinkers who struggle with spelling (Einstein was one of them). I'll be meeting with a few children to let them know that they will need to put extra time and receive extra help in spelling, and that together, we can make huge progress. Meanwhile, these children need to be reminded that although their progress in spelling matters and merits attention, they need to also work toward other goals as well. Like all children, I'll encourage these youngsters to write a lot and to write with voice and detail. I look forward to supporting and studying your children's progress toward writing more correct and more effective pieces of writing.

Sincerely,

This sample letter to parents is also available on the CD-ROM.

In general, there are principles that can guide you as you and your colleagues devise an approach to spelling that can be publicized. First, you need to convey to the parents and to your children that you recognize that spelling matters. If you show parents that you value their child's progress in spelling, they will be more apt to trust you. Since you certainly do care about the children's progress in spelling, among other areas of writing, your letter to parents should convey this.

Second, it should be a priority to help children spell high-frequency words with ease and automaticity. Fifty percent of the words children write come from a list of the thirty-six most common words, so helping children master those words has a great payoff.

Also, it is important to teach children strategies for tackling tough words so they aren't hesitant or ill-equipped to do so. That is, the job is not only to teach lists of words; the job is also to teach tools and strategies for spelling. One strategy you'll teach is that you'll help children know they can approximate a spelling and return to it later to problem solve. If a child believes she has misspelled a word, suggest she look at what she's written and think, "What part of this seems right? What part seems wrong?" This is helpful because it gives the child a sense of control. The child who is writing "international" may believe she's spelled "inter" and "na" correctly. So now she's working only on one or two problematic syllables. Finally, suggest that writers think, "What other words do I know that can help me spell the hard parts of this word?"

"Fifty percent of the words children write come from a list of the thirty-six most common words, so helping children master those words has a great payoff."

This session ends, however, not with a focus on spelling, but with you teaching students that after collecting entries for a while, after letting the water run until it runs clear, writers stop collecting and instead reread to choose one entry to develop into a published piece of writing. This share session, then, readies students for an upcoming week of work.

Editing as We Go
Making Sure Others Can Read Our Writing

CONNECTION

Channel students to list the things they know by heart—including words they know how to spell. Note that some kids know how to spell high-frequency words correctly and yet don't do it.

"Writers, I'm glad to see you sitting with your partner! Thanks for remembering to do that.

"Writers, there are many things you may know by heart: addition facts, your phone number, the lineup and batting averages for the New York Yankees, the Pledge of Allegiance, your best friend's email address, the words of a favorite song, and so on. Right now, tell your partner three things you know by heart. Go!"

After half a minute, I reconvened the class. "Writers, I didn't hear many of you saying, 'I know how to spell *spectacular*,' but my hunch is that there are many words you can spell by heart. This time, turn and tell your partner some of the words you can spell by heart."

As I listened in, I did a quick assessment, noting words to add to the word wall. "Writers, some of the words you mentioned are words that kids use all the time. Did you know that half the words kids write are the same thirty-six words? Some of the words you say you know by heart are those really important thirty-six words. Many of you know words like *when*, *said*, *then*, *finally*, *because*, and of course *there*, *their*, and *they're*. Here's the amazing thing. Lots of kids—including lots of you—know how to spell those thirty-six words by heart, but then, some people just don't do it. They know how to spell a word like *when*, but then they drop the *h* when writing in their writer's notebook!"

❖ **Name the teaching point.**

"Writers, today I want to teach you that you don't have to wait until you're finished with your writing to ask, 'Am I correctly spelling the words I know by heart?' Because you want people to read your writing, you take an extra second to think, 'Wait! I know that word,' and then you spell the word correctly by thinking about how the word looks."

Ten minutes a day of explicit and systematic spelling instruction will improve students' reading and writing. You may want to study Pat Cunningham's work with high-frequency words and word walls. If you explicitly teach spelling outside writing time, during writing time you can help students transfer and apply that work.

Perhaps the most important thing you are conveying in this minilesson is this: spelling matters. And spelling will be a big deal for a large proportion of your class. Third graders have reached that age where invented spellings aren't 'cute'— they're distracting. You still and always will want children to be fearless spellers, but you also want them to be skilled spellers. A big part of this involves teaching them that spelling matters and is within their grasp.

TEACHING

Tell children that it helps to invent ways to remind oneself to spell correctly the words one almost knows by heart.

"Writers, we need to add to our goals."

I'm going to take a second to spell correctly the words I almost know by heart.

"The thing is, I can't teach you *how* to do this in one minilesson. That's why we have a time to study spelling outside the writing workshop. Today's minilesson can't really have any teaching section in it, because you know what words you know and what words you still need to learn, and there is no one list of words or way to remember spellings that works for most writers. *You* need to invent your own list of words to work on, and your own ways to work on your spelling.

"What I can do is to tell you that every writer in the whole world has a list of errors that we remind ourselves to avoid and a list of 'to dos,' as well. Famous writers probably don't have to worry about how to spell *because*—that has become a habit for them—but they have a list of things to remember *and* ways to remember those things.

"As a writer, you aren't just the author of your writing. You are also the author of your life. And as part of that, you need to author plans that will work for yourself. Do you want to tie yarn around your finger so you remember that *when* has an *h* in it? To make a little tent-sized word wall and prop it up beside you as you write? Do you want to come up with little sayings that will help you with the tricky words—like *said* has to be spelled with an *a* (not an *e*) because 'I s*a*y, I said?' Or like, when *there* is a place, there has *here* inside of it? Or *lonely* has *one* inside of it?"

ACTIVE ENGAGEMENT

Ask children to think about ways they can remind themselves of words they know and to share their ideas with their partners and the class.

"Right now, please talk with each other and see if you can come up with a strategy that you think might help you remember to take an extra second on some words that you almost know by heart."

After a minute, I reconvened the writers. "Takeshi decided he is going to put word cards holding the words he 'uses but confuses' onto a key ring. Ellie says she is going to keep a tiny word wall—her very own word wall, not the class one—near her as she writes. So both Takeshi and Ellie have added spelling to their list of goals.

"They need to plan more ways to work on spelling, and so do the rest of you. How will your new writing partner help? Right now, partners, talk together. How are you going to remind each other and check on each other so this actually happens? Turn and talk."

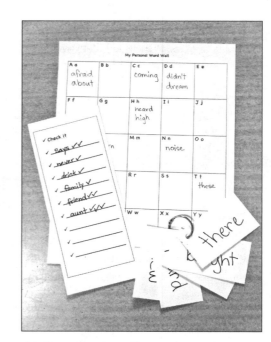

FIG. 6–1   Sample spelling tools used by students

A few minutes later, children were bursting with resolve.

"What are some ways you are going to help each other remember what you can do to help yourself spell words the best you can?"

"You can look at the word wall and copy the right spelling," Ellie offered.

"I always close my eyes and try to see the word," Felix added.

"You can ask Michela or Olivia 'cause they are really good spellers," Simeon suggested.

Debrief, emphasizing that the important thing is for the children to support each other in working with resolve.

"Wow, you all know so many ways you can make sure you spell words the best you can, and more importantly, you realize you don't have to feel alone. You know there are people and tools in this room that can help you should you ever need help. But the first person to go to is you! You know a lot, and you can use all you know to help yourself spell most words you will ever need."

LINK

Reiterate the importance of taking a few seconds to reach for correct spelling, and remind writers that the goal is neither perfection nor an obsession with correctness.

"So, writers, do you think it would be a good idea to spend every minute of today thinking about spelling?

"No way! In any day's writing workshop, you need to live like a professional writer, and that means the first thing you do is reread your writing, thinking, 'What do I need to do next? Should I add on to or change the entry I just wrote? Should I start a new entry?' And if you are starting a new entry and you are stuck on what to write about, show your partner a part of the chart that will help you get a topic." They did. "And what if you think, 'Wait, I want to make this a beautiful, powerful story?' Point to the parts of our charts that can help you do this.

"So today some of you will start new entries, and others will work on entries that are halfway done. And here's the new message of today: as you write (not just *after* you write, but *as* you write) you will want to use whatever means work for you to remember to take half a second to spell correctly the words you almost know by heart. You can pause as you write and ask, 'Does that look right?' and you can check the word wall. Later, partners can check over each other's work."

Once again I offer children several options for them to choose from rather than assign them all to fill out a personal word wall. Some children might like words written individually on word cards. Others might find a column of words listed on a bookmark to be more useful. It helps to leave some space for children to invent their own tools.

It is important to notice that today's minilesson focuses on spelling, but the writers will be drawing on their full repertoire of strategies to continue whatever their work is for today. All minilessons are meant to add to writers' repertoire—today's accentuates this.

Making Spelling Personal and Purposeful

IN ADDITION to conferring with your students about the content of their pieces, you will also want to use your conferring to support their use of conventions. When conferring about conventions, some of the overarching questions to ask yourself are these: Are my children generally on track in their spelling development? In their control of punctuation? In their use of standard English syntax and grammar? In their sentence complexity? In their vocabulary development?

To answer these questions, you need general guidelines. Here are some of my recommendations for finding or setting guidelines around spelling.

◆ **Assess your students' knowledge of high-frequency words.** Pat Cunningham has a recommended list of high-frequency words for each elementary grade level. For third grade, the list includes some review words from second grade (*said*, *about*, *before*) and introduces some new words to master by fourth grade (*question*, *through*). The third-grade list includes *discover*, *friendly*, *terrible*, *city*, *school*, *I'm*, *that's*. It's worth obtaining Cunningham's lists of high-frequency words and determining which grade-level list is aligned to most of your children. Ask yourself, "Do 80 percent of my third-graders spell the second-grade words correctly when they write?" If the answer is no, then it is fair to say that your kids are not on course as spellers and will need you to give this extra attention! Ask yourself whether the majority of your third-graders are able to spell some of the words on the third-grade suggested list. This will give you one indication of how you can assess your children's spelling and will also suggest starting points for their continued growth.

◆ **Help students break unknown words into syllables to approximate the spelling.** By third grade, children should be able to tackle a word they do not know how to spell—say, *substitution*—and their spellings should reflect that they have broken the word into syllables and used a knowledge of how those syllables are usually spelled to produce an approximation: *substitusion*, *substitootion*, or perhaps *substatushun*. They should know that each syllable

MID-WORKSHOP TEACHING
Writers Also Write with Periods and Capitals

"Writers, eyes up here. You've been writing up a storm! How many of you have been making a movie in your mind and telling stories step by step? That's great. How many of you *also* remembered to take an extra second to spell correctly the words you almost know by heart?" Everyone signaled they'd done this. "Right now, will you and your partner look together at each other's writing from today to check those easy-to-miss, all-important words?"

After only a few minutes, I reconvened the class. "Writers, I know you aren't done; in the end, you'll need to check your own spelling. For now, I want to give you one more tip about writing in ways that make it easy for people to read. Writers *also* take a second to write with periods and capitals.

"Some of you might be thinking that it is only during editing, right before you publish, that writers worry about adding periods and stuff like that. You are right that writers don't worry whether their writing is perfect when they are just getting ideas onto the page. But actually, even then, writers write with periods. Writers don't write unpunctuated text and then sprinkle periods in like they are adding jelly beans to a field of grass. Instead, published writers *write in sentences* from the start.

"The thing that messes some writers up is writing too slowly. This is what some of you do that *doesn't* work for you." I picked up my pen and wrote a phrase, and then stopped.

I was standing

Then I paused, looked around, shook out my hand, and resumed writing another phrase.

in the middle of the playground

I again paused and then shifted out of the role-play. "That's not writing in sentences. That's writing in phrases. That's robot writing: 'I was standing / in the middle of the playground.'"

To contrast, I said, "Watch a way of writing that *does* work, that helps a person write with periods and capitals." And then I thought aloud, acting as if I was mulling over what my first sentence would be. My head cocked and my eyes looking upward, I said, "'I was standing in the middle of the playground.'"

I wrote that sentence quickly and fluidly, and as I thumped in a period, I said, "Period." "What next?" I again mused, "'Everybody wanted me to buy candy for them.'

"Writers, am I going to write, 'Everybody / wanted me / to buy candy / for them'? No!" I again took up my pen and wrote the whole sentence, quickly, and voiced, "Period.

"Writers, back to your work. Remember to take a second as you write to spell words you know by heart and to write whole sentences with periods and capitals."

contains a vowel and should spell common word endings, prefixes, and suffixes (-ly, -tion, pre-).

◆ **Set your students on course to develop skills for finding correct spellings of unknown words.** Sandra Wilde, author of many books on spelling, once told me this rule of thumb: By the time children are in fifth grade, 90 percent of the words on their rough drafts should be spelled correctly, and children should also have the skills necessary to find correct spellings for many of the misspelled words.

You might convene a small group of students and begin in the following way: "Writers, you are using strategies that grown-up professional writers use. What I want to remind you now is that when you are writing for readers, it is important to spell common words as correctly as you can. That way, everyone can understand you easily.

"So when you are writing, take a second to spell the words on our word wall (and other words you know) correctly. Right now, reread what you've written so far, and if you find a word wall word that you've misspelled, please fix it. If you aren't sure how to spell it, check the word wall. But instead of copying the word letter for letter when you look at the word wall, go through all the steps we go through when we are learning new words. Look at the word. Think about what you notice about it. Now try to imprint the word on your mind. Close your eyes and try to see the letters in your imagination. Say the letters aloud. Now open your eyes and check to see if you were right. When you have the correct spelling fixed in your brain, write it. Check that you were right.

"And after this, for the rest of this year and for the whole of your life, remember that it's important to get into the habit of correctly spelling the words you use a lot. If you are writing a word and you think, 'This is on our word wall,' and you aren't quite sure how to spell it, take an extra fifteen seconds to try to spell (and write) like a pro!

"I've also noticed that some of you are getting stuck when you come to a word that you know is spelled wrong, but you're not quite sure how to fix it. I want to remind you that when you come to words like this, you can give them your best try. I want to teach you a few things to remember to do when you are trying out new spellings. You might:

◆ Circle words you think are spelled incorrectly.

◆ Think about what is right and what is wrong with the word you spelled.

◆ Try to spell it a few different ways by asking yourself, "Are there other words I know that can help me with this word?"

◆ After you've spelled it a few different ways, decide which way looks the best. Change the word in your piece to match your best try. Then keep writing your draft.

"Brave writers still use words in their writing that they are not sure how to spell. They give these words their best try, and then they move on in their piece, even if they aren't sure of the spelling. Fortunately, writers reread their work often, and when they reread, one of the things they do is take another try at spelling these tricky or unfamiliar words.

"Right now, try rereading least three entries. Circle words you think you have misspelled. Ask yourself, 'What seems right here? What seems wrong here?' Next, you'll find space in the margins of the page to give the spelling a couple more tries. You can then pick the try that seems to be most correct and change the spelling in your piece."

Choosing a Seed Idea

Suggest that children search through their notebooks, considering which entry, of all they have written, they want to develop into a finished piece.

After children convened, with partners sitting beside each other, I said, "You've been collecting the stories of your lives in your notebooks, recording one moment and another and then another. I have one new thing to tell you. Writers don't just write story after story after story. Instead, after collecting stories for a while, writers reread them and find one that for *some reason* snags their attention, suggesting that just maybe it could become something more. And then writers rewrite that one story, that one entry, all over again, this time trying to make it feel like a published book.

"This will be a working share session, because right now, you have some important work to do. I want each of you to reread your notebook, asking, 'Of all that's here, which one story do I want to develop into a publishable book?' You may want to develop a system for doing this—like putting one star or two or three beside different entries and then looking at which are your three-star entries. Get started."

As children worked, I voiced over. "I love that you aren't just rereading your entries like this," and I flipped mindlessly through my pages. "You aren't just flip, flip, flipping through your notebooks. You are taking the time to reread thoughtfully, like real writers do.

"You have a few more minutes to do this, and then you'll have time to talk to your partner.

"Right now, take just a minute to talk to your partner about other things you might do to choose an idea. As you talk, I am going to give each of you a paper clip so you can mark your entry—we'll call it your 'seed idea' because we are going to grow the entry, like one grows a seed, into something wonderful!"

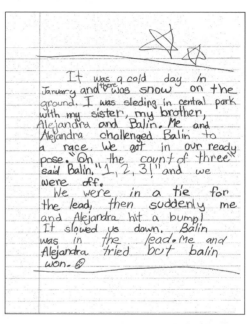

FIG. 6–2 Olivia has starred the entry she has chosen to be her seed idea.

Rehearsing
Storytelling and Leads

IN THIS SESSION, you'll teach students to rehearse for writing by teaching them that writers story-tell and generate alternate leads as ways to rehearse a story.

GETTING READY

✔ Students' writer's notebooks with their seed story paper-clipped, to be brought to the meeting area. Students should sit with their partners.

✔ Four- to five-page drafting booklets and a pocket folder for each child and one for you to model using

✔ Extra drafting booklets in the writing center

✔ Your own story to story-tell (and sketch) across the pages of a drafting booklet (see Teaching)

✔ "To Write a True Story" chart (see Link)

✔ Mentor text, *Come On, Rain!* by Karen Hesse, or another familiar book with a great lead

✔ "Leads Sometimes Include . . ." chart, to be created with students (see Share)

COMMON CORE STATE STANDARDS: W.3.10, W.3.3.a,b,c,d; W.3.4, W.3.5, W.3.8, W.4.3.a, RL.3.4, RL.3.5, RL.3.7, SL.3.6, SL.3.4, SL.3.6, SL.4.4, L.3.3.a,b; L.3.6, L.3.1

S INCE THE START OF THIS UNIT, your children have spent their writing time collecting one entry after another. At the end of the previous session, they made the turn from collecting toward developing entries: they chose a seed idea. In today's session, you'll help writers begin what will be a several-day process of developing their seed ideas. Another way to say this is that today writers begin taking an entry through the stages of the writing process, starting with rehearsal.

Remember that earlier you taught your children strategies for coming up with story ideas? In a similar manner, today you will teach writers several strategies for rehearsing for writing. Again, you'll be teaching in ways that provide them with a repertoire of strategies they can draw upon, and again, you'll end the session hoping that writers do the big thing—rehearse prior to writing—but you won't necessarily care whether writers engage in any one particular kind of rehearsal.

Because one of your goals throughout this unit is to support storytelling and the closely related skill of showing, not telling, you'll suggest that one way to rehearse for writing is to re-experience an event by telling the story over and over, to oneself and others. Many writers do this. As one engages in repeated storytelling, the story changes. The storyteller can sense the parts that are juicy and can embellish those parts even more. Although it is sometimes hard to explain this to third-graders, whether writers are deliberately aware of this or not, as a storyteller watches an audience's reaction to a story, it is natural for the storyteller to revise the story to bring out whatever response the storyteller aims to achieve: building tension, increasing suspense, developing sympathy.

Later in this session, you'll teach writers a second form of rehearsal—trying different leads. In some ways, using the word *lead* to describe that first sentence or first paragraph of a piece of writing is so misleading! A better word might be grab, pull, or yank. Writers of every genre know that the first bit of text on a page must cajole, beg, or even jerk the reader into the text so that he will invest the time and attention it takes to finish, to appreciate, the story.

Inexperienced writers often become paralyzed when writing the first words or sentences of a story because the words represent a huge mental decision: out of all the information that I have swimming about in my head, where do I start? I tell students that it's like standing on a high diving board, looking down that scary distance to the water. It seems impossible to step off, yet once we do it, we realize it's not that hard; in fact it's a blast, and we can't wait to climb up the ladder to dive again!

"One way to rehearse for writing is to re-experience an event by telling the story over and over, to oneself and others."

In this session, teach children that writers don't pick up the pen and write a new draft. Instead they first tell the story several times, each time trying to make it sound more story-like.

That is, writers rehearse their stories by remembering how the story started, picturing how it went, step by step, and thinking about how they want the reader or listener to feel as the story unfolds. Some writers start a story by describing small actions, some by showing what the character says, and some by showing the setting.

Rehearsing
Storytelling Again and Again

CONNECTION

Set children up to story-tell their seed ideas to partners in such a way that they elicit a reaction.

"Writers, as you come to the meeting area today, I'll be giving each one of you a story booklet and a pocket folder for the writing you'll do today." Once children were settled, books in hand, I said, "This is an exciting day! Each of you has chosen one entry from your notebook, one seed idea, that you will turn into a published book. Today you'll be able to write the story you have chosen—writing it as if it will be a book in the library (and it might become that!).

"Right now, quickly turn to your partner, and Partner 2, *tell the story* that you will be writing today. Tell it long. Tell it in ways that give your listener goose bumps."

During these early days of getting the writing workshop up and going, you have choices to make that will ultimately affect the tone and the energy that will drive the workshop forward throughout the year. If children think their stories are insignificant, they will not be able to sustain the energy necessary to be writers.

I listened in as children told their stories, moving among the children prompting, "Don't stop. What happened next? Keep going." I listened as Olivia told her story of sledding to Ellie, building up tension as the story progressed to a climactic end!

"Writers, let me stop you. Your stories are incredible! And it seemed as if in the middle of a story, many of you started remembering more stuff about it. Is that what happened?" Children nodded, and I confirmed, "That's exactly why we often story-tell before we write."

Don't feel that you need both partners to tell their stories. Partner 1 will have a turn later in the minilesson, and in any case, both the talking and the listening partner benefit.

❖ Name the teaching point.

"Listen up—this is important. Most writers don't just pick an idea and then bingo, write the book. Just as a choir rehearses for a concert, writers *rehearse* for writing. One of the best ways they rehearse a story is to story-tell their story—and to do so repeatedly in lots of different ways."

TEACHING

Model how to tell a story across the pages of a drafting booklet, reliving the moment and then assuming the role of storyteller.

"Robert Munsch, author of *'Thomas' Snowsuit'* (2007), says that he never writes a story until he has told it at least a hundred times! Obviously you won't tell your own stories that many times, but you will tell your story a lot of times, and you'll make your story better each time you tell it.

"For now, watch while I rehearse my story about buying candy for the kids at school. Notice that to story-tell well, we have to go back to that time, to imagine, to put ourselves in the situation. For my story, I need to put myself into my ten-year-old shoes. Let me think. How did it start? (I always ask myself that question.) Oh, I remember. On the playground, the kids gave me money to get them candy." I stared up at the ceiling, as if musing about the moment.

Switching over to the role of a storyteller, I picked up a story booklet and tapped the first page. I began telling my story, conveying as I did both that these might be the words that I'd actually write and that I was lost in the memory of the moment.

> Six or seven kids crowded near me. Ginny told me she wanted me to get Junior Mints and Juicy Fruit, and she gave me a dollar. Phil told me he wanted the same as always, which meant Mars Bars, as many as I could get. Joey told me he wanted a giant-sized box of Dots. Amy Jo wanted red licorice. I stuffed their dollars into my parka pocket. I didn't have time to write a list, because I had to get to the store and back before the teachers realized I was gone. I raced to the edge of the playground. Then I looked back over my shoulder to be sure the recess teacher wasn't watching, and zoomed out of the school lot and down the block to Gates' Deli.

I turned to the second page of the booklet and tapped it. Then I continued the story.

> I pushed open the door and the lady at the checkout counter smiled and asked, "Can I help you?" I said I knew where to find things, and I quickly turned to the candy shelves. I found the candy the kids had wanted, though it was hard to hold it all in my arms.

Name the replicable moves you made as a writer, asking the children to give a thumbs up for each one they noticed.

"I'll pause there. Writers, quickly turn and tell your partner one thing you noticed me doing right now."

I gave them just thirty seconds to do so and then said, "Thumbs up if you noticed that I told a lot of details—more than last time I told the story, right? I don't really remember which kids ordered what candy, but I juiced up the story to make it good." Then I added, "Thumbs up if you noticed that I said the start of the story—the part on the playground—on page 1 of the booklet, and I told the second part, getting the candy, on the second page."

Notice that before I slip into the role of writer and demonstrate, I usually frame the demonstration with remarks meant to orient children so they know what they are watching, and what they're expected to do with what they see.

When you demonstrate, as in this instance, be sure your intonation and gestures suggest you are mulling over, thinking aloud. You aren't talking to the children. Your eyes aren't on them. Instead you are thinking aloud, letting children eavesdrop on your thinking. But don't look at the children or direct these remarks to them.

"Did you notice I even tapped each new page as I turned to the next part of my story? That's sort of a silly thing I do, I guess, but it helps me remember to chunk my story into different parts and put just one chunk on a page: on the playground on one page, at the store on another page, my mother catching me in the act on another page—like that. Tapping each page isn't crucial, but everyone makes up their own little tricks for how to story-tell, just like we do for how to spell.

"Here is a really important thing. Thumbs up if you noticed that I was making a movie in my mind, picturing it all, and if you noticed that I told it bit by bit so you could picture it too." They signaled with thumbs up. "Thumbs up if you noticed I didn't even look back at the old entry that I wrote about this in my writer's notebook."

ACTIVE ENGAGEMENT

Set children up to tell each other their stories, touching pages of a booklet as they proceed through the chronology. As they do this, call out coaching tips.

"Partner 1, story-tell your story right now, and Partner 2, listen like a writing teacher does, in ways that help the storyteller say more. Storytellers, think about where, in the sequence of your story, you'll start the story." I gave them a second. "Think about what, exactly, you were doing or saying." I gave them another few seconds to locate themselves. "When you're ready, tap your first page and start storytelling."

As children told their stories, I listened in, sometimes whispering in and sometimes calling out coaching tips.

"Remember to use a storyteller's voice. Think about what you want your reader to feel, and pump up the parts that can get the reader feeling that!

"Don't forget to tell your story in small steps. This is a *story*, not a summary, not a news report.

"Listen to how Ashley's story can sweep her listener up," and I repeated the opening of the story, giving Ashley's words grandeur and flair.

"Do you hear how Ashley is telling her story bit by bit by including describing the exact actions and responses to those actions? It's like a movie we can hear and see unfolding before our very eyes on the big screen."

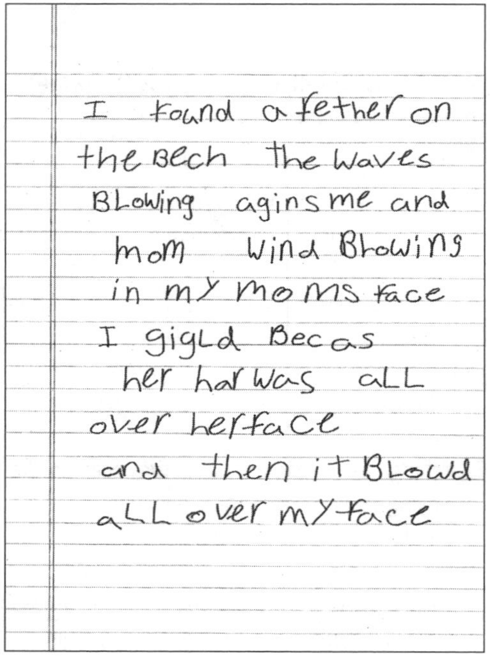

> I found a fether on
> the Bech the waves
> BLowing agins me and
> mom wind Blowing
> in my moms face
> I gigLd Becas
> her har was aLL
> over herface
> and then it BLowd
> aLL over my face

I found a feather on the beach. The waves blowing against me and Mom. The wind blowing in my Mom's face. I giggled because her hair was all over her face and then it blowed all over my face.

FIG. 7–1 Ashley's spelling is a problem—reading her work aloud to celebrate its strengths is a big deal.

LINK

Restate your teaching point. Send children off to rehearse their stories by storytelling them first. Then suggest sketching as a way to hold onto the oral story.

"Writers, when you want to do something well, always remember that rehearsal matters. Whether you are hoping to put on a terrific show or to pull off a great party or to write a great story—all of us, teachers, children, moms and dads, published authors, rehearse the things we plan to do. We go over them in our mind, and our ideas change as we go over them.

"Although usually at the end of a minilesson, I remind you that you are the boss of your writing and suggest you choose the work you want to do, today I think it will really help if each one of you rehearses. And I'm going to add one last tip. Today try sketching out the sequence of your story in teeny tiny sketches on one small corner of each page, and then touch not only each page, but also each sketch as you story-tell that page." I quickly drew a tiny sketch on two pages of my sample drafting booklet to illustrate what I meant. "Once you have sketched out and story-told one sequence, you can do it again, tons better. Or you can sketch out a different way the same story could be laid out across pages and do the same thing again. So for now, you are stretching and storytelling—not writing."

Years ago, I suggested kids "nurture" their seed ideas in their notebooks for several weeks before beginning a draft. I have come to believe, however, that until youngsters have had a lot of experience with the writing process, they can be swamped if they collect too much loosely related material. I don't want children to lose hold of their organizational structure or their focused message. So during the first units of study, I keep this "nurturing one's seed idea" phase streamlined. It will become longer and more elaborate in later units in this series.

To Write a True Story

- Find story ideas that are focused and important to you and write lots of entries.
- Make a mental movie of what happened, telling it in small detail, bit by bit.
  - Detail the actions.
  - Include the dialogue.
- Remember your self-assessments of your narrative writing and your goals.
- Rehearse for your writing by storytelling the story repeatedly.

FIG. 7–2

Helping Writers See They Have Stories to Tell and the Language with Which to Tell Them

I OFTEN REMIND CHILDREN that on any given day, their work during the writing workshop should draw not just on that day's minilesson, but on all the strategies they've learned. Similarly, your teaching needs to draw upon all the strategies you've taught. Today, however, is a bit of an exception because everyone will be doing the same work—storytelling and studying and drafting leads.

In your conferences and small-group work today, you'll aim to do a few things in particular. First, you'll want to rally behind the seed ideas that writers have chosen. Because all your students will have just reread all their entries to select just one to develop and are now sketching the storyline across pages in their booklet and telling the story to themselves, they will tend to be tentative about their choices. "This one? Is this good?" they ask, looking for confirmation.

"It's a hugely important one, isn't it?" I will respond. I will say this, acting on faith, even before the evidence is there on the page. After all, out of all the child's life, he earlier made the decision to record this story in an entry, and now, out of all the entries, the child has chosen this one. The significance is not always apparent to us, but I find that if I confirm the entry's importance and then lean in to listen, saying, "Tell me all about it. How, exactly, did it start?" I can help the child tell the story with engagement.

MID-WORKSHOP TEACHING Storytelling and Then Starting to Draft

"Writers, can I have your attention? Don't forget what Robert Munsch said: stories get much better if we tell them again and again, trying to tell them in ways that really affect listeners and readers. Do you want to make people shiver with fear, laugh aloud, gasp, wince? Each time you practice telling your story, you can make it affect readers in the way you want to affect them. And often, you want readers to feel one thing at the start of a story, then another thing later in the story, so you should be clear what you are wanting to make your readers (or your listeners) feel at each part of the story.

Right now, will you and your partner work together? First reread your story to figure out what feeling you are trying to give readers at different parts of it. Then Partner 2, tell your story to Partner 1, really building up the parts that get those feelings across. As you do this, storytellers, watch to see if you can make your listeners' mouths drop open in surprise or get them to lean in closer. Make your listeners feel whatever you want them to feel. And listeners, listen in a way that lets your partner's story affect you. Okay, go to it!"

As I listened in, I noticed animated faces and gestures. "Writers, can I stop you for a moment? Jill wasn't just reading her story about fighting with her sister over who got to sit next to the window on the train, she actually acted it out. And you should have seen her partner's face. Amanda's eyes opened wide, and she even gasped! That's what writers live for—to make their readers react.

"Let's get back to writing stories that will make readers gasp. You story-told in ways that are *way* better than the entry you wrote last week. You have fifteen minutes now to get started writing the first page of your booklet, writing it so that you draw your listeners in."

Of course, we can't listen respectfully and offer generous amounts of time and focus to every single child! This is one day when I am especially apt to make appointments to confer at lunch or recess; it is also a day when I set children up to listen well to each other. "Now that you have your seed idea chosen," I'll say to one writer, "will you listen to Robbie like I listened to you? Get him to tell you the whole story and to tell it with detail. Help him tell it in a way that gives you goose bumps."

You can enter today's writing workshop anticipating that some children will tell a story and then produce a three-line lead and want to call it a day. Be ready to help those children understand that revision can start now. It is easier to revise a lead than to revise an entire piece—and often, the effect is equally powerful because front-end revisions allow the writer to take a draft through a succession of possible plans. The revision can be large scale: where in the sequence of the event will the story begin? When a writer varies the starting point for a story, this has profound implications.

You may end up teaching some children that it helps to start with actions that are close to the main event of the story or that it is important to show not only what the character is doing but also how she does it or that it helps to select actions that reveal what the character cares about and that set us up to understand the character's main struggles.

But revisions can be small ones, too, as writers work to set the right tone and achieve the right cadence.

If you are going to be successful at luring your writers to revise anything—starting with their leads—it will be important for you to put aside any distaste you may have for revision and at least pretend to be a writer who loves revision. Like most other writers, the truth is I absolutely love tinkering with sentences until they are just right. I listen to the sounds of the words, fiddle with the punctuation, syntax, and word choice until the sentence sounds pleasing. I say my sentences aloud, testing them for sound just like I say proposed names for a newborn baby aloud. I mimic the sentences of writers I admire. Act as if you can't possibly imagine how it could be that a child doesn't love this work. Try it yourself. You'll see!

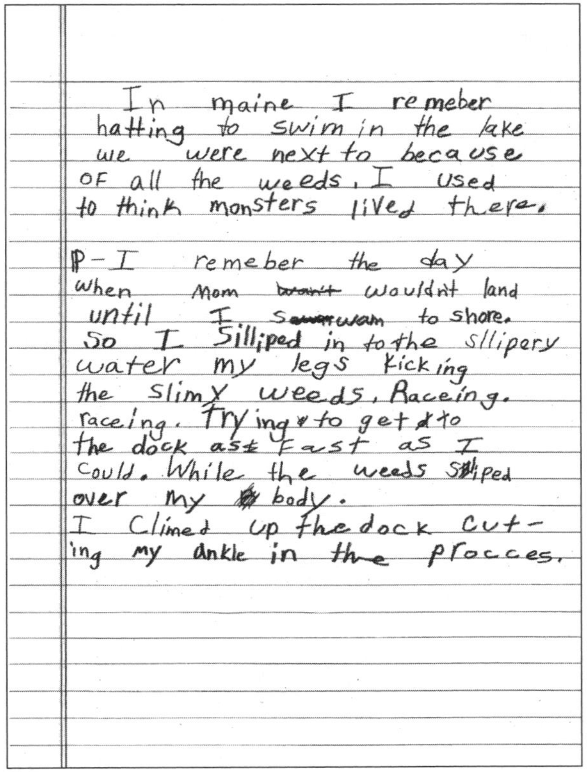
In maine I remeber hatting to swim in the lake we were next to because OF all the weeds. I used to think monsters lived there.

P-I remeber the day when Mom ~~wasn't~~ wouldn't land until I ~~s~~wam to shore. So I Silliped in to the sllipery water my legs kicking the slimy weeds. Raceing. raceing. Trying to get to the dock as Fast as I Could. While the weeds slliped over my body. I Climed up the dock cut-ing my ankle in the procces.

FIG. 7–3 Mile's entry about rowing on a summer day

Trying Leads on for Size

Convene children. Tell them that writers try out different leads to rehearse for writing.

"Writers, something magical happened in this classroom just now. Your stories came to life! During the mid-workshop, your stories all started to sound like literature. I want to share something Lizzie just noticed while everyone was working. She tugged on my sleeve, all excited, and said, 'When I made my story start in a different place, it was like the rest just poured out.'

"That is such a smart observation. And it made me realize that all of you are ready to learn something else that authors do to rehearse for writing—something that helps make stories flow.

"Authors try out different leads. They know, just as all of you do, that a lead in a story matters. A great lead sets us up to write a great story. And great writers know, as Lizzie found, that the lead of a story helps the rest of the story 'pour out.' One way to learn to do something, as writers, is to see how famous writers do whatever it is that we want to do. So let's look again at what Karen Hesse has done to get a good lead for her world-famous book, *Come On, Rain!* We talked about this earlier. Let's look at this again and think, 'What's this author doing at the start, the lead, of her story?'"

> *"Come on, rain!" I say, squinting into the endless heat.*
>
> *Mama lifts a listless vine and sighs.*
>
> *"Three weeks and not a drop," she says, sagging over her parched plants.*
>
> *The sound of a heavy truck rumbles past. Uneasy, Mamma looks over to me.*
>
> *"Is that thunder, Tessie?" she asks.*
>
> *Mamma hates thunder. I climb up the steps for a better look.*
>
> *"It's just a truck, Mamma," I say.*

I reread the lead. "I'm thinking, 'What has Karen Hesse done that I could do?'" I muttered to myself.

I believe that children are well served by working on their leads early in their writing process. The leads can bring life and possibility to their writing—they can lift the level of the whole piece of writing to follow. Leads can also point out new directions stories can take, and it's much easier to explore those directions before the whole draft is written than it is afterward.

Channel students to think about great leads, first by noting what Hesse has done to start her story and then encouraging them to try similar techniques.

"The first thing I'm noticing is that Karen Hesse has Tessie doing a small action in the very first line. She is saying, 'Come on, rain!' while squinting into the endless heat. If this were a play, as soon as the curtain opened, the main character would be up on stage doing something.

"So what I'm noticing is that leads sometimes include," I held up my fist and began listing across my fingers, "the main character saying or thinking something and doing a specific action. The other thing I noticed is that Hesse really plops us right into the story by including the exact actions of Tessie's mother as she responds to Tessie.

"Is there anything else that Hesse does in her lead that we could try? Let me read it to you again, and then you'll have time to tell your partner, 'One thing I notice that she did that I could try is. . . .' So listen up." I reread the lead.

"What are you noticing that Hesse has done to get a good lead? Turn and talk!" Talk erupted, and after a minute I convened the class.

Caitlyn said, "Well, she doesn't just have Tessie do something. Her mother does something, too."

Terrance added, "What I notice is that she didn't just tell all about it. She showed it, like she had a movie in her mind. And she showed what Tessie did first and then she showed what happened next, with the talking and everything."

I nodded. "As I jot some of the things we have noticed Karen Hesse doing at the start of her story, will you, in your writer's notebook, to try a couple different leads to your story? You can get started on those leads right now." As children started to write, I scrawled a fast "Leads Sometimes Include . . ." chart.

End by asking students to try different leads and then come to class tomorrow with a lead chosen.

In a voiceover, as children scrawled, I called out, "Try a few different leads. If you first start with an action that hooks the reader into the story's events right away, then next you might begin with a bit of dialogue, just like Karen Hesse did, that tells us something about *who* is in this story.

"As you work, see what feels right to you. And tonight, at home, choose the lead that you think works best to set up your story. You'll have a number of different leads to choose from, and if you get stuck, think about what Karen Hesse did to start her story or think about how leads can include actions or dialogue. I can't wait to hear what each of you chooses for your lead."

Leads Sometimes Include . . .

- The main characters doing an action ("Come on, rain!" I say, squinting into the endless heat.)
- Each character is doing not just one action, but the next and the next. (Mamma lifts a listless vine and sighs. "Three weeks and not a drop," she says, sagging over her parched plants.)
- The main characters are talking, with the exact dialogue included. ("It's just a truck, Mamma," I say.)
- The story starts midway through a whole chain of actions but you know what already happened.

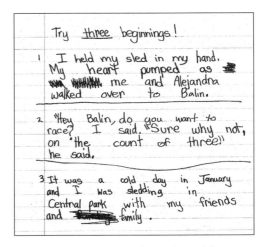

FIG. 7–4 Olivia has tried out three different leads in her notebook.

Writing Discovery Drafts

IN THIS SESSION, you'll teach students that writers draft by writing fast and furiously, working to capture the mental movie on the page.

GETTING READY

✔ Students' folders with their drafting booklets, to be brought to the meeting area

✔ Sample student writing, preferably a flash draft, to project on overhead or document camera

✔ "To Write a True Story" chart (see Link)

✔ Your own writer's notebook, drafting booklet, and folder to use while conferring

✔ Mentor text, *Come On, Rain!*, to use as a teaching tool during conferring

I'VE HELPED THOUSANDS OF TEACHERS launch writing workshops, and there is a dazzling array of options for how one might proceed into drafting. Do you begin by teaching children to make a timeline of the event and then tell the story following that timeline? Do you begin by studying a touchstone text closely and then encouraging children to write in the same fashion or with the same structure? Do you start the year with an emphasis on content only? "Tell your readers the true story of what happened," you could say, postponing discussion about craft until later.

The world is bursting with options, but a writer and a teacher both must reach into the hurly-burly of life and select just one teaching point, then the next. Out of all the options, I've chosen to channel children toward writing well-structured, chronological, focused narratives because I think structure is fundamental to good writing. And I've chosen to emphasize show-not-tell and storytelling because I believe these are essential to narrative writing.

Writers often say that narrative writing is almost like drama, on the page. "Don't say the old lady screamed," Mark Twain said. "Bring her on and let her scream." The task of teaching youngsters to dramatize as they write, to let their story unfold on the page rather than chatting and commenting about it, will span this entire unit and will continue to be a challenge well into middle school. Today, you'll help children storytell by teaching them that writing a rough draft works best when writers write fast and furiously, keeping their eyes on the subject and trying to put that subject onto the page.

You'll teach children that when writing a first draft, it is best to write long and strong, not stopping.

There may be one or two unusual children who carve their words into the page like a sculptor carves into marble, but for the vast majority of writers, a draft is much stronger, more cohesive, and more vital if the writer focuses on reliving life, putting the whole of it on the paper. Even children who have regarded themselves as struggling writers often find an

COMMON CORE STATE STANDARDS: W.3.3.a, W.3.4, W.3.10, W.3.5, RL.3.1, RL.3.3, RFS.3.4, SL.3.1, SL.3.4, SL.4.4, L.3.6, L.3.1

internal source of power when they rehearse their writing by storytelling, then think carefully about where in the sequence of events they'll start the story, and then pick up the pen and write with passion, lost in the story.

Then, too, a lesson on fast-drafting sets the stage for a later lesson on large-scale, dramatic revision because children who write quickly are more willing to revise in large-scale ways.

"Writing a rough draft works best when writers write fast and furiously, keeping their eyes on the subject and trying to put that subject on the page."

Writing Discovery Drafts

CONNECTION

Remind children of the work they've done so far in the process of drafting, and tell them they are ready to go one step further.

"Writers, can I have your eyes and your attention? You are on the brink of beginning your first draft. You've selected the entry you want to write as literature in a book, and you've rehearsed for your writing, sketching what happens, bit by bit, across the pages of your booklet and then using that booklet to support you storytelling your way through the pages. You've also selected a lead you like. You know a lot about getting ready to write."

❖ **Name the teaching point.**

"Today I'm going to teach you that after carefully crafting each word of a lead, it's good to fix your eyes on your subject and to write your story fast and furious, without stopping.

TEACHING

Use a metaphor to tell children that writers sometimes fast-write a discovery draft. Model how this is done and show an example.

"Today you'll write fast and furious, writing the same stories (only better) that you told each other yesterday.

"Remember that earlier you learned to make a movie in your mind of how the story unfolds, starting by thinking, 'Where was I?' 'What, exactly, was I doing?'

"Well, a friend of mine is studying to be an artist, and in her class on painting portraits, her professor has taught her that one way to get unbelievable power into her drawing is to look at her subject, and to sketch what she sees *without even looking down at her paper*. She keeps her eyes on the person and sketches with the goal of putting down the truth of what she sees—all of it—onto the page.

"Writers do something similar. They fill themselves with the true thing that happened to them. They remember the very start of the episode and story-tell what happened first (only they scrawl the story onto the paper rather than tell it),

Notice that whenever I summarize the work children have done to date, I try to name parts of the writing process I hope they will cycle through again and again. I know that when children first progress through the writing process, they sometimes proceed with tunnel vision, seeing only the next step. In the movie Platoon, *a character says that war means putting one foot in front of the other, trying to see three inches in front of us. By retelling the broad vista of the writing process, I help children gain a greater sense of control.*

The friend I am referring to here is the writer Georgia Heard. She writes about this technique in her book Writing Toward Home *(1995).*

and then, without worrying much about perfect spelling or word choice or anything, they keep their minds fixed on everything that happened and write fast and long without stopping.

"Let me show you Felix's flash draft. It isn't spelled all that well, and it isn't perfect—but listen to the power of this fast-write." (See Figure 8–1.)

> "Felix, wake up, we have to go to the church." We went to the church. I started seeing all my family members. I did not know what was happening. Then I saw a big box coming out of the church. My grandma laid her head against the big brown box and started crying. I tugged on her shirt, "Grandma, grandma what's in there?"
>
> "Just look."
>
> I stared through the screen. It was my grandfather. He was as pale as glue. "Grandfather get out of there, come and help me make the paper airplanes you make! Don't go. Don't! I am sorry about what I said to you." I knocked on the screen. It did not help. He would not wake up. "I want to see my grandfather now." I knew now what was going on. My grandfather had just died. I did not know what to say to myself. I felt scared. What was I going to do without my grandpa?
>
> No no no. There's no paper airplanes that he's going to make me. Who is going to say the funny stories everyday? Who's going to put a smile on me everyday? I stop. A tear runs through my face. I stomp over to my grandfather but my uncle holds me back. I see his white face. His hard boney hands on his sides.
>
> "Grandpa, let's go to the window and throw the paper airplanes." I see him coming, his pale white face grinning at me. He slowly starts walking with a long brown stick, his weak hands holding on the stick.

"Do you feel slightly breathless from being right there in the moment with Felix? Did you notice how he did that by including the exact words he said, what he saw, what he thought, what he felt? All this made us feel like we were riding right along with Felix during this most memorable moment in his life."

ACTIVE ENGAGEMENT

Recruit children to be willing to write discovery drafts and channel them toward being ready to start this work.

"Writers, get ready to try this right now. To get started, be sure your lead is on page 1 of your drafting booklet and that you've sketched little pictures to remind you of what part of your story goes on each page. Then reread the lead, touch each page of the booklet, and say the part you'll write on that page. Do this for the whole story, telling it fast and furious." As the children started, I walked around prompting them to get back into the story, retelling it bit by bit.

Felix has gone through school with the reputation of being a struggling writer. Like some other children with this reputation, Felix is in fact a very powerful writer—but one who struggles with the conventions of written language. He needs explicit instruction in these conventions, but more important, he needs a teacher who can see the power of his work. This piece reveals his difficulties with the surface mechanics of language, yet it also reveals his willingness to write honestly, with deep emotion, and his enviable gift for simile: "pale as glue." I want children to see Felix's handwriting and spelling errors because I want every child in the classroom to realize that powerful, honest writing is within grasp. Spelling well does not necessarily correlate with writing well. Both are important. Children who care about writing and believe they have something to say will be much more willing to do the work of becoming more effective spellers.

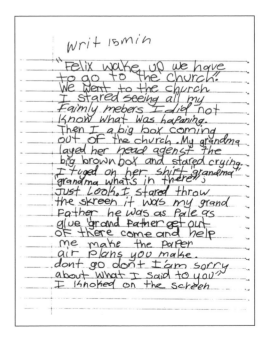

FIG. 8–1   The first page of Felix's draft

"Don't forget to include your exact actions—what you said, what you were thinking," I voiced over as they told their stories to themselves. As I noticed children coming to the end of their drafting booklets, I called them back together.

"Wow, I could really feel the energy created when you told your stories fast and furious. Partner 2, right now, go back to page 1. Reread your lead and remember the beginning of the event. Story-tell the story to your partner. Make your partner feel whatever you want him to feel. Start with your lead, then turn the page of your drafting booklet as you continue taking your partner along with you into the world of your story."

Partners huddled together holding their drafting booklets and telling their stories. As pages turned and children told their stories, I listened for fluency and expressive language and noted which children's stories flowed and which seemed tentative. This research helped me develop some ideas about who I might follow up with while conferring or pulling small groups.

LINK

Remind writers of what you've taught today, and tell them they can use this new strategy for the rest of their lives.

"Get started writing while you are here on the carpet, and write fast, keeping your eyes on the true story. Once you feel like you are really imagining the story as it unfolded and you are writing fast and furiously, then get up and go to your seat to keep on writing."

To Write a True Story

- Find story ideas that are focused and important to you and write lots of entries.
- Make a mental movie of what happened, telling it in small detail, bit by bit.
  - Detail the actions.
  - Include the dialogue.
- Remember your self-assessments of your narrative writing and your goals.
- Rehearse for your writing by storytelling the story repeatedly.
- Try different leads for your story (Action? Dialogue?).
- Write a flash draft, writing fast and furious, eyes on the mental movie.

The poet and novelist Naomi Shihab Nye says it this way: "Write luxuriously, abundantly, fill whole pages, making little notes to yourself in the margins. Don't worry about saying it perfectly" (Flynn and McPhillips 2000, p. 46).

Don't worry that every writer needs a turn storytelling, and don't give children time enough to get past their first page or two.

Writing with Fluency

WHEN THE CHILDREN IN YOUR ROOM are writing discovery drafts, trying to write quickly and for a long time, your conferring will probably be a little different than usual. Whereas most days when you confer, you won't hesitate to interrupt children at work since you know that your interruption—your conference—will provide a strategy to help them strengthen their work, today's situation is a bit different. Today, many of the children will be pushing themselves to write without interruption—to write fast and long. Interrupting them to determine if there is a way to help them write without interruption might seem like a contradiction. On the other hand, there are telltale signs that signal children could use help.

◆ If a child is staring into space instead of writing, you might teach the child that he can get a running start into writing by going to the first page of the booklet and storytelling the part that belongs on that page, then shift into writing.

◆ If a child is stopping to erase, you might teach the child to put a light line through the part of the writing that is leading her astray and simply keep writing.

◆ If a child is thinking and rethinking how any given part of the draft goes, teach that child to make marginal notes about alternatives to how he's written the draft and just keep going.

◆ If a child is judging every sentence, encourage the child to think, "Oh well, I'll just do the best I can and keep going."

◆ If a youngster's story is about a giant swath of time, not a focused episode, or if the writer is summarizing rather than storytelling, you might decide to intervene.

I decided, for example, to interrupt Nicole's writing. In the first page of her booklet, she told all about ballet: how she felt doing ballet, what she did to learn ballet. Parts of her writing were lovely. But nevertheless, I needed her to understand clearly that she was actually not writing a story at all but instead, an all-about text. "Nicole," I said, "I want to stop you before you get any farther. Later this year, you and your classmates will be writing all-about books, and the page you have written about ballet would be a great

---

MID-WORKSHOP TEACHING
Rereading to Build Writing Stamina

"Writers, can I have your eyes and your attention? When I feel myself lagging in energy, I reread my writing. But I reread in a special way. I reread it to myself as if the story is an utter masterpiece.

"I don't fuss over the details; if a word is awry, I mentally fix it and keep going because I want to read with a rapt focus on my content, filling myself with the story. When I come to the last word I've written, I just pick up my pen and write for dear life, scrawling down the page.

"So, writers, if you are lagging in energy and want to give yourself a second wind, pause, and reread. Reread your own writing as if it is a masterpiece, and let your rereading give you a boost for more writing."

---

page for an all-about-ballet book. But for now, we are writing stories, like, 'One day, when I got to ballet class, my teacher said to me . . . ' Right now, will you think of one particular thing that happened at ballet that made you feel happy, or made you sad."

I waited. Nicole thought for a bit, then said, "I know!" Soon she'd begun a new booklet, this time writing a story.

I also intervened to speak with a few writers who were copying their notebook entries into their drafting booklets. I pointed out that when writers turn a notebook entry into a draft, they usually enlarge and elaborate on the entry. "Writers, the entry is like an artist's sketch.

(continues)

The sketch gives an idea of what the painting will look like, where everything will go, the size and shape of things, but when the painting is actually being done you can begin to see all the details, like the colors, the subtle shading, the thickness of the brushstrokes. That's what happens when you move from your entry to your drafting booklet." I'd soon convinced these writers to put aside their entries and write from their mental movies.

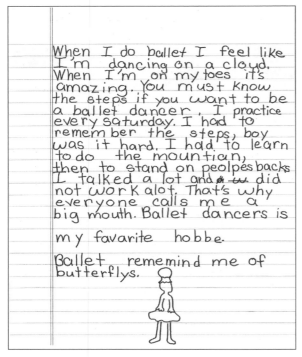

When I do ballet I feel like I'm dancing on a cloud. When I'm on my toes it's amazing. You must know the steps if you want to be a ballet dancer. I practice every saturday. I had to remember the steps, boy was it hard. I had to learn to do the mountian, then to stand on peolpes backs I talked a lot and did not work alot. That's why everyone calls me a big mouth. Ballet dancers is

my favarite hobbe.

Ballet rememind me of butterflys.

FIG. 8–2   The first page of Nicole's booklet

A Symphony Share

Remind writers of the strategies they already know for writing with stamina.

"Writers, earlier some of you reread your writing to yourselves, rereading your drafts like they are masterpieces, and I could tell that helped you get a second wind. Do that often when you write. You needn't reread the whole draft. Sometimes I go directly to the parts of my writing that I am proud of. When I do this rereading at home, if I am all alone, I pretend I'm on a stage, reading that particular part of my writing out loud to an audience. I use my best reading voice; I even give the characters different voices. I slow way down when I come to the dramatic parts; I speed my voice up when I come to exciting parts. So do this sort of rereading whenever you need a second wind."

Ask students to try this strategy by reading favorite parts to the whole class.

"Of course, it also helps to listen to other people's writing. Right now, choose a line or two that you particularly like from your writing, and in a moment I'm going to ask you to read it aloud to others. Thumbs up when you have found a little bit to read." I waited until a good many thumbs were up. "I'll be the conductor, and you be the instruments in a symphony. When I tip my imaginary baton at you, please read your part out to everyone—no discussion, just read them with power. Let your words sing out. You ready?"

I tipped my baton toward Amanda. She read, "The trees were swaying back and forth like they were dancing." Now I gestured to Brooke. She read, "When I took the swim test, my stomach felt like it had butterflies in it."

I smiled and nodded toward Song Moo. He read, "The cake was mush." A few more children read.

Voice your appreciation for the writing the children have read aloud. Remind children to use this strategy when they need writing energy.

"Wow, can you feel the writing energy in the room right now? When you read your writing aloud, the words come to life. They have power. From now on, remember you can take a moment to read your writing aloud to yourself so you can hear what you have written and go from there."

Setting

I walked through the door and I yelled "Snowy" I took here out and started to play with her.

I went back from school and came in. I thought Snowy would bark and she did.

I took her out of the gate and yelled "Snowy!"

She went on top of me and started to lick me I thought to myself I love dogs. I also thought all she did was licking me but... She WAS peing on me. "SNOWY SCobert!!

"Why did you pee on me?!" "Bark Bark" Snowy replied.

After that She Just layed with me and went to sleep.

FIG. 8–3 This student's two-page booklet contains a particularly dramatic moment!

Revising by Studying What Other Authors Have Done

IN THIS SESSION, you'll teach students that one way writers revise is by studying other authors' craft and naming what the author does so they can try it in their own writing.

GETTING READY

✔ Mentor text, *Come On, Rain!*, to introduce today's lesson

✔ Copies of a few excerpts or pages from *Come On, Rain!* that show powerful descriptive language. Distribute a page or two to each child before the minilesson.

✔ Post-its and pens for highlighting craft moves during the minilesson

✔ "What Hesse Did to Make Her Storytelling Voice So Good in *Come On, Rain!*" chart, with heading prewritten (see Teaching)

✔ Additional picture books that show a variety of craft moves (see Conferring and Small-Group Work)

✔ Narrative Writing Checklist, Grades 3 and 4 from Session 5 (see Share). You may also decide to make individual copies of the checklist for students to use and keep in their writing folders as well.

COMMON CORE STATE STANDARDS: W.3.3.b,c; W.3.5, W.4.3.d, RL.3.4, RL.3.5, RL.3.7, RL.4.2, RL.4.4, SL.3.1.c,d; L.3.3, L.3.5.a,b,c

I F YOUR EDUCATION in the qualities of good writing was anything like mine, you'll probably find that you are learning about qualities of strong narrative writing right alongside your children. When I was in school, I was taught to write with my five senses, to use adjectives and adverbs, and to include similes and alliteration. But I was not taught anything else about narrative writing until I was out of graduate school and teaching third-graders. I wanted to write an article about my students and therefore got hold of Donald Murray's *A Writer Teaches Writing* (1985), and the rest is history.

I strongly advise you to read some books on good writing, and talk with colleagues about these books. Try Katherine Bomer's *Writing a Life* (2005), Ralph Fletcher's *What a Writer Needs* (1992), Murray's *A Writer Teaches Writing*, William Zinsser's *On Writing Well* (1998), or Natalie Goldberg's *Writing Down the Bones* (1986).

The stories that other authors have written will also help teach you qualities of good writing. Try to name things the author has done in Kate DiCamillo's *Because of Winn-Dixie* (2004), Patricia MacLachlan's *Journey* (1993), and "Mr. Entwhistle" in Jean Little's *Hey World, Here I Am* (1990). And push yourself beyond clichés toward words that are more precise, exact, and replicable: What *exactly* has the author done that you could try?

Once you name the technique, try it yourself. Pull out the entry you began earlier and see how your sentences turn out, rewritten under the influence of Karen Hesse, Julie Brinckloe, or Alma Flor Ada. Then tell the children about what you learned. Your own experience, writing under the influence of a great author, can set the stage for this lesson in which you invite children to do likewise. Your experience will be a precious resource when you go to teach this session.

Today's minilesson does not follow the usual structure. Instead of teaching by demonstrating and providing opportunities for guided practice, you will use the minilesson as an opportunity for youngsters to learn through an inquiry approach by returning to *Come On, Rain!* Expect that the entire infrastructure of the minilesson will differ from most—and watch to see how you and your children take to this structure!

Revising by Studying What Other Authors Have Done

CONNECTION

Establish the reason for the teaching point, or in this case, the inquiry question. You want to know what makes *Come On, Rain!* so good—and plan to use what you learn in your own writing.

"Writers, last night I sat down to make changes to my draft. I wanted to make it the best piece of writing I've ever done. The best piece in the world. As good as *Come On, Rain!*, even! So I sharpened my pencil and sat down at my desk and started to revise my piece. But it was tough to figure out how to make my piece as good as *Come On, Rain!* I started wondering, What makes *Come On, Rain!* so good? We have already noticed how she uses a storytelling voice to show, not tell. But so many people have loved that story for so many years. What makes it so wonderful?

"I started thinking that today we could all work together to figure that out. We all want to make our stories as wonderful as Karen Hesse's story. We all want to make our readers laugh and gasp and pull closer the way Hesse does."

❖ **Name a question that will guide the inquiry.**

"Writers, today we are going to do an inquiry. We are going to investigate the question, 'What does Karen Hesse do to make *Come On, Rain!* so powerful and meaningful?' And then we'll be able to ask, 'How can we do some of that in our own writing?'"

TEACHING: GUIDED INQUIRY

Set writers up to investigate *Come On, Rain!* by guiding them through a series of steps that help them answer the larger, overarching question. Then listen in and coach, eliciting and collecting their comments.

"Okay, writers, so to investigate this big question, first we are going to look at the places we love the most in *Come On, Rain!* I'm going to give each of you an excerpt from Karen Hesse's book. Right now, find a part that makes you pull a little closer to the story, makes you pause, or reread, or that really gets that movie in your mind going strong. When you find a part like that, put a big star or heart in the margin next to it."

◆ COACHING

This minilesson is best taught after children have written a good portion of their first draft. If your children got off to a slow start on their writing, you may want to insert a day for writing non-stop before you teach this lesson on revision under the influence of an author.

When you set children up to do an inquiry, you empower them by giving them space and time to explore, question, and hypothesize, which in turn lifts student engagement and energy around this work.

"Now, writers, here comes the really important part. You're going to ask yourselves a huge question. You're going to ask yourself *why* you love that part so much. Look closely. Think about what Karen Hesse did to make that part effective. Reread the passage and ask yourselves, 'What exactly did Hesse do in this part to make it so powerful?' On a Post-it, jot what exactly Hesse did in that part."

Coach into children's work, prompting them to study Hesse's use of language carefully.

As children worked, I voiced over.

"Reread the passage a few times and keep asking, 'What did she do?' Think, 'What is it about this passage that made me notice it?'"

"Writers, notice particular words. What other word could she have used? Why did she choose this word?"

After a few minutes, I said, "Writers, put a thumb up if you have ideas about what Karen Hesse has done." Across the rug thumbs popped up. "Writers, be sure you've used Post-its to name precisely what Hesse did to make you pause. Stick the Post-its on the special parts." After a bit, I said, "Turn and tell your partner what you noticed."

Listen in and highlight observations that students make. Repeat their observations using more precise language and record these on a chart.

"Writers, I'm going to make a list of all of the things you noticed."

Isaiah said, "I like the words. Her words make the story so good."

"Okay, Isaiah, that's a start. Now try to ask yourself, 'What *specifically* was it that Hesse did?' We'll help you. Can you take us to an exact part where you like the words, and we'll all try to name what she is doing that works so well."

Isaiah turned to the page where he had drawn a star and read, "'Is there thunder?' Mamma asks. 'No thunder,' I say."

"Isaiah, it's great that you went back to the text and said the exact words that Hesse wrote. That really helps us. Now, we have to figure out why the words work so well."

"Well, it's good because she tells us what they say to each other," said Isaiah.

"Yes!" I said. "Karen Hesse doesn't just tell us that the narrator and her mother talked about the rain. She put in the exact words that the characters said. Very precise observation. Let's use that to get our chart started."

Abraham raised his thumb, and I gestured for him to share what he had found.

By asking students to reread a mentor text, examining the language the author used, the choices the author made, you are supporting the close, analytic reading that is valued in the CCSS. Although this is the writing workshop, you are teaching reading standards RL.4.5 and RL.4.6

Notice that over and over, I point out good work and then name what is good about the work in a way that is generalizable to another day and another piece.

Whenever you make a strategy chart, include examples with each strategy so students can use them as models for their own writing.

"Right here on this page, it says, '"Jackie-Joyce?" I breathe, pressing my nose against her screen.' I like this part," he said.

"Hmm . . . So everyone, let's help Abraham think. What is it about that line that works so well?

"'Cause it tells *how* she said it," said Abraham. And he acted out Tessie leaning forward and whispering, "Jackie-Joyce" in a breathy voice.

I nodded. "So one thing that makes this book so special is that Hesse shows not only *what* her characters say, but also *how* they say it?" Abraham nodded.

Olivia shouted out, "Here she says, 'I whisper.' That's another place where she does the same thing!"

Isaiah added, "And on this page it says 'It's about time,' she murmurs."

"Great. Let's put that on our chart too, and later you'll have a chance to see if you can show *how* characters say something in your writing as well. What else, writers?"

Soon the group had identified that Hesse writes with descriptive details, as in this excerpt.

> *Mamma sinks onto a kitchen chair and sweeps off her hat. Sweat trickles down her neck and wets the front of her dress and under her arms. Mamma presses the ice-chilled glass against her skin.*

"Let's again think, 'She could have written . . . But instead she wrote . . .'" I said, and channeled the students to think about that.

Soon Carl proposed, "She could have just said, 'Mamma sat down and got a drink,' but instead she says a lot more: sinks onto a kitchen chair, sweeps off her hat, presses the ice-chilled glass against her skin. She really describes things, like ice-chilled glass. And she says all of the things that Mamma did."

"Fascinating, Carl," I said, taking his lovely observation and repeating it in more precise language. "So what you are saying is that she uses descriptive details, and she tells the story bit by bit, writing exactly what Mamma did. Those are two powerful things we can add to the chart."

In that fashion, we started a chart that I finished later.

FIG. 9–1 The finished chart, with examples from *Come On, Rain!*

ACTIVE ENGAGEMENT AND LINK

Set writers up to try out one of these techniques on their own writing.

"Writers, this is a nice long list! I'm starting to see what makes *Come On, Rain!* so wonderful. I don't know about you, but I feel as if I could put some of these things in my own story. Do any of you feel that way?

"I could try teaching you how I do that, but you all just invented this whole list. How 'bout if you invent ways to do some of this cool stuff in your own writing? You game? I am not sure how you could go about changing your writing around. I know some of you were asking me if we had any tape or staplers or scissors, but I'm not totally sure *what* you have in mind. How about if I just leave this totally up to each of you to figure out what you want to do to make your writing the best it can be using what we have learned from Karen Hesse and how you might go about doing that. Then later we could learn from each other's inventions."

Teaching Children to Read Like Writers

THIS DAY MARKS THE HALFWAY POINT of the unit, and the children are revising their first draft. As children do this they also begin to solidify the language writers use to talk about the writing process and ultimately about their own writing. Teaching children to talk well about their writing, not just retell their story, is something to strive toward. Creating small writing groups is one place to start.

One group of children that can particularly benefit from being part of a writing group are those children who are proficient at writing, who pick up each thing you teach and fly with it. Teachers often tell me that these are the students they fear most when conferring. They ask me, "What do I teach when they are already doing everything I have taught?" The tendency is to leave these students to fend for themselves or to ask them to help others in need of support. As teachers we must be cognizant that these children need support and attention, too. The good news is that you do have some coteachers in the classroom to draw upon for support. Professional authors can be coteachers, as can other children in the class. Put these two together and you have a win-win situation. The children can explore books for craft moves, looking particularly at how word choice impacts the tone of the story or how the author chose to structure the text, share what they discover with others, and talk about what they have tried or still want to try. They can also use the charts to reflect, analyze their own writing just as readers analyze texts, and develop their own charts based on the goals they create.

You may decide to convene a small group, telling children, "Cynthia Rylant once said, 'I learned how to write from writers. I didn't know any personally. But I read.' She is not alone. Writers all agree that they learned to write from other authors. It is totally exciting to me that right now, each of you is spending some time not just writing and rewriting, but also reading like a writer. When you read like a writer, you notice not only what authors *say*, but also *how they say it*. And I was thinking that you might work as a study group to think together about what writers do to write such great literature."

Then you could set out one or two books that contain lots of examples of craft and structure and invite the children to explore them. *(continues)*

MID-WORKSHOP TEACHING
"What Do I Want My Readers to Feel?"

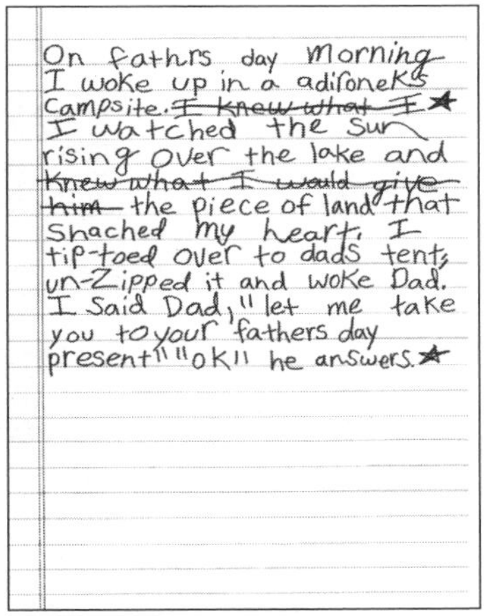

FIG. 9–2 Miles reread this, then tried to add more descriptive details.

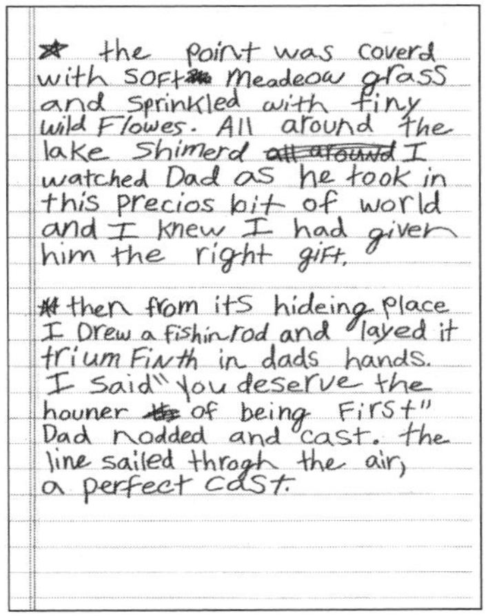

FIG. 9–3 These are Miles's additions.

"Writers, I want to suggest one more thing that'll make a world of difference to your writing. Ask yourself this: 'What am I trying to make my listeners *feel*?' Are you writing a slow, sad story or a funny story? Or is your piece one of those sit-on-the-edge-of-the-seat stories, where readers are nervously chewing their nails as they read? When published authors write their stories, they often do so knowing the tone—the mood—they're hoping to convey."

"I've chosen a few books that have amazing craft moves that I bet you could try in your own writing. All of these books were written by authors who set out to create a particular tone or used a particular structure. You may want to spend a little time thinking, 'What did this author do that I might try too?'

"Will you read and reread a page or two 'til you get the sound in your bones? A man named Edward Hirsch said, in an article he wrote, 'I feel words creating a rhythm, a music, a spell, a mood, a shape, a form' (2006). You'll want to bookmark places in these books where an author has used a technique you'd like to try, and then see if you can feel the words creating a rhythm, a music, a spell."

Pulling a group of children who will not only support, but also inspire each other, is a great way to keep their engagement high.

You can convene a second group, and approach reading–writing connections differently. "Writers, earlier you set some goals for yourself. Will you look back at those goals right now?" Then, after they've reread their goals, you could say, "What I want to suggest is that *Come on Rain!* can probably help you meet some of your goals. If your goal is to show readers where the story occurs, *Come on Rain!* can give you ideas. If your goal is to paragraph better. . . . Guess what? You are right. This book can help. Will you work with each other, your goals, and this book while I watch and coach in to help?"

Outgrowing Ourselves as Writers

Convene writers and channel them to study the work a classmate has done, just as they've studied a text written by a published author.

"Writers, earlier we looked closely at Karen Hesse's writing to learn what she did that we could try. Let's now study Song Moo's writing and think, 'Is there something I can learn from Song Moo that might help me in my own writing?'" (See Figure 9–4.)

"Turn and talk to your partner about what Song Moo did that you could try in your own stories. As you do this, it might help to use the narrative checklist to help you notice particular things he has done."

FIG. 9–4 Song Moo wrote on notebook paper rather than in a story booklet.

Soon, the room was filled with conversation, with the children making observations, like:

"He showed the talking between the friends."

"He included descriptive details. Like wiggling in six pieces."

"He told the story bit by bit, just like we learned before."

"He used words that sound good together like 'worms wiggling.'"

Ask children to meet with their partners to assess their work, noticing ways they have and have not met the goals they set earlier.

"Writers, you noticed the powerful ways Karen Hesse wrote, and tried some of those ways of writing in your narratives. Some of you focused on using a storytelling voice, while others added descriptive details and dialogue. It seems like a good time to look back at your Narrative Writing Checklist and your goals to see how much progress you've made on those goals and to perhaps create a few new goals.

We have chosen this halfway point in the unit to introduce the Level 4 checklist, so that all students have ambitious goals to work toward. If you find yourself saying, "Wait! My children aren't ready for Level 4 yet!," then don't fret—you'll simply introduce the new level later in the unit, or with small groups of children who are in need of an extra challenge.

"And this time, let's look at the fourth-grade checklist as well as the third-grade one. The fourth-grade checklist includes some of the new things you have been learning. Will you look back and forth between your writing and the checklist? What are you already doing as a writer? How have you done with meeting your goals? What will your next big goals be?" This checklist is available on the CD-ROM. After a few minutes of quiet work, I said, "Turn and tell your partner your thoughts." After listening in for a bit, I convened the group.

"Writers, can I have your eyes and your attention? I heard wonderful partner conversations. Many of you helped your partner name more goals to work toward. Will you talk now about how you'll make your goals actually translate into improved work?"

Narrative Writing Checklist

	Grade 3	NOT YET	STARTING TO	YES!	Grade 4	NOT YET	STARTING TO	YES!
	Structure				**Structure**			
Overall	I told the story bit by bit.	☐	☐	☐	I wrote the important part of an event bit by bit and took out unimportant parts.	☐	☐	☐
Lead	I wrote a beginning in which I helped readers know who the characters were and what the setting was in my story.	☐	☐	☐	I wrote a beginning in which I showed what was happening and where, getting readers into the world of the story.	☐	☐	☐
Transitions	I told my story in order by using phrases such as *a little later* and *after that.*	☐	☐	☐	I showed how much time went by with words and phrases that mark time such as *just then* and *suddenly* (to show when things happened quickly) or *after a while* and *a little later* (to show when a little time passed).	☐	☐	☐
Ending	I chose the action, talk, or feeling that would make a good ending and worked to write it well.	☐	☐	☐	I wrote an ending that connected to the beginning or the middle of the story. I used action, dialogue, or feeling to bring my story to a close.	☐	☐	☐
Organization	I used paragraphs and skipped lines to separate what happened first from what happened later (and finally) in my story.	☐	☐	☐	I used paragraphs to separate the different parts or times of the story or to show when a new character was speaking.	☐	☐	☐
	Development				**Development**			
Elaboration	I worked to show what happened to (and in) my characters.	☐	☐	☐	I added more to the heart of my story, including not only actions and dialogue but also thought and feelings.	☐	☐	☐

Storytellers Develop the Heart of a Story

THE DAY the very first copies of my book *The Art of Teaching Reading* (1994) arrived, a few teachers were beside me watching while I, with trembling hands, opened the box and brought out one copy of the book. My hand ran over the glossy cover with delight. I clasped the book against me, loving its heft. "I can't imagine you wrote all those words!" one of the teachers said. I remember thinking, "If she only knew." The words that I held with such pride were just the tip of the iceberg. In making that one book, I had written hundreds of thousands of words that no one would ever see. When people build houses, they fill a truck-sized trailer with the rejected materials. When I write, I need one of those trailers parked next to my desk.

In life, I am often aware that the things I say and do go out into the world, good or bad, as they are. In life, I can't take back my words. As I move through my days, if I am clumsy or hurtful or obscure, I can't rewind and make myself into a more agile or lucid or savvy person. I can't call back a speech I have given, a workshop I have led, a meeting I have facilitated, a conversation I have participated in. But the effort I'm participating in now—redoing two giant best-selling series of books—brings home the fact that as a writer, I can call back my writing. I can take whatever I've done and make it much, much better. Revising my writing (and in doing so, revising myself) is a great and powerful opportunity. Revision is my favorite part of the writing process. It is pure pleasure to be able to stand back, scan what I've written, and think, "How can I make my best work better?"

Children, however, often come into our classrooms dreading revision. Quite often, children are unsure of what revising actually *is*. Most children have been asked by teachers to add details since first grade, but adding details is vague and signals for many children that they just need to write more and more, which is not an easy task for any writer and does not necessarily improve the draft they are working on. You cannot tarry a moment, then, before giving children very tangible revision strategies so they tackle their fast drafts with focus and control and a very clear understanding of what to do next. In this session you

IN THIS SESSION, you will teach students that writers revise by asking, "What's the most important part of this story?" and developing that section.

GETTING READY

✔ "To Write A True Story" chart (see Connection and Share)

✔ Two copies of a child's draft, one they wrote before you conferred with them and the revised draft after the conference on elaborating the most important part of a story (the heart of the story) (see Teaching)

✔ Shared class story from Session 4 or another shared writing story you have written on chart paper (see Active Engagement)

✔ Scissors, strips of paper, tape, staplers, and colored pens and pencils

COMMON CORE STATE STANDARDS: W.3.3.a,b,c; W.3.4, W.3.5, W.4.3.c,d; RL.3.3, RL.4.3, SL.3.6, L.3.3.a,b; L.3.1

let children know that revision begins with selection. Writers reread and say, "This part of the story is the most important part." And then they give that part of the text the compliment of revision.

You cannot tarry a moment before giving children very tangible revision strategies so they tackle their fast drafts with focus and control and a very clear understanding of what to do next.

In addition to focusing children on specific revision strategies, you can also find ways to entice children into revising with the tools you make readily available. Colorful strips of paper, tape, scissors, and fancy markers can all make a big difference in the number of risks children are willing to take as they reread their stories and think about ways they can make them even more exciting. And what is more exciting than seeing one's writing physically grow or become multicolored with each and every revision made?

Revision itself is all about giving a piece of writing the respect, the listening attention, that will allow that piece to become even stronger. The most important thing I do when I revise is find the life in my piece and create space for it. I say, "This is beautiful." When children see their own work become dramatically stronger through revision, sermons on the importance of revision are not necessary. That is the work in today's session.

Storytellers Develop the Heart of a Story

CONNECTION

Remind students that revision is a compliment to their writing. Use a story to illustrate the importance of revising in a way that draws out the heart of their writing.

"Writers, yesterday you did the all-important work of revising your writing using Karen Hesse's *Come On, Rain!* for inspiration. But when listening to your partnerships, I found that a few of you don't like to revise. Horrors! I think somehow you've gotten the idea—a very wrong idea—that revision is a sign that the writing is bad. It is actually just the opposite. Writers revise because a piece of writing has potential. When your writing is lousy, you throw it out. When your writing is full of potential, you revise it. Revision is a compliment to good writing!

"I want to tell you something about running that relates to revision. You know how you wrote this draft, fast and furious? That's how I run, most of the time. Usually when I run, I'm so focused on my pace that I don't really pay attention to my surroundings. But sometimes, when there is something important on the roadside—like a tree in full bloom— I slow down and pay attention. Master storytellers are the same way. They recognize that somewhere in each story is a point that needs them to s . . . l . . . o . . . w down. They don't do this at any old part in the story. They slow down at the most important part, at the part where they want the reader to pay greater attention. This might be the saddest or the funniest or the strangest or the most breathtaking part. It might be the part where they want their reader to sit up and listen closer, thinking, 'This is what the story is about.' Storytellers call this the *heart of the story*.

"I want you to take a minute to place your hand over your own heart. Under your hand, beneath all the layers of tissue and muscle, is the heart that keeps you alive. The heart of a story is the same way. It is the most important part because it gives life to the rest of the story."

❖ Name the teaching point.

"This brings me to the thing I want to teach you today, so listen carefully. Revision is not about fixing errors; it is about finding and developing potentially great writing, sometimes by adding more to the heart of the story." I pointed to the chart as I went over what we learned yesterday.

Stories often begin with the author putting a character into a setting and, in a sense, this minilesson (like so many others) establishes the setting, the context, for today's teaching. If your students seem to have no resistance around revision, you will not want to begin the minilesson this way. If they have no reason to have reservations about revision, why offer them any? On the other hand, if you know there is resistance to revision in the air, acknowledging it may be the best way to begin.

To Write a True Story

- Find story ideas that are focused and important to you and write lots of entries.
- Make a mental movie of what happened, telling it in small detail, bit by bit.
  - Detail the actions.
  - Include the dialogue.
- Remember your self-assessments of your narrative writing and your goals.
- Rehearse for your writing by storytelling the story repeatedly.
- Try different leads for your story (Action? Dialogue?).
- Write a flash draft, writing fast and furious, eyes on the mental movie.
- Revise.
  - Try what other authors have done.
  - Develop the heart of the story.

FIG. 10–1

TEACHING

Spotlight what one child did in a way that illustrates the teaching point. Retell the story of the process.

"Writers, you've been revisiting your drafts and revising your work. Revising is all about finding and developing powerful writing. One way you develop writing is by adding more to the important parts of the story. Yesterday, Gregory did some powerful revision work that was inspired by Karen Hesse's *Come On, Rain!* I want to tell you the story of his revision because some of you may want to follow his example. Be researchers and listen, seeing if you can list the lessons you learn about revision on your fingers. Pay attention because then you'll chance to try out some of these lessons.

"When I pulled my chair alongside Gregory, he'd already written a quick draft about the day he learned that his fish, Al, had died. I told him that what I usually do after I've finished a draft is reread it, thinking, 'What's the most important part of this story? What's the heart of this story?' So Gregory reread his draft, looking for the most important part. I copied it onto chart paper so you can see it." (See Figure 10–2.)

Al is What!

Dead. Ever since I had fish, I had Al: the best algae-eater in the world. Once I heard he was dead, I did not cry. I just was still. Then I asked, "Where is he?" My dad said, "In the trash." I asked to see him. I saw it was true. My dad put him back. For a second, I thought, then I said,

By now you have seen that there are several common methods you can use in the teaching component of a minilesson. You can write publicly or bring in writing you have done at home. You can tell children about a published author's process or show the author's work. You can reenact a conference you had with a child, or you can retell the story of a child's process. Another option is to invite the child to be a guest speaker, telling the class what he did to make his writing better. Knowing this list of options should enable you to invent minilessons more easily, and to realize that you could teach the same content about writing in any one of many different ways. In this teaching component, I retell the story of one child's process of revision.

Notice that I copied this story onto chart paper for the purposes of this minilesson.

"We can give him a funeral." My dad looked doubtful for a minute but I picked him up and said, "He was special." Then I cried. Al was gone.

"Gregory motioned to a line in the middle of the draft where he'd described seeing the dead fish in the trash."

I asked to see him. I saw it was true.

"Gregory said, 'That's the most important part. That was the saddest part.'

"'So, Gregory,' I said. 'You have just done the first step in revision. You have located the heart of your story.'" I stopped and looked at the children. "You should be listing lessons that you are learning about revision. Think about what Gregory did first. Then I said to Gregory, 'I notice something: that most-important part of your story is pretty short, isn't it. You definitely don't stretch it out.'

"Then I added, 'What I do when I find the most important section in a story is this: I add some more paper right into my draft by scissoring the page apart, like this.'"

At this point I started cutting the chart paper version of his story into two at the place Gregory had identified as the heart of his story. "Then I tape a lot more paper into that important section of the draft." I taped a half page of paper into his story. I stopped again. "Writers, are you noticing lessons for revision? Do you notice how after Gregory found the most important part of his story, he added more paper right into that part? Keep listening to hear what comes next because it is the most important part.

To Gregory I said, "Then I reread the first part of my story, up to where there's space for more writing. I try to make a movie in my mind of exactly what happened." I told him that we can make a movie in our minds and at that important part, slow the movie down to make that part last longer. Sort of like we see it happening in slow motion."

To help Gregory get himself started, I read his draft aloud to him, stopping at the section he'd identified. 'Make a movie in your mind of just this part, Gregory,' I told him. I reread, "then I asked, 'Where is he?' my dad said, 'In the trash.' Then, imagining the missing section of the story, I added, "'I walked over to the trash can and looked in. I saw . . .' and let the sentence hang signaling for Gregory to carry on. He said "I looked in the trash can and saw . . . lots of trash."

"'Be exact. What exactly did you see? If you can't remember, make it up,' I said, and repeated 'I walked over to the trash can and looked in. I saw . . .' to give him a new jump start.

"Gregory repeated the last line of the story and then added on to it. 'I walked over to the trash can and I opened it. I looked in and saw . . . wet paper towels, orange peels, and a pile of coffee grounds. On the top of it, I saw Al!

"'Keep going. What exactly did you do?' I said. Holding his hand out, as if it contained a dead fish, Gregory said, 'I picked up Al.'

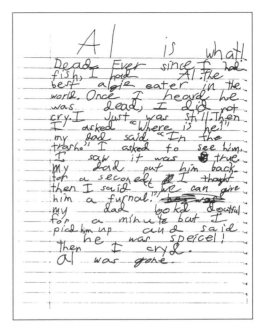

FIG. 10–2 Gregory's first draft

This draft is a great favorite of mine. Read it aloud well. Your children should get goose bumps!

Details are magic. These details transform this story. Notice that my interjections are lean. I do not want to overwhelm his story. But my prompts are calculated. I shift Gregory from generalizations to specifics of what he saw, what he did, what he said.

"'Be exact. What *exactly* did you do? What did you say?'

"'I flicked off the coffee grounds and said, 'Al, I'm gonna miss you.''"

Debrief. Point out what the one child did to find and develop the heart of his story.

"Class, do you see what Gregory did? He reread his story, determined that this part about looking in the trash can and seeing his beloved fish was the heart of the story, and then he added a chunk of paper right at that section of the story. He went back, made a movie in his mind to recall exactly what happened, then story-told and wrote that section with much more detail. Look at the difference now." I put a copy of Gregory's revised story with the inset written next to the first draft.

> Dead. Ever since I had fish, I had Al: the best algae-eater in the world. Once I heard he was dead, I did not cry. I was just still. Then I asked, "Where is he?" My dad said, "In the trash."
>
> I asked to see him. I walked over to the trash can and I opened it. I looked in and saw wet paper towels, orange peels and a pile of coffee grounds. On the top of the coffee grounds, I saw Al. I picked up Al.
>
> I flicked the coffee grounds, and said, "Al, my friend. I'm gonna miss you." My dad put him back.
>
> For a second, I thought, then I said, "We can give him a funeral." My dad looked doubtful for a minute but I picked him up and said, "He was special." Then I cried. Al was gone.

"So, do you see, writers, that after you finish a draft, it helps to reread it, thinking, 'What's the heart of my story?' and then to think, 'How can I slow this part down, adding descriptive detail and using my storytelling voice to add significance to this important moment?'"

ACTIVE ENGAGEMENT

Set children up to do similar work on the shared class story.

"Let's practice it. Let's revisit one of our class stories about the dragonfly and develop the heart of it. I've written a version of that dragonfly story on this chart paper. Would you each pretend it is your personal story and reread it, trying to find the heart of it? Then think how you could tell that one part with more detail, using our Hesse storytelling chart to help remind you of all you can do to make your storytelling strong. Let me read it aloud."

> Our teacher opened <u>Because of Winn-Dixie</u> and began to read. We were so quiet, we could probably have heard ants crawling along the floor. Then our teacher lowered the book. We were about to say, 'No! Read it!' But she was looking at a blur of wings that flew between us. What was that?

When you shift from the demonstration to debriefing, students should feel the different moves you are making just by the way your intonation and posture change. After most demonstrations, there will be a time for you to debrief, and that's a time when you are no longer acting like a writer. You are the teacher who has been watching the demonstration and now turns to talk, eye to eye with kids, asking if they noticed this or that during the previous portion of the minilesson.

I love this revision strategy because essentially we are asking children to do what they've worked hard to learn to do—make a movie in their mind, telling the story in a step-by-step way. But now they're doing this to expand a moment within the moment. They should have a lot of success with this.

By explaining that every child in the room can follow in Gregory's path, finding the heart of a story and expanding on it as Gregory has done, I show children that Gregory's work is replicable and worth replicating—and it is! This revision strategy has proven to be accessible and powerful.

Sam called, "Dragonflies," and sure enough, we saw them now: three dragonflies hoevered over our heads.

"They want to hear the story!" we said, and our teacher began to read.

"Tell your partners where the heart of this story might be for you. Make a movie in your mind of what happened at that part and story-tell to your partner how you'd stretch that part out. Write it in the air with details." I gave them a few minutes to do this.

"Okay, writers, can I have your eyes and your attention? Most of you felt that the heart of this story when the whole class saw the dragonflies. You stretched that part out to each other. Felix, you said."

The dragonflies hung over our heads.

"Terrance, you added this next bit."

We could see their big eyes.

"What else could we add?"

Amanda dictated, "They twinkled like tinfoil."

I nodded and transcribed as directed. Then I said, "I think we should tell what we did. Did we say something or do something?"

"The dragonflies were so beautiful that we all smiled," Song Moo said. I added this and then read the entire story aloud again, starting from the very beginning.

LINK

Summarize the lesson in a way that directs children through the steps of using this strategy.

"Writers, you really revised this story! You reread it, found the heart of it, made a movie in your mind, and added more detail to the part where readers should really sit up and take note. That's what writers do all the time when they revise! You can do that every time you have a really deserving draft in front of you. I can't wait to see how you stretch out the heart of the story to revise—if you decide you need to do that!"

Of course, there is no one right answer to the question "What is the heart of this story?" If children choose a part and have reasons for their choice, they could certainly take the story in that direction.

When I say, "Write-in-the-air" I am asking children to dictate to a partner the exact words they would write if they were writing instead of talking. I take some time to explicitly teach children what this injunction means.

We are not obligated to include every child's suggestion every time. If we elaborate on the heart of this class story with empty words and cumbersome phrases, the whole lesson falls flat. If children can feel the story improve, if they can feel that this kind of revision helps, then they will be drawn to the strategy. If you worry that the suggestions for revision of the class story that kids make won't be strong, ask them to turn and talk with their partners about what they'd add. Walk among them, listening in for suggestions to take. If there are none, let that inform your teaching for tomorrow! In the meantime, make up great suggestions yourself!

Remind children to help themselves.

"Remember that you need to help yourself and figure out what you need to do to make your story the best it can be. You may decide to find the heart of your story and then make a movie of it in your mind, adding details to stretch it out, bit by bit, making your storytelling voices stronger, like Karen Hesse does." I pointed to the Hesse storytelling chart. "You may have other ideas for how to make this story so, so much better. You are the kind of writers who can look at your story and know what it needs next. Okay, writers, get going."

Notice that in this minilesson, as in most minilessons, I leave children aware of their options for the day ahead. Just because I've taught something in a minilesson doesn't mean everyone must spend the workshop doing the content of that day's minilesson.

Getting Children Off to a Strong Start

NOW THAT YOUR CHILDREN ARE WORKING with increased independence, you will want to build on the show, not tell, work you started in Session 4 and continue to do some longer, complex conferences, developing the heart of a story, making movies in students' minds, and storytelling bit by bit. This means taking some time to research the writers, observing what they are doing and starting to do, then deciding what to teach next, and recording these observations and decisions. In the Teachers College Reading and Writing Project community, this type of conference is referred to as the research, decide, teach conference. It has been a staple of our teaching for decades.

When I asked Amanda what she'd been working on, she told me she'd been trying to show, not tell, her story. That sounded like a great goal, but when I read her most recent draft, I needed her to know she was still summarizing. This is what she'd written:

> I was 4 and my brother wanted to play Capture the flag with me. It took me about 20 minutes to finally understand how. He got frustrated from all my questions and threw a snowball at my face.

"Amanda, can you show me what part of this seems like it's showing the story?" Amanda pointed to the final detail about the snowball in her face. I nodded. "You are right that telling us this action helps. But this is still a summary of what happened. You are telling readers all about it, like a news reporter, but you don't quite yet allow us to be standing there with you, experiencing what happened first, next, next. To let your reader see and hear what happened, you need more snowballs, but you need more of the real details of what happened first and next and next." I proceeded to take her back to the start of the episodes. "Amanda, can you remember exactly how this started? Where you were at the beginning? What happened, exactly?"

Once she began to tell the episode, I repeated the story back to her as she told it to me and then coached her to get the words on the page, almost dictating the start of the story verbatim. This time the story went like this.

MID-WORKSHOP TEACHING
Inserting Paper to Help Revision

"Writers, can I have your eyes and your attention? As I watch you work today, cutting your draft apart and adding more space into it, I am reminded that writing is more like playing in clay than inscribing in marble. You are all realizing that drafts can be cut and spliced. Ellie did something smart. She realized that she didn't like her lead sentence, so she wrote a new lead and taped it on top of the old one! And Isaiah realized that he needed to expand not just one section of his draft (the heart of it), but also another section where things weren't that clear. So he sliced open his draft in two different places, inserting some extra paper into both spaces.

"You can do something similar, if you want. Don't forget that scissors, strips, tape, and revision pens can always be found in the writing center.

"Okay, writers, you can return to your work now."

> I was at the kitchen table eating macaroni. My big brother, Chris, came in and said, 'You gotta play Capture the Flag with me and Nate. You are on my team.' I followed him out to the front lawn . . .

Then I set up the other writers at the Amanda's table to be the "audience." I told Amanda, "Tell your story, and tell it so that you can see your listeners' mouths drop open in surprise or get them to chuckle or get them to lean in closer." I prompted the other writers at the table to try to do the same thing with their own drafts, saying aloud the exact details of how their episodes started and telling it bit by bit.

Above all, you will teach writers to make the gigantic leap from summarizing to storytelling. You will teach them that the writer, like the reader, must be transported to another time and another place and must relive the event whenever writing a narrative.

Writing Not Just the External, but the Internal Story, Too

Highlight a child who took the minilesson to heart. Tell the story of that child's work in a way others can learn from.

"Writers, today many of you tried to find and develop the heart of your story. Let me show you how Michela stretched out the important part of her story. First she wrote her story bit by bit. Listen to this first draft." (See Figure 10–3.)

"Then Michela realized she'd rushed past an important part—the suspense of opening the box. So she rewrote that section of the story. What I want you to notice is that Michela stretched out the important section of her story by telling not only what she and her mother did, but also what she thought. This is an important strategy writers use often. They don't only tell the external story, the sequence of actions. They also tell the internal story, as Michela does in this instance. Listen for how she shows what she thought as she stared at the box in her mother's hands." (See Figure 10–4.)

> What could be in that box? I wondered.
>
> "Pitter pat, pitter pat!" a noise came from the box.
>
> "Pitter pat, pitter pat!" There it was again for a second time. Something was moving inside that box." Maybe there's a monster in there!" I thought. "A mini one!" I started backing away slowly.
>
> "What's in the box, Mommy?" I asked. "A monster?"
>
> "No, no," said my mom.

"This is such important work that, writers, I'm going to ask you to reread the heart of your story, this time seeing a place where you could add the internal story. Try using phrases like, 'I noticed . . .' 'I wanted to say . . .'" I left some silence and then said, "Tomorrow you may decide to add some of the internal story. And for the rest of your life, always remember that writers write not only the external story, but also the internal story."

To Write a True Story

- Find story ideas that are focused and important to you and write lots of entries.
- Make a mental movie of what happened, telling it in small detail, bit by bit.
  - Detail the actions.
  - Include the dialogue.
- Remember your self-assessments of your narrative writing and your goals.
- Rehearse for your writing by storytelling the story repeatedly.
- Try different leads for your story (Action? Dialogue?).
- Write a flash draft, writing fast and furious, eyes on the mental movie.
- Revise.
  - Try what other authors have done.
  - Develop the heart of the story.
- Bring out the internal story ('I noticed . . . ' 'I wondered . . . ' 'I thought . . . ').

When I got My bird

It was the night before Halloween, my Mom comes in the door. "Mommy, Mommy, Mommy!" I shout. I run to her giving her a hug and a Kiss. Then I notice she's carrying a little tiny brown box. "Pitter Pat, Pitter Pat" Something's moving around inside of the box! I squeeze her arm. "What is it Mommy, What is it?" My Mom slowly opens the box as if she was afraid Something would pop out. I peer into the box. A animal with black beady little eyes, a small orange beak and a pair of wings looks up at me with it's head cocked to one side. "It's a bird!" I shout. "A bird?" My sister Alex, comes running. She peers into the box. "He is soooo cute" says Alex. "What should we name him?" I ask. "I've got the perfect name, we'll name him twinkle!" Twinkle wistles. "Then twinkle it is!" say's Alex. Then we Hurry of to bed and go to sleep, dreaming of our new pet.

FIG. 10–3   Michela's first draft—she later deleted the boxed out section, substituting in the writing shown in Figure 10–4.

I was about to drag her in when I noticed she was carrying a little brown box.
What could be in that box? I wondered.
"Pitter pat, pitter pat!" a noise came from the box.
"Pitter pat, pitter pat!" There it was again for a second time.
Something was moving inside that box.
"Mabey there's a monster in there!" I thought. "A mini one!"
I started backing away slowly.
"Whats in the box, Mommy?" I asked.
"A monster?"
"No, No" said my Mom.
My Mom slowly opened the box. I peeked inside very, very coutiously.

FIG. 10–4   Michela's insert

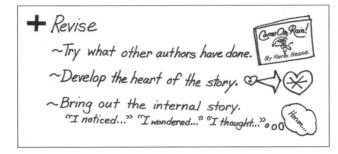

+ Revise
~Try what other authors have done.
~Develop the heart of the story.
~Bring out the internal story.
"I noticed..." "I wondered..." "I thought..."

FIG. 10–5

Paragraphing to Support Sequencing, Dialogue, and Elaboration

IN THIS SESSION, you'll show students how writers can revise their stories by grouping related sentences into paragraphs and then elaborating on those paragraphs.

GETTING READY

✔ Examples from students' drafts that illustrate how some writers are stretching out the heart of their stories (see Connection)

✔ "When to Start a New Paragraph" chart (see Connection)

✔ An excerpt from a child's draft with two or three subtopics written all together without paragraphs and that same excerpt written in paragraph form (see Teaching)

✔ Copies of another child's draft where paragraphs have been used. You can also use your own writing as an example (see Active Engagement).

✔ Sample student work that demonstrates creative and useful ways for indicating places to paragraph, for example adding numbers or symbols or adding another page (see Share)

✔ Narrative Writing Checklist, Grades 3 and 4, from Sessions 5 and 9 (see Conferring and Small-Group Work)

COMMON CORE STATE STANDARDS: W.3.3.a,b,c,d; W.3.4, W.3.5, W.3.10, W.4.2.a, W.4.3.a,b,c,d; RL.3.3, SL.3.1.a,b,c,d; L.3.2.c

IN THIS SESSION, you will teach students to chunk their drafts into paragraphs as a way to help readers. You'll let them know that writers often paragraph when there is a new subtopic, a new person speaking, or when time has moved forward. The goal of this teaching, of course, is not just paragraphing. It is to help kids consider ways to polish their pieces for readers.

But this lesson on paragraphing is also a lesson on elaboration. Once children realize that whenever time moves forward it is helpful to paragraph, many of them start realizing that their writing has been written as a necklace of teeny tiny underdeveloped paragraphs. A natural next step, then, is to teach elaboration.

Inexperienced writers tend to write in what Mina Shaughnessy (1977) calls "sentences of thought" instead of "passages of thought." They write one sentence when a more skilled writer would be apt to write three sentences—or ten. When a child writes, "I sat on the bench at the ball game. Then the game started. The first player made it to first base," we need to teach the child that the draft would be much stronger, allowing the reader to put herself in the narrator's place, if the child wrote two sentences for every one. "I sat on the bench at the ball game. It was still damp and the water soaked through my pants. Then the game started. People stopped talking and started watching."

Think about news stories you remember, and think why you remember them. Thirty-three miners are trapped underground for two months. Because the world learns the littlest details about how those miners are spending their time—praying together, organizing their own system of government, watching a live soccer game via a projector snaked down through a bore hole—the whole world waits with bated breath each day, each week, each month as the rescue operation drags on. Yet, across the globe, there are countless people trapped in terrible situations, and no one notices. It's only when we know the details of a person's story that we empathize.

Elaborating is important for more pedestrian reasons as well. *The New York Times* ("SAT Essay Test Rewards Length and Ignores Errors," May 4, 2005) recently showcased research that showed that by considering length alone, one can accurately predict the score a student will receive on the new writing component of the SAT exam. The longer the answer, the higher the score. The Educational Testing Service, the designer of the test, has hastened to challenge that claim, but the research stands. On standardized tests, length matters. Elaboration matters.

If children begin to group their thinking in clusters of sentences, whole passages of thought, rather than in smaller clusters of words, they will draw more language, more thoughts, out of themselves and onto the page.

I believe that one way to help children develop the habit of elaborating is to encourage them to think and write in paragraphs rather than sentences. If children begin to group their thinking in clusters of sentences, whole passages of thought, rather than in smaller clusters of words, they will draw more language, more thoughts, out of themselves and onto the page. Although in this session, paragraphing is an afterthought, a postwriting organizational structure, it will be very important to teach writers that from here on in, paragraphing becomes something they do during first-draft writing. They write, not edit, in paragraphs.

Paragraphing to Support Sequencing, Dialogue, and Elaboration

CONNECTION

Celebrate all of the work that children are doing to bring out the hearts of their stories.

"Writers, I love the way you are bringing out the hearts of your stories. Some of you are stretching out the heart of your story by telling step by step what happened. Others are adding the internal story. Many of you are doing both. Carl knew he wanted to write about his first checker game, so he made a tiny thumbnail sketch on his paper to remind himself of the topic for that page. He *could* have written, 'My opponent and I sat down and began to play.' Instead, what Carl did was he transported himself back to that moment, the moment that felt most important to the heart of his story. Then he played a movie in his mind of what happened at the very start of the checkers game, and then he told the story as though he was right there doing it all over again. Listen."
(See Figure 11–1.)

I am always pleased when minilessons dovetail together as this one does with others around it. This minilesson extends the teaching share from last session and leans toward the minilesson in the next session.

> At my first game of checkers I sat down on my chair. I was getting ready for my match. I took a deep breath. I rubbed my hands together. Then I had my eyes glued to my opponent like I was going to murder him. He sat down with me. We started to shake hands to one another. I said may the best man win. My opponent had a strange little smile on his face.

It makes sense that children will need additional scaffolding to have success with what we teach. So, in this instance, you'll tell children that when their writing involves lots of tiny paragraphs, this is a signal that they need to elaborate more. Teach them that at the very least, elaborating means writing two sentences instead of one.

"Many of you, like Carl, are taking the time to relive the moments you are writing about, and that's great for your writing!"

Use an analogy to illustrate that writers use paragraphing to help readers know which parts fit together.

"Writers, today I want to remind you that writers are always working on more than one thing. While you are finding and stretching out the heart of your story, you also need to keep an awareness in your mind that paragraphing matters, just like spelling and punctuation

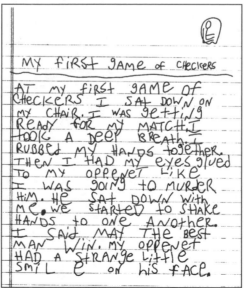

FIG. 11–1 Carl's thumbnail sketch and elaborated entry to stretch out the heart of his story

We can learn some qualities of good writing from the expert authors who write books on the topic—but some of the lessons that will matter for children will come simply from looking at children's work and thinking, "What next step might I suggest for this writer?"

matter. Words can be like books—I bet you agree with me that when every inch of a bookshelf space is crammed with books and you can't see how they are organized, it's hard to appreciate any of them. We pass them by.

"On the other hand, if a bookstore has its books nicely grouped—a round table featuring a selection of mysteries, a special shelf of biographies, and a display of store favorites—and if each of these groups is set out carefully with space around it, then it's easier to take the books in, to decide which ones to read.

"Writers, we need to make sure people's eyes don't fly right past our words and our ideas like they fly past books when they are crammed too close together with no organization!"

❖ Name the teaching point.

"Today, as you edit your drafts, I want to teach you that there are a few places where writers typically begin new paragraphs. Keeping these places in mind can help us know when to start a new paragraph. Some of those typical places are when there is a new subtopic, when time has moved forward, and when a new person is speaking."

TEACHING

Tell the story of one child's writing in a way that demonstrates how a writer might do this work.

"Writers, let's take a look at Abraham's story so I can show you what I mean. Abraham is writing a story about his cat, Ginger. As he was revising his draft, he realized that his story had different sections in it, almost like different chapters. Listen closely and think about what you would do if you were Abraham. This is what he'd written," I said, reading from the projected copy of his story.

> Ginger stretched out on the carpet and yawned. I scratched behind her ears and she leaned her head into my hand. She purred. My mom was in the kitchen baking cookies. She was singing a Spanish song. She always sings when she's in the kitchen.

"Think about what you notice, writers." After a few moments, I said, "Abraham realized that his piece really had two parts: one about his cat and one about his mom. Abraham was really smart because when he saw he had two topics, he paused and thought, 'If I have two topics, does this mean I have two stories? Or do they really fit together into one small moment, just not in one paragraph?' In this instance, he decided they belong in the same story because they are both parts of a longer story about Ginger eating one of his mom's chocolate chip cookies and getting sick. Watch me as I show you how he added a code that signified a new subtopic and therefore a new paragraph," I said, and added the paragraph sign at the appropriate place.

> Ginger stretched out on the carpet and yawned. I scratched behind her ears and she leaned her head into my hand. She purred. ¶ My mom was in the kitchen baking cookies. She was singing a Spanish song. She always sings when she's in the kitchen.

FIG. 11–2   Tips for when to start a new paragraph

I selected an example that isn't subtle, and abbreviated it for this purpose. Minilessons aren't times to be subtle—the message goes by children too quickly.

Paragraphs are more important than many people realize. When children learn to paragraph as they write, they are on their way toward internalizing the importance of structure in writing. If a child who is writing a narrative knows that each new step forward in time probably merits a new paragraph, this internalized feel for how writing goes will nudge the child to expand on rather than simply mention each incident. The child will know that writing in one-sentence paragraphs is not a reasonable option.

"On Abraham's next draft, he'll start a new line and will begin the first sentence of the new paragraph about a finger space away from the line, like this. That will give us, as readers, a chance to get ready for a part that is a little bit new or different."

Ginger stretched out on the carpet and yawned. I scratched behind her ears and she leaned her head into my hand. She purred.

My mom was in the kitchen baking cookies. She was singing a Spanish song. She always sings when she's in the kitchen.

"In Abraham's story, the need for a new paragraph came from a new subtopic, but remember, sometimes the need for a new paragraph comes because time has moved forward, and sometimes it comes because a new person is speaking."

ACTIVE ENGAGEMENT

Set children up to practice what you've taught. In this case, help them practice thinking about how to group sentences to alleviate dense, unbroken text.

"Writers, let's try this out using someone else's draft. I'm going to give each partnership a copy of Michela's draft. You will see that she is working on paragraphs, so she has boxed her story in ways that reflect the paragraph divisions she thinks will work, which is another way to show where you will start new paragraphs. Each time she starts a new paragraph, I want you and your partner to think, 'Why does she think this is a new paragraph? Is there a new subtopic? Has time moved forward? Is someone new talking?' Work with your partner to decide and jot the reason for the new paragraph beside the paragraph box that she made. There may be places where you disagree with her judgments. If so, write, 'We disagree because . . .' alongside the box and mark the text the way you would paragraph it." (See Figure 11–3.)

Getting ready to go to California

"Beep, Beep, Beep" the alarm clock went off. It was 4:00 in the morning.

"Go, Go, Go!" I screamed. We peeled off our pajamas and jumped into our clothes as fast as we could.

"Get the toothbrushes, get the suitcases!" yelled my mom.

"Get the entertainment, get the extra pillows!" bellowed my dad.

"Where's my cell phone?" screamed my sister.

"Get everything!" I yelled.

"Honk, Honk!"

"The car service is here," I said, hitting my head with my palm. We bolted out the door and slammed it behind us.

The car door opened with a creak and we hopped inside.

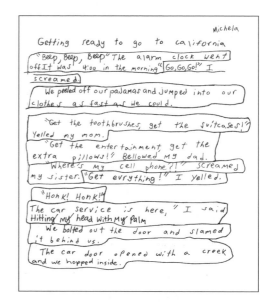

FIG. 11–3   Michela's story with paragraphs blocked out

As the children read and marked the paragraphs in Michela's draft, I listened in. "Writers, I heard you doing some smart work as you read Michela's draft. You noticed lots of reasons for using paragraphs. Some of you noticed reasons for paragraphing we haven't even mentioned yet! I heard Adam say that another reason to start a new paragraph might be when it feels like the story has turned a corner or is going in a different direction. Remember from now on as you write to use these reasons to group your thoughts in paragraphs."

LINK

Remind children that, as they revise and edit, they should be on the lookout for places where a new paragraph would be helpful.

"Writers, when you go off to write today and every day, remember to be on the lookout for places a new paragraph might help your reader. These places include when your story changes subtopic, moves forward in time, or when there is a new speaker. Today you will be looking for places in your draft where a new paragraph would help your reader. Use some of the editing marks we talked about to show where you would add paragraphs if you were writing another draft of your story. In the future, when you start a new piece of writing, you can make paragraphs as you go.

"Of course, you know other work that you can do as well to edit. You know that you can check for capital letters and ending punctuation. And, of course, you know that you can check to see that all of your words are spelled correctly, especially the ones you know by heart. Most importantly, remember that writers are always revising and editing as they go along."

You need to remember the importance of helping children speak in paragraphs, rather than in short phrases or single sentences. We often settle for the first words a child expresses. Just think how much more we might hear by simply asking each child to say more. Of course we will want to teach some explicit strategies for elaboration, such as remembering exact actions, dialogue, descriptions, and thoughts. But by helping children speak in paragraphs rather than short expressions or individual words, we help increase not only their fluency but their confidence as well.

Supporting Sequencing and Elaboration

As YOU CONFER and lead small-group work with your writers, you will want to keep in mind not just the goal of this session—organizing sentences into paragraphs—but bigger goals borne out of the qualities of good personal narrative writing. On the surface, it will look like your writers are figuring out where to add paragraphs, but they will really be doing much more than that—sorting out the chronology of their stories, adding dialogue, and considering the twists and turns their stories make.

You might notice that some writers are struggling with the chronology of their stories as they attempt to chunk the text into paragraphs. They might struggle to find places where the piece moves forward in time, because it might seem to these writers that the whole piece is from the same "time." It may be helpful to gather these writers into a small group and teach them to go back to a familiar planning tool, planning in booklets. After writers have planned their stories, you can show how this informs paragraphing. "The micro-event that happens first in your story—the first page of your booklet—is probably one chunk of sentences. For now, you can teach them to mark a box around the sentences that they think go into a chunk. If their chunks are very small, you can help them add another sentence or two into each one.

You might want to have on hand the narrative writing checklist from Session 9 that includes the different ways narrative writers elaborate. Carrying the checklist with you is also a good way to teach into how to use this tool to self-assess. With your checklist in hand, you can pinpoint the kinds of elaboration individual writers are already using and which they are not. For example, if most of the writer's mini-paragraphs are descriptions of actions, you would want to compliment this, and then perhaps teach the writer to include some dialogue to not only show what the characters are doing, but also what they are saying. Or, if most of the writer's mini-paragraphs are snippets of dialogue without much else, you would want to compliment her brave use of dialogue and then teach her other ways to elaborate to support the dialogue, such as adding some setting details, some actions, or some internal thoughts.

MID-WORKSHOP TEACHING   **Point Out to Children that Many of Their Paragraphs Are Tiny, a Signal that Their Texts Are Underdeveloped**

"Writers, I'm noticing as I'm watching you work is that a lot of you have zillions of tiny paragraphs! Now, on the one hand, that's wonderful, because that means you have zillions of small, step-by-step actions, and narrative writers want to spell out the small steps in a progression! But, on the other hand, it's almost always true that your paragraphs deserve more than just one quick, thin sentence in them. Probably, each new micro-moment in your story needs more words and sentences.

When your piece has lots of tiny paragraphs, this is a sign that you need to elaborate more. It means you need to say more about a topic, a moment, a scene before you move to the next paragraph. Remember some of what we noticed when we studied *Come On, Rain!* Whenever Karen Hesse makes a statement like, 'We make such a racket,' she always says more by describing the action. She adds what people do and say. 'Miz Glick rushes out on her porch. Miz Grace and Miz Vera come next, and then comes Mamma. They run from their kitchens and skid to a stop.'

We noticed that good narratives are told bit by bit, have exact words people say, and have descriptive details. You could elaborate on your paragraphs today by adding actions, dialogue, descriptions, and thoughts, just like Karen Hesse does."

Adding More

Spotlight one child's revisions in a way that illustrates elaboration.

"Earlier, we looked at how Michela boxed her writing into paragraphs. As she was working, Michela realized she had lots of tiny paragraphs in her draft. So she inserted little numbers in her draft where she thought she could say more, and then on another sheet of paper, she wrote those numbers and additional sentences that could elaborate on her initial writing. Michela realized that in her first draft, she tended to write conversations but not actions or descriptions. In her revised version, she wrote not only what people say but also what they do, and she described the scene. (See Figures 11–4 and 11–5.) Notice her first draft and the page of insertions."

Use the final moment of today's share as a micro-celebration.

"Writers, we've studied the drafts that a few of you have written—and your revisions. I'd really like to study all your work. Right now, will you look over your goals, your progress, your revisions, and make marginal stars and smiling faces beside the work you've done that you are proud of." I gave children five minutes for this. "Leave your work on your desk as you go to gym because I'm going to study—glory in—your accomplishments."

Then I said, "Next time we meet for a writing workshop, you will start a new story. You'll want to use paragraphs to help readers sense the different chunks, the different parts, of your draft. You'll want to write in paragraphs from the start. And if you feel yourself indenting every sentence or two, that will be a sign to you that you need to

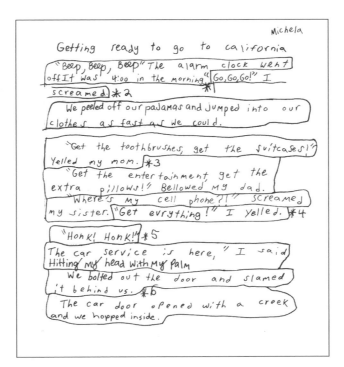

FIG. 11–4 Michela's first draft with numbers inserted where she added more text

I like using Michela as an example because her original draft isn't especially developed or strong, and yet she does an extraordinary amount of work on it. The model, then, conveys to all children that this work is doable.

FIG. 11–5 Michela plans for the additions she will make.

elaborate, progressing through the event in tinier steps, or you need to add more of the internal story—like you did as you stretched out the heart of your story.

"Meanwhile, you have just finished—for now, anyhow—this year's first piece of writing! This is a cause for celebration. Just like we did at our New Year's celebration on the very first day of writing workshop, let's get our horns, our confetti, and our glasses ready. When I give you the signal, blare your horns, clang your glasses, and throw your confetti. Ready? Let's celebrate!"

To Write a True Story

- Find story ideas that are focused and important to you and write lots of entries.
- Make a mental movie of what happened, telling it in small detail, bit by bit.
  - Detail the actions.
  - Include the dialogue.
- Remember your self-assessments of your narrative writing and your goals.
- Rehearse for your writing by storytelling the story repeatedly.
- Try different leads for your story (Action? Dialogue?).
- Write a flash draft, writing fast and furious, eyes on the mental movie.
- Revise.
  - Try what other authors have done.
  - Develop the heart of the story.
- Bring out the internal story ('I noticed . . .' 'I wondered . . .' 'I thought . . .').

Someday, you'll want to help children cull through all the details they could add to choose the most meaningful ones—leaving the others behind. Someday, you'll explain to children that authors include (and exclude) different kinds of information for different reasons—dialogue has its place and time, as does description. For now, we want to banish kids' censors and loosen their inhibitions about writing. To write well, kids first need to write voluminously, not worrying whether the writing is marvelous or not.

Becoming One's Own Job Captain

Starting a Second Piece, Working with New Independence

IN THIS SESSION, you'll emphasize that writers draw on all they have learned to become their own job captains.

GETTING READY

✔ Children's revised stories on hand for the celebration

✔ Students' writer's notebooks and writing folders, to be brought to the meeting area

✔ A copy of the "To Write a True Story: Monitoring My Process" guidesheet (see Active Engagement) in each student's writing folder ✪

✔ "Finding Ideas for True Stories" chart (see Minilesson and Share)

✔ "What Hesse Did to Make Her Storytelling Voice so Good in *Come On, Rain!*" chart (see Share)

COMMON CORE STATE STANDARDS: W.3.3.a,b,c; W.3.5, W.3.10, W.3.4, W.4.4, RL.3.3, SL.3.6, SL.3.3, L.3.1, L.3.2, L.3.3

T
HIS SESSION REPRESENTS A NEW BEND in the road of this unit and new expectations for the nature of the work students will be doing. Always, it is important to approach our teaching with clear expectations about the sort of work students will be doing, (not just with ideas on what we will be teaching, as the two are not the same). Whereas in the last bend of the unit, each day you taught students a new step in the process of writing narratives and expected your class to progress somewhat in sync through that process, the unit has now turned a bend, and starting today, you'll ask students to plan their own schedules, to become their own job captains. This push for students to become more self-directed writers is especially important considering the Common Core State Standards' call for increased student independence. This bend in the unit supports this call, setting students on a path to become co-constructors of their own learning.

Before proceeding into this bend, you will want to think about your students' progress thus far and make sure you think they'll profit from the invitation to take the reins in their own hands. It could be that your students never really did the strategies you tried to teach last week, in which case you may decide to keep them working in sync, working in a step-by-step way that mirrors last week. Many of these sessions need only be tweaked to support that work. Then again, you could feel your students' narrative writing is exceptionally strong and time is especially pressing, leading you to decide to skip the entire upcoming bend, moving on to Bend IV, where you might spend time supporting more extensive revisions and editing.

If you are a bit worried at the prospect of granting your students some leeway to make decisions and chart their own course, pause to think about instances in your own life when people in leadership roles have said, "I think you are ready to step up, to take more leadership, to share some of the decisions." Chances are that this show of faith led you to invest more and to work with new zeal. Your students are not all that different than you.

Over decades of teaching writing, we've found time and again that if students feel as if they are the authors of their own writerly lives, they step into this role with enormous seriousness. So we encourage you to create some fanfare around this upcoming bend. Act as if it is a very big deal that students will be deciding on their own work flow, moving themselves through the process.

If students feel as if they are the authors of their own writerly lives, they step into this role with enormous seriousness.

The truth is that you aren't really, truly stepping that far back! Although the words of this minilesson emphasize independence, in truth, it is a limited sort of independence. You'll be teaching students to draw on the charts you have made together and the strategies you have learned together as they progress through the process of writing. You'll be removing some of the scaffolds you provided in the last bend, yes, but you'll remove those scaffolds gradually.

Becoming One's Own Job Captain
Starting a Second Piece, Working with New Independence

CONNECTION

Celebrate your children's rough drafts.

"Writers, I have been reading the stories you wrote last week every chance I get. When you were at music earlier this morning, I didn't go to the faculty room. I just sat here with your stories. I read about how violins sound when you first try to play them; I laughed about the pigeon with the wink that Ray saw on the sidewalk. Then I looked up and saw I was out of time! I was so disappointed! When I had to stop reading, I felt like someone was taking a prize right out of my hands. You are turning into such strong writers. Congratulations!

"Until now, you've all walked through the writing process together, in sync with each other, with each of you doing the same sort of work each day. But as I looked over the work you have done so far, it became clear to me that you are ready to graduate. You are ready to become job captains of your own writing. This week, then, each of you will write a whole new story—a personal narrative again. But this week, I'm not going to tell you, 'Do this, do this.' This week, *you* will be the boss of your own writing. What I *am* going to tell you is that you need to produce about a page of writing (or of rewriting) each day. You need to experience the writing process. And your piece needs to be done five days from now."

❖ **Name the teaching point.**

"Today I want to teach you that when writers are in charge of their own writing, they think back over everything they know how to do and they make a work plan for their writing. Writers sometimes use charts *and* their own writing to remind them of stuff they know how to do."

TEACHING

Create added fanfare around students assuming responsibility for their writing, and point out that they'll make decisions based on judging their emerging writing.

"One child whom I taught once said, 'I am the mother of my own story. No one else can tell me, "Do this with your story" or "Do that with your story" because I am the mother of my story.' And it is true. Each one of you is the parent (or the boss or the job captain) of your own writing.

◆ COACHING

Time and again you will notice that I try to convey general messages through details. Madeleine L'Engle, the great fiction writer, once told me, "If you say, 'I once saw some flying elephants,' that isn't particularly believable. But it feels more believable if you say, 'Last Tuesday, when I walked from the school to my car, I saw something flying over the far parking lot. At first I thought it was a blimp but then I looked again and it was two pinkish purple elephants, with a baby elephant trailing behind them.' Because I want children to believe me when I say that I have really, truly enjoyed reading their writing, I don't rely on generalizations, saying only, "I have enjoyed reading your writing. The stories are really great." Instead I try to use details that will make my words more convincing.

"This week you do not need to come to me and ask, 'Should I start by collecting more entries in my notebook, or should I go back and choose another entry that I liked to become my seed idea?' You'll need to decide! And if you decide to generate more entries first, you won't need to come to me asking, 'How do I go about finding ideas for my entries?' because you know where to find ideas for stories on our class charts. You'll be making the choices that are right for you.

"But—here is my suggestion. You need to realize that writers make decisions by listening to their own writing. They let their writing lead the way."

Illustrate the contingent nature of their process decisions by asking, "What if . . . ? What process decisions would you make then?"

"I'll show you what I mean." Pointing to bullets on the anchor chart, I said, "Pretend you have an amazing seed idea that you've been wishing you'd written on last week because you know it would make a great story. Would you decide to start your work this week by writing a bunch of entries on a bunch of different stories, or would you start by storytelling your story across the pages of a booklet and writing different leads?"

The children all chimed that they'd start by storytelling.

"And if last week, your writing only felt so-so because your story idea wasn't that great—it happened so long ago you could hardly remember it, and really, you didn't care about it anyhow—which part of this process (I gestured to the anchor chart) would you especially work on this time? Tell your partner."

The partners conferred, and then I quickly reconvened the class and we agreed that in such an instance, the right decision would be to take some time finding story ideas and writing a bunch of new entries. I pointed also to the "Finding Ideas for True Stories" chart hanging nearby.

Debrief, emphasizing the teaching point.

"The important thing is that when you are your own job captain, you need to try to make wise decisions about what your process of work will be like—using our charts *and* your writing to help you make your decisions."

ACTIVE ENGAGEMENT

Set children up to begin planning their process, using a chart to keep tabs.

"When I'm organizing my writing life, I keep tabs on my progress. I know my writing process usually involves certain steps, so I have a system for checking off when I have completed each step or decided to skip one. That helps me know what to try next."

This is perfect, isn't it? It easily could have been part of the teaching point.

You may find it surprising that the children are suddenly done with one piece of writing and back at the rehearsal stage. I think the opportunity to cycle through the process again right away, this time accumulating new strategies and knowledge for each phase, is an important one. Before long children will have written two narratives, and then I'll ask them to select their best and revise and edit it.

It is very important to teach children the way in which a writing curriculum cumulates, leaving the writer with a repertoire of skills and strategies. Today gives you a chance to convey the cumulative nature of your teaching.

When you shift to debriefing, students should feel the different moves you are making just by the way your intonation and posture change.

Set children up to start planning their own writing process for the day, using charts and the writing process guide sheet for support.

"I've put a guide sheet like this inside each of your writing folders. You won't be able to think about your process, however, until you have thought about the possible stories you might write this week. The first item on the checklist is 'Find focused ideas and write entries,' so right now, while we are sitting here, let's each of us take a minute to sift through our minds, trying to see if *we* have a story idea, lying right there, ready for us to go with. Let's have absolute quiet so we can jot possibilities. I'll be doing this too."

I sat at the front of the room and thought, flipping through the pages of my memories. The children did this as well.

I quietly voiced over their thinking. "You're going to want to think of a moment that mattered to you—one that gives you strong feelings, even now as you recall it. Flipping through the pages of your writer's notebook can also spark story ideas." After a minute I said, "I know you'll zoom in on a story, a focused story."

"I'm going to stop you. Right now, before we head off to work, think about what you need to do today. Touch the boxes on your guide sheet that show what work you'll do today.

LINK

Get children started being job captains for themselves, and then send them off to write.

"There are some other charts in our room that may help you. Look at 'Finding Ideas for True Stories,' and use your thumb to signal if this will be a chart you use (thumb up) or don't use (thumb down)." After they signaled, I said, "What about this one?" and pointed to, 'What Hesse Did to Make Her Storytelling Voice So Good in *Come On, Rain!*,' Again, children signaled. "How about the Narrative Writing Checklist in your writing folder?

"Tell your partner what work you will do today, what strategies you'll use, *and* what your goals will be for yourself." I let children talk.

For now and for the rest of your life, keep in mind that you are job captains for your own writing. You will make decisions based on what your writing needs—and based on what you as a writer need. But always, draw on resources like our charts and writing strategies so you don't forget things you have learned to do. Job captains—off you go!"

Some teachers keep a whole-class, wall-sized version of the checklist, with each child moving his or her magnetic plaque along on a white board chart. You'll need to decide whether this checklist is an individual one kept in writing folders or a whole-class one, displayed on a wall, or both.

To Write a True Story: *Monitoring My Process*

☐ Find focused story ideas and write entries.

☐ For each make mental movies, tell bit by bit.

☐ Remember goals.

☐ Choose one to develop.

☐ Rehearse 'seed idea.'
- Storytelling
- Leads

☐ Booklet? Notebook paper?

☐ Flash draft with paragraphs.

☐ Revise
- Emulate other authors
- Develop heart
- Bring out internal story

☐ Edit
- Spelling
- Punctuation

FIG. 12–1   A writing progress guide sheet

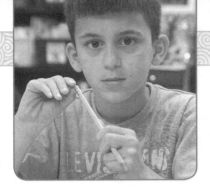

Encouraging Independent Problem Solving

IN YOUR CONFERRING TODAY, try to teach independence. Invite children to identify and solve their own writing problems. As teachers, we love to feel useful, and we love to feel as if we are teaching something, so we often rush to suggest solutions to every problem. It's wise to remember, however, that our job is to put ourselves out of a job. More importantly, you are teaching children to be resilient when faced with a problem. Today, enter the workshop planning to turn issues back to the child. So if a child says that he has nothing to write about, instead of generating a list of five things the writer could do next, plan to restate the problem and commiserate with it, then turn it back to the writer. Say, "I know that feeling of being empty-handed, of feeling as if I have nothing to say. I know when I am stuck, I usually reach out for a strategy that could help me, so why don't you try doing that? Reach out for one of the strategies that you have in your mental strategy kit, and see if that helps. I'm going to check back with you in five minutes and see how things are going." When you expect the writer to find his way out of a predicament, you will find that he or she usually rises to the occasion.

So guard against being the problem solver. For today, anyhow, if the writer expresses a problem, try mulling the problem over aloud, as if you are thinking of a solution: "Hmm, I'm trying to think of what writers do when we encounter this problem. Hmm . . ." The writer will probably supply a possible course of action. Go with it! "So are you suggesting . . . ?" you can say, and as you retell what the child has suggested, sneak in a few little tips of your own.

Keep a copy of the "Monitoring My Writing Process" guide sheet in hand as you confer. If a writer isn't certain what he or she might do next, help him or her use the guide to find possibilities: "Where are you in the process? This guide might help you plan what you will do next."

MID-WORKSHOP TEACHING   "There's Not One Teacher in This Classroom, but Twenty-Four of You"

At one point in the workshop, I had a line of about six children following me, each hoping to get help. This is a predictable situation, and I'm ready for it with a mid-workshop teaching point that is perfect for the occasion. "Writers, can I have your eyes and your attention? Look what I have following me!" I gestured to the line of children trailing me.

"Writers, listen while I talk with each of the writers who are in line for help. Listen closely, because this could be you lined up for help."

Then I said to the first child, "What is it you are wanting?" The child explained that he was done with one entry and wasn't sure what to do next. I kindly but firmly asked if he thought he could figure that out, and he admitted that he probably could. "Okay, off you go then," I said.

The next child wanted to know if I liked his lead. "Hmm, is it vitally important to know whether I like your lead? Do *you* like it?" The writer confessed that he really wasn't that fond of it. "So I bet you can figure out what to do next, can't you?" and he, too, went on his way. After one more child went back to handle his own problem, I turned to the class.

"Writers, do you get my point? You need to become your own job captains and make your own decisions. I can't be the person who decides what every one of you should be doing. From this day on, when you feel like coming to me for help, take a second to think, 'Do I really need help? Could I solve this on my own?' One thing you can always do is use the tools you have around you for help, like the charts in the classroom, your previous work in your writer's notebook, and each other."

(continues)

There is a thin line between supporting a writer's independence, and supporting a writer's engagement in the process of writing. After all, the goal really is not for students to whip through one draft only while writing with great independence. Instead, the goal is for writers to become metacognitive, strategic, resourceful, critical problem solvers, internalizing many of the roles that teachers have often played (the role of assessor, of assigner, etc.). Turning the metacognitive work over to students is important. For example, many writers don't pause to plan their writing work before diving into it. They sit in front of the page, pick up a pen, and instead of thinking, "Where am I in my work?" and "What should I do next?" they think, "Where am I in *my story*?" and then simply pick up where they left off. It is a big deal, therefore, to teach writers to take some time to plan their writing process. Teach students that in an upper corner on their actual drafts, they can sometimes jot little planning boxes. You might, in a conference, say to a writer, "Adam, here's the important thing. Writers do not just plan what they are going to write about. They also plan how they're going to go about writing. Right now, please reread what you've written, look over our class charts, and think, 'How will I go about writing my next entry?' If you haven't already reused a strategy from earlier in the unit of study, pick one to reuse today. And before you write (today and from this day on), make and fill in a planning box for yourself in your notebook."

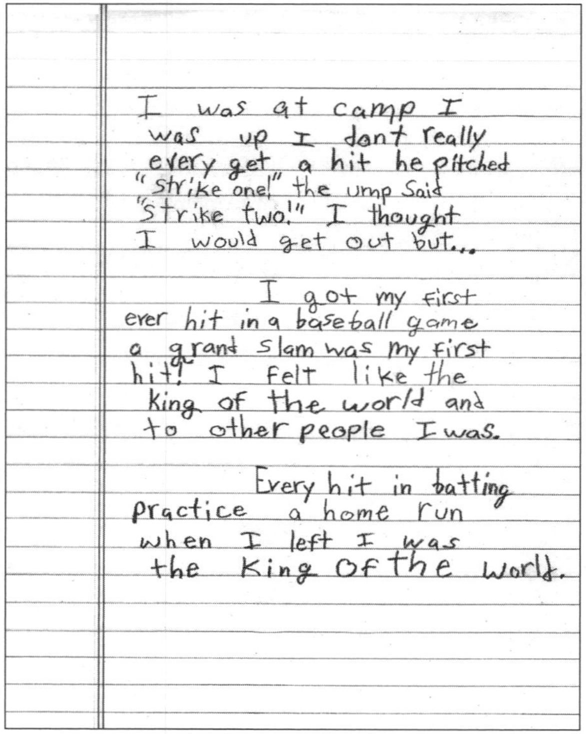

I was at camp I was up I dont really every get a hit he pitched "strike one!" the ump Said "Strike two!" I thought I would get out but...

I got my first ever hit in a baseball game a grand slam was my first hit! I felt like the King of the world and to other people I was.

Every hit in batting practice a home run when I left I was the King of the world.

FIG. 12–2 Sam's entry

I glared at the pitcher, he glared back, I Said to my Self I'm going to get a hit, I'm going to get a hit I held the bat. "Strike One! he yelled I held the bat tighter, "Strike two!" I held the bat tighter and... kaboom! I whacked the ball over.

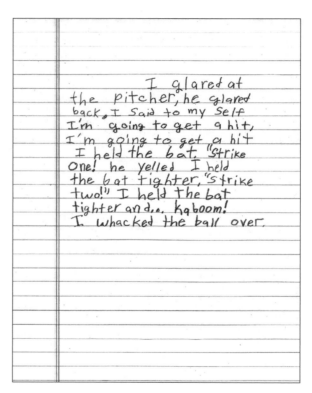

FIG. 12–3 Sam's later effort to develop the heart of his story: this gets inserted after his first paragraph.

Remembering to Carry Forward All We Know

Convene children. Ask writers to examine their work for examples of some qualities of good writing from the class chart.

"Writers, I was really blown away today to see each of you making responsible decisions. Many of you resumed gathering narrative entries in your notebooks and did this without needing me to tell you what to do. You also wrote those entries much more quickly than you wrote them earlier this year. *But*—some of you remembered qualities of good writing that we learned earlier, and some of you seemed to totally forget stuff you have learned. Right now, look at the finished piece that you wrote last week. I'm going to read off our chart that lists the qualities of good writing we learned from Karen Hesse. Give me a thumbs up for each of these things if your final piece from last week illustrates this quality." I read each of the bullets below, pausing at the end of each bullet for children to signal yea or nay.

Most children had done most of these things in the final draft that culminated last week's work. "Writers, most of you have done a lot of these things in last week's writing. Terrific. Give yourselves a pat on the back. Stand and take a bow!"

Have students work with partners to set new goals for their writing.

"But here is the problem. Listen up because it is serious. What I noticed today is that a lot of you did *not* do those things in the writing you did today. I know that is hard to believe, because we just established you can do this work. But let me read the items on the chart again, and you'll look at what you wrote today with honest eyes and signal yes, no, or maybe." I adjusted my thumb to illustrate each signal.

This time, many writers agreed they had not done many of the things they know how to do.

"So, writers, I have to say this really confuses me. You know how to write putting in the exact words people say and how they say it. You know about using descriptive details and telling a story bit by bit. So what is keeping you from doing these things?

"Will you talk with your partner? Talk about which of the qualities of good writing you didn't remember, and talk about what your work plans will be for tomorrow. My hunch is that many of you are going to begin by rewriting some of your entries—if you like them—so that your notebook doesn't contain work that is so much below the best you can do. But that, of course, will be up to you."

FIG. 12–4 The qualities of good writing learned from Hesse

Rally children to use the classroom charts as they begin new stories, and highlight one student whose work reflects one item on the chart.

"Writers, as we begin to work on new pieces of writing, I want to remind you that *you already know* strategies for coming up with stories that make readers sigh and laugh and pull in to read more. As writers, you each carry with you an invisible backpack full of all the strategies you've ever learned, and you pull them out as needed. It's not an accident that the charts we made when we wrote our first story are still in the room. You'll look at those charts often as you write your next story to remind you of strategies you've already learned."

Then, pointing to one item on the chart, I asked the writers, "Did you write with descriptive details? Right now, find a particularly nice detail in the writing you did today and share it with your partner." After a minute of talk, I said, "Isaiah found a lot of details in his writing. Let's listen to it and see if we agree that he has written with true, descriptive details." (See Figure 12–5.)

> I looked inside the tank. There he was, Hissy, my beloved pet snake. I looked at my mom eagerly. The moment I had been waiting for was almost here. The time to take Hissy out of his tank. I watched excitedly as my mom took Hissy out. I held out my hands. They were a little shaky but I was still excited. Mom gave Hissy to me.

"Isaiah, you have definitely zoomed in on one moment, and you stretched the moment out so much that I feel as if I am right there with you, leaning over the tank." Then I asked the class, "Do you think Isaiah wrote with true and descriptive details?" When children confirmed that he'd done this, I said, "As you continue working tomorrow and for the rest of your life, remember to keep in mind these qualities of good writing, as well as this sequence of writing work from your monitoring checklist."

You will notice that throughout this unit I am constantly having children reflect on their writing by using the tools we have created, like the charts and checklists. Then, having the children make goals or "work plans" reminds them of what they are learning to do as writers while handing over to them the responsibility of setting those expectations.

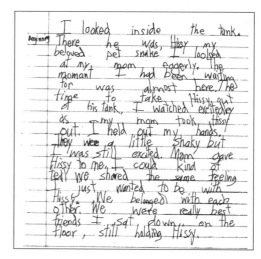

FIG. 12–5   Isaiah writes with true, descriptive details.

Revision Happens throughout the Writing Process

ear Teachers,

I will not be writing out the exact transcript of the teaching that I did on this day but will instead aim to help you and your colleagues design your own minilesson, conferring, mid-workshop teaching, and share. This scaffolds your increasing independence while you, in turn, scaffold your students' increasing independence. I hope this also helps you extract enduring principles from all the teaching you've read about in the preceding sessions. You are the authors of your own teaching, and my rationale is not very different from the rationale for this bend of the unit.

MINILESSON

In this letter, I will help you imagine the teaching you might do today. Usually the connection in a minilesson harkens back to the preceding work that undergirds the new instruction. Certainly, the previous share session will have brought to light a realization that you probably want to spotlight at the start of your minilesson. Many students worked through the process once, ostensibly learning all sorts of things about the qualities of effective narrative writing, but now, when given a chance to create some new narratives, it is as if all that learning has been lost. You will want to teach students that the work writers do during revision and editing stages of the writing process for one piece then moves forward and becomes work that writers do right from the start, the next time they write. So the paragraphs that writers added as a final formatting process in their work with the earlier piece should now be part of what writers do as they draft their entries.

Of course, writers will also need to be reminded of all they learned previously about drafting—including the importance of writing fast and furiously, not stopping, of keeping their eyes on the mental movie and showing, not telling, and of writing with periods, right from the start. This is a lot to keep in mind, and drafts are called rough drafts for a

COMMON CORE STATE STANDARDS: W.3.5, W.3.3.b, W.4.3.b, W.3.4, RL.3.5, SL.3.1, SL.3.6, L.3.2.c,e,f; L.3.3.a,b reason. Your writers will not pull off all they aspire to do, but it will be important to teach them to draw on all they know as they write.

After recalling that lesson, you will shift toward the teaching point for today. Take some time to draft and revise a teaching point that is concise and clear and that follows the format of others in this book. There is an art form to writing teaching points! One of the things to be aware of is the tendency to write teaching points as if they are assignments for the day, rather than points that writers can draw on always. Instead of saying something like, "Today I want to teach you to go back and revise the entries you wrote yesterday, using all that you learned about good writing," you will want to word your teaching point as a lesson that is meant to last a lifetime. "Today I want to teach you that always, writers try to remember that the qualities of good writing they learned during revision in one piece become qualities of good writing they then think of at the very start of their work with another piece. To make the start of a piece show all the writer knows about good writing, writers often pause after just a bit of writing to ask, 'Does this show everything I know?' And then they revise."

One possible way to teach this might be to show a very bad example of narrative writing—one that contains all the mess-ups you see in many of your children's entries—and to then ask children to join you in pretending this is your piece of writing and in helping you do the work of being a job captain. You could then reread the piece to see if it reflects all that you and the class know (it won't). And then you could recruit the class to join you in pretending you were each job captains of the piece, and work to make plans for how to fix the piece and then get started on some early revision. That revision could be done through writing in the air. If you decide to do that, you definitely will not want to show one of your own students' very bad pieces! You might pretend that you have been teaching writing to a neighborhood boy—give the kid a name—and show a piece that you pretend is his. "Can you and I think together about what we'll suggest Petey does with this?" you can say.

Of course, when it comes to the link of your minilesson, you absolutely cannot send children off to do a set of specific actions. After all, yesterday you were full of talk about how the kids have now become job captains. So instead, when you send children off, remind them of their options. They should probably fill in their chart, marking where they are in the process, and then you can mention options that are before them. Some will revise an entry they wrote the previous day. Others will write new entries, hopefully using the reminders to lift the quality of those entries. Still others will be choosing their seed ideas and getting started storytelling them or writing different leads. You might send children off to work by saying, "Those of you who will be doing . . . , get started." Then, after those children disperse, you can say, "Those of you who will be. . . ." and send off another group. You may want, as the final prompt, to say, "Those of you who are not sure what you are doing, stay here, and why don't you help each other?" This, then, collects all the lost souls and allows you to give them the support they are signaling they need.

CONFERRING AND SMALL-GROUP WORK

Don't forget to plan your small groups and your conferring. Your children will be at the stages of work that you supported during Sessions 5, 6, and 7 of this unit, so scan the conferring write-ups from those sessions for ideas. You may want to convene all the writers who are choosing seed ideas, suggesting they remind each other of what they know about doing this, and do the same to support writers who are working on various forms of rehearsal. If children are working on leads, remind them that writers need (at the very least) to decide where in the sequence of events they will begin their story. The work with leads can overlap with the work on showing, not telling. For example, you may want to teach writers to take a few minutes to envision the place in which the story is set. Teach them that it helps to go back to the beginning of the story and to think, "Where was I exactly?" If the writer's first thought is a general one such as "I was in the park," teach the child that it is important to press on for more specifics, for example, "I was sitting on the bench under the giant willow tree in Central Park." Then you can teach children that writers sometimes take a second to sketch the place, and do so thinking, "What can I put in my story that will help readers see the scene clearly?" Of course, the challenge will be to paint the picture using not a drawing but words. You could also, in small groups, return to the mentor text and help writers remember that they can try starting a narrative using dialogue or small actions or setting. Remind children that not only can they weigh different ways to start a story, but they can also tell the story aloud in different ways. If some children are ready to write a draft, you'll definitely want to help them scrawl a draft, writing fast and long.

MID-WORKSHOP TEACHING

To set up your mid-workshop teaching, you might confer with one writer in a way that you think could be broadly applicable to the whole class. For example, you might suggest one writer keep either his last final draft, the class's mentor text, his goals, or the narrative checklist out on the desk as he writes, referring often to that example. "Your notebook is like a writer's workbench," you could say. "Workers keep their tools on hand." Then for your mid-workshop teaching, you could tell the entire class about the great idea this one youngster came up with (giving the child the credit, which gives your idea the social power). If your instinct tells you that children need an interlude for talk, you could suggest that each partnership decide on the tools they especially want to draw upon—and put those resources out beside them (have small copies of the charts on hand). Partners could then talk about how those tools will help the work they are just about to do.

SHARE

For your share, look back on previous shares and see if the format of one feels applicable to the work your writers are doing today. You may want to use the share session to set writers up to choose a seed idea if they haven't done so already, just as you did at the end of Session 6. In this case, you will likely want to draw on the Session 6 share as a model.

Good luck!!

Lucy and Marjorie

Drafting

Writing from Inside a Memory

IN THIS SESSION, you'll teach students that writers replay life events in ways that let readers feel the experience.

GETTING READY

✔ Students' writer's notebooks and writing folders, to be brought to the meeting area. Students should sit with their partners.

✔ A favorite book or a time you have become lost in the story, to show there is a thin line between reading and imagining (see Connection)

✔ A moment seared into your memory so you can relive the moment bit by bit like it was happening again (see Teaching). Plan for what you might write and where you might model getting into trouble, and how you might find your way out of trouble.

✔ Story prompts that encourage children to practice writing from a recent memory, reliving the moment, remembering how it started, what was said, and what was done (see Active Engagement)

✔ Monitoring My Writing Process checklist on document camera or on chart paper (see Mid-Workshop Teaching)

✔ Chart paper and/or document camera to model writing in front of students

✔ Narrative Writing Checklist, Grades 3 and 4 (see Share)

COMMON CORE STATE STANDARDS: W.3.3.a,b,c; W.3.4, W.3.8, W.3.10, W.3.5, W.4.3.b, RL.3.5, RL.4.6, SL.3.1, L.3.2.c,e,f; L.3.3.a,b; L3.6

T ODAY'S SESSION aims to help children understand that to write an effective narrative, after weighing possible plans, a writer commits himself or herself to one trajectory and then relives that story, holding onto the unfolding storyline with the same rapt attention a reader might give when lost in a book.

The fiction writer John Gardner, in *The Art of Fiction* (1991), pointed out that when reading, we first see letters on the page. But soon we are seeing not ink marks on a page but a train rushing through a Russian countryside or rain pelting down on a ramshackle house. "We read on, we dream on," he says.

But here is the secret. Readers can only see a train hurtling through the Russian countryside or rain pelting down on a ramshackle house if first, we as writers have seen those scenes. We must first write, seeing not words on the page but the events of our lives. We see these events, relive these events, so that readers can, in turn, do the same. To this end, Gardner offers this: "Preliminary good advice might be—write as if you were a movie camera. Get exactly what is there . . . the trick is to bring it out, get it down. Getting it down precisely, what you really care about . . . setting down what you, the writer, really noticed."

If you don't actually do this work on the page, do it in your conversations with friends, and notice yourself doing it. The other day my husband brought me to the window to look out at what had been a small garden and was now a patch of scorched earth. "You know what happened?" John asked and launched into this story. "Matt told me that every spring, he burns his dead plants, and new growth shoots up," he said. "So I brought out the garden hose and left the water running into the lawn, just to be safe. Then I took a match and set fire to the dried grasses we used to have in the center of the garden. It smoldered. I wondered if it would catch fire. I blew on the sparks. Then I glanced away. Out of the corner of my eye, I saw an explosion of fire. The whole garden was wreathed in flames. I grabbed for the hose, but the little stream of water seemed like nothing! I thought the house was going to burn down!" As John retold the escapade, he relived it in Technicolor and I, in turn, felt as if I had been right there with him. For both of us, the story made our hearts leap. I didn't tell him the whole event was great for my book!

As novelist Joseph Conrad once described the writer's job, "My task which I am trying to achieve is, by the power of the written word, to make you hear, to make you feel—it is, before all, to make you see. That, and no more, and it is everything." In this session, you will teach your young writers to relive the moments they are writing about so that they too may make their readers hear, feel, and, above all, see.

In this session, you will teach your young writers to relive the moments they are writing about so that they too may make their readers hear, feel, and, above all, see.

This work should feel reminiscent of Session 4, when you taught children to use a "storytelling voice" rather than summarizing their memories and to show, not tell. Here, you're aiming to strengthen children's sense of effective storytelling with the hope that they do this work with increasing independence as they revise rapidly written first drafts.

Drafting

Writing from Inside a Memory

CONNECTION

Put today's work into the context of the writing process so that children can see how today's work fits into the cycle of rehearsing, drafting, revising, and editing. Then give an example of the power of writing to help us step inside a moment.

"Writers, I am thrilled to see the ways you are becoming your own job captains. You are monitoring your own writing process, asking yourselves questions like 'Am I using a strong storytelling voice as I gather entries in my notebook and plan my drafts? Do I have enough entries to choose a seed idea? How should I rehearse for my draft?' Many of you have collected some entries in your notebooks and have chosen a seed idea. Many of you are getting ready to rehearse for drafting, and then I know you will write fast and furious, as you did earlier in this unit.

"Last night, I began reading *The Lion, the Witch and the Wardrobe*. I opened the book, and soon I was hiding in that wardrobe, and then I was pushing past the furry coats to get to the back of the wardrobe and suddenly, I felt something cold brush against me, and it was snow. I looked down and saw I was standing in snow, and all around were trees, their boughs heavy with snow, and from far away I heard the jingle of sleigh bells, and soon a sleigh drew close.

"For me, and for all of you, there is a thin line between reading and imagining. I begin reading words, and soon I am in another world. You could say that I become the character in a play, acting out the drama."

❧ **Name the teaching point.**

Tell children that writing involves reenacting their own experiences. "I am telling you this because writers, like readers, get lost in a story. They pick up the pen and step into another time, another place. As they get ready to draft, they can relive that event, reexperience that time."

So far this year, children have inched along through the writing process. In this connection, I'm helping them to look back over the terrain they've traveled as if they're finally standing on a hilltop, surveying the route they've traveled. By helping them trace the path they've taken, I'm teaching toward independence. I want them to understand that whenever they write, they'll make a similar journey. It is important, then, that they see all the steps of the process as a single trail of work.

TEACHING

Point out to children that we all have memories that are seared into our minds forever. Give examples.

"Writers, each of you already has moments from your life that are really easy for you to imagine. You can replay those moments in your mind easily. Sometimes those are the hard moments, the moments we do not want to relive. For every one of us, there are moments in our lives that are seared into our memories forever. For me, one of those is the time I heard that a second plane had just flown into the World Trade Center towers, and all of a sudden the awareness flooded into me that the plane hitting the World Trade Center was not an accident. I can close my eyes and relive where I was in that moment, what I heard on the radio, what I thought, what I looked at, what I said, what I did. I can, and I do, go back to my experience of that event and replay it.

"As a writer, I have come to realize that I can go back and relive not only the traumatic, life-changing events, but also little moments that for some reason have mattered to me. You already know that before writers start to story-tell, they make a movie in their minds. But now, I'm going to tell you that they don't just watch the movie. They are a part of it. Whenever I write a personal narrative, I relive my own experiences. I act as if I am living that moment again."

Demonstrate to show that you write by reliving.

"Let me show you how I go about doing this kind of writing, and then we'll try it together. I'm going to choose a story that I've already told you—the time I skipped recess to go to Gates' Deli to buy candy for the other kids and my mom caught me. So I'm going to make a movie of that time in my mind. But this time, instead of just watching the movie in my mind, I'm going to actually put myself inside the movie. I'm going to close my eyes and relive what happened. You watch me, because soon you will try this.

"We already worked on the start—remember?" I reread the beginning of the story, which ended:

> I raced to the edge of the playground. Then I looked over my shoulder to be sure the recess teacher wasn't watching, and zoomed out of the school lot and down the block to Gates' Deli. I pushed open the door and the lady at the checkout counter smiled and asked, "Can I help you?" I said I knew where to find things . . .

"Let me relive what happened next in my mind." I was quiet for just a moment, eyes closed, inside my memory, wanting the students to see my process. "I want to see what I saw and hear what I heard then. If I can't remember something, I'll picture how it might have gone and write that. I'm going to try to stay specific. Showing, not telling." I jotted on the chart paper next to me.

> I grabbed Mars bars, licorice, Dots, cradling them in my arm. I added a few Nestle's Crunch bars. Then I hurried to the checkout counter.

The juxtaposition of these distinct stories is no accident. By showing children that there are many episodes in our lives that for some reason are seared into our memories, I emphasize the power writing has to imbue small moments with meaning. It is through writing that we discover the particularities of how and why moments matter.

Notice that when I write in front of children, I generally work on just a tiny excerpt of text. I think aloud, letting children in on the thoughts as I weigh them. I deliberately show myself struggling in ways that resemble the struggles children also encounter.

"I don't remember what I got that day, I'm making it up," I confessed.

> I spilled my goods onto the counter. Just then the door squeaked open. I glanced up. What? My mom? I froze.

I stopped to interject a quick aside. "Writers, do you see the way I'm reliving what happened and seeing and hearing everything again as if I was there? Let me keep going."

> . . . I froze. I was very worried she'd be mad at me.

I stopped again. "Oh no. That last part 'I was very worried she'd be mad—that's not writing from inside the memory. That's not writing if I was there. That's just telling about it. I'll cross that last part out and again." I crossed it out. "Let me relive the memory again and try to see and hear and feel what happened."

> . . . I froze. "Oh no," I thought. "Oh no!" Blood rushed to my face. I stepped back from the candy, wanting to pretend it wasn't mine.

"Writers, do you see how much stronger that is now? Do you see how I'm inside the memory, reliving it again? I'm not giving you information about what happened. I'm not reporting. I'm there again—remembering what I saw, heard, thought. And if I don't remember what happened exactly, I'm picturing what probably happened and writing that."

ACTIVE ENGAGEMENT

Ask kids to try the strategy you've introduced. In this case, have them relive an important moment from the day before and write it down as they lived it. Then share one child's writing as an example.

"To practice, think of something important that happened to you yesterday. For now, maybe you want to recall a time when you entered or left a place, because the sequence of events should be clear. For example, recall how you entered the lunchroom and found a seat, or how you left school at the end of the day and boarded the bus. Some small episode. Now remember how it started. Where were you? Put yourself back in the memory. What did you do? What did you say? Thumbs up if you can recall what you did and said, what you heard and felt."

When most thumbs were up, I said, "So, quickly, scrawl that small moment down in your notebook, just as I wrote mine on the easel. Imagine yourself right inside the story. Use a strong storytelling voice. Stay detailed, specific, and true to the story. This is just a practice exercise; it won't be a draft you develop."

After a few minutes, I asked children to share what they had written with partners. Then, calling the children back together, I said, "Listen for the details in Ellie's." (See Figure 14–1.)

Watch the way I move kids quickly past topic indecision, shepherding them along so they have a moment in mind and can proceed to learn from my pointers on how to write about that moment.

As the year unfurls, there will be more and more times when you ask children to stop and jot in lieu of turning and talking with partners. This is the first such time, and you may need to take special care to help children realize that they're simply creating a tiny exercise-text. You aren't looking for a class full of lunchtime or bus line publications!

"Oh man! I am late to lunch," I said as I glanced at my watch. I rushed through the quiet hall, clutching my lunch bag in my right hand. I wove through the Kindergarteners with my arm stretched like a football player ready to push the wood door open. My other hand gripped my paper bag lunch.

"Do you hear how Ellie got right inside the moment and wrote the exact actions she took at that moment and wrote the things she saw at that moment? She was really reliving it as she wrote, wasn't she?"

LINK

Remind children of the different choices they might make as job captains in charge of their own writing.

"Before you get started, writers, will you think for a moment about the work you will do today? There are probably some of you who began your draft yesterday and have decided you're going to start over on a new sheet of notebook paper or in a new drafting booklet, revising like writers revise, so that you really live inside your story. Some of you haven't yet begun your draft. Remember that you are job captains for your own writing lives. I can't wait to see what you decide to do today. And remember to relive the episode as you write it. This is how we make our writing intense and real."

> "Oh man! I am late to lunch" I said as I glanced at my watch. I rushed through the quiet hall, clutching my lunch bag in my right hand. I wove through the Kindergarterners, with my arm stretched like a football player ready to push the wood door open. my other hand gripped my paper bag lunch.

FIG. 14–1 Ellie's quick practice exercise written in her notebook

Conferring Effectively: Targeted Questions and Planning for Predictable Struggles

BY NOW, YOUR KIDS are probably engaged enough in their writing that you can think less about simply getting them going and more about conferring well. As I mentioned earlier, I recommend that teachers generally begin a writing conference by learning what it is the child has been trying to do as a writer. If we know the writer's intention, we can support that intention by equipping the writer to do what he wants to do, or we can explain why we think he should be aiming toward a different goal.

I recommend opening most writing conferences by asking, "What are you working on as a writer?" At first, children will answer by telling you about the topic. If the child does that, ask a follow-up question: "And what exactly are you trying to do as a writer? What strategies have you been using?" Sometimes you will need to show the child the sort of answer you have in mind. You can do this by looking over the child's draft and then answering your question yourself, saying, for example, "It looks like you have been experimenting with different leads, and some include dialogue and some include the setting. Is that right?"

Once you and the child have established whatever it is that the child has been trying to do, I recommend saying to the child, "Can you show me where you have done that?" Then I look at what the child has already done, not just recently, but over time. As I look, I am trying to think of what I can compliment. I try to compliment something that I hope writers will do another day in another piece, which means I need to find something transferable. "I love the way you described where you were when you were bowling," I said to one writer. "Always remember that it is smart to bring out the setting for your story like you did just now." In a writing conference, after I've complimented the child, I tell the child that there is one thing I'd like to teach. Then I name the teaching point and teach it, just as if this were a brief minilesson. The teaching point often contains a bit of critique. "I know you said you are, but actually I think you aren't yet doing that . . ." And the teaching always contains suggested next steps.

MID-WORKSHOP TEACHING
Writers Keep an Eye on Deadlines

This mid-workshop teaching brings up a critical point for writers the world over: writers need deadlines. My writing teacher Donald Murray even wrote a whole book on the subject called, *Writing to Deadline* (2000). As a journalist he came to understand the reality of writing long and fast in the midst of a busy newsroom with a paper that published daily. When Murray was asked, "How do you get the writing done?" he answered, "I have a deadline." When asked, "How do you know a piece of writing is finished?" he answered, "When I get to the deadline."

"Writers, can I have your eyes and your attention? Today is Day Three of you being your own job captains, the boss of your own writing, making decisions about what you are doing and how you are doing it. But here's the thing. We also have a deadline looming. In two days we said we would finish a second story, from notebook to draft, from revision to final edit. Deadlines are a part of every writer's life.

"So this means that right now you need to take out your 'Monitoring My Process' guide sheet and take a look at where you are in the writing process. Ask yourself, 'What do I need to do to get ready to finish my second story two days from now?' Then you need to make a plan, give yourself some deadlines of your own, like 'I need to be finished with my first draft by tonight so I can start revising tomorrow.' Make notes about what you plan to do right now."

Before any one day's writing workshop, it helps to anticipate the sort of things you might find yourself teaching. Your list of possibilities will be cumulative and will pertain to many days in addition to the teaching you did that day. On this day, your list of possible teaching ideas for a conference might look like this.

- ◆ Narrative writers don't tell all about a time. They're more apt to focus on a small moment. It helps to remember an exact time you did something or something happened.

- ◆ Writers envision how the event rolled out. Instead of talking about the time, reporting on it, writers relive it so readers can, too.

- ◆ Writers write with specifics, so that instead of saying "I played a game," the writer names the game.

- ◆ Writers include exact speech.

- ◆ Writers spell word wall words correctly.

- ◆ Writers punctuate as they write.

- ◆ Writers write with paragraphs, paragraphing when time moves forward or when the place changes.

- ◆ Writers sometimes pretend to be a stranger, rereading their own draft and thinking, "Can I follow this? Does it all make sense?"

- ◆ Writers sometimes recruit readers who can tell them places where their draft is confusing.

- ◆ Writers try to solve their own problems, inventing solutions rather than simply lining up behind the teacher.

- ◆ Writers don't tell each part of the story with equal emphasis. They skip past some parts, and they stretch out the heart of their stories.

Keep in mind that the purpose of conferring is to give writers individualized support by targeting their area of greatest need. Often, you will pull alongside a writer who is not yet ready for the teaching point of the day's minilesson. For example, if you pull alongside a writer who is not yet writing about a tightly focused event, you will have time to intervene before she gets too far in the revision process. Rely on the standard questions: "Of all the things that you did while at your grandma's, what's the one particular event that you most remember?" "How did that start?" "What exactly were you doing at the start?"

On the other hand, you might find that the child you pull alongside is trying out the strategy you taught that day but needs some fine-tuning. If the child you are conferring with did focus on a specific event, and is making a movie in her mind, you might check to see if the piece feels balanced. In some cases, you will find that the draft is detailed and lively but it is swamped by dialogue.

I pulled alongside one such writer, Danielle, whose draft showed evidence of instruction: it was focused, chronological, detailed, and included direct dialogue. But I noticed that Danielle's draft read like a sound track of a film, without any actions!

When I conferred with Danielle, I celebrated the fact that she clearly had made a movie in her mind and recorded that movie (see Figure 14–2).

I pointed out, however, that because *she* knows the people, the place, and the actions, she only paid attention to the sound track in her movie. For the sake of her reader, she needs to play that mental movie to record not only the dialogue, but also the actions, including who spoke and how they spoke, and what her characters did along with what they said. Before I showed her how to do that, I first asked her to show me where she might add more actions. This move helped me determine whether she needed more modeling or just more coaching.

I was in the Pool and me and my sister's was Playing water fit so I was skard because I thote that I was going to Drawn so my sister siad you are not going to Drawn I got you Dont worry I have you. so I siad ok and she siad to go on her Bake and she was going to 7 Feet and I had my eye's close and I was telling My sister Plec Dont Jrup me Plec Dont Jrupeme and she siad Im not going to Jrupeyou iP you Keep saying that Im going to Jrupe you. and I siad OK so we whent Bake to 3 Feet and I was learning how to swemre by my sister and she taild me to Put my to Feet in the water and Let your Bady Flot and keep your hands up and she siad now swime swime and I was swimeing now I Know how to swime and it was Fun.

FIG. 14–2 Danielle's revised draft

Setting Goals for Future Writing

Explain that writers can make goals for themselves by looking at their past writing and deciding what to aim for in future writing. Share the story of one child who did that.

"Writers, I've been watching you as you move through the writing process with greater independence. One thing I'm so excited about is the way you are making decisions for yourselves. I told you earlier that you need to be job captains of your writing, deciding when it is time for you to start this second piece of writing. Well, you also need to decide on a goal and give yourself reminders that will help you do your best work.

"You can glean those reminders from looking back at your first piece and the 'Narrative Writing Checklist' and thinking, 'What did I do in this piece of writing that I want to always do as a writer?' Then jot yourself a reminder on a sticky note, and put it beside you as you write. Perhaps you remembered to write with periods and capitals. Well, you definitely don't want to go back to the old days before you did that! So write a reminder.

"Danielle realized by looking at her first piece that she wrote what one person said and the next person said, but her writing was like a sound track. It told what people said but didn't show the actions or say where they were, so she's written herself a note that says, 'Not just a sound track!'

"Meanwhile, Maria's story has dialogue only at the very start of it, when her grandfather asks, 'Do you want to make smoothies?' She's going to remember the whole story, putting in more specific dialogue and actions."

"Right now, get with your partner. Look over each other's first pieces, and create some goals together for your future writing, starting with this next piece."

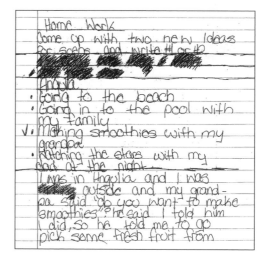

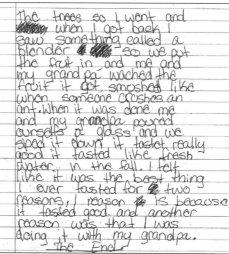

FIG. 14–3   Maria resolves to rewrite this with more details.

Session 15

Revision

Balancing Kinds of Details

ear Teachers,

Today is another day on which I turn the reins over to you. Once again, I will help you imagine the teaching you might do.

MINILESSON

As you know, in your connection, you will remind kids to bring forward what they already know to support them in the work they will learn today. Today's session will be about revision, but your connection is a good opportunity to remind kids that they are their own job captains, that they know all of the steps in the writing process, and that they can make decisions about how and when to cycle through them.

Just as your writers are learning to make choices about their own process as writers, so, too, they are learning to make choices about the details they include to fill up their stories. One powerful revision strategy you might teach today is that writers balance the kinds of details in their stories. In other words, they take care to not let one kind of detail overwhelm the piece. Of course, plan teaching that meets the needs of your writers.

As always, make sure your teaching point is worded so that it is not an assignment for the day, but rather a strategy that students can use always and forever in their writing lives. You might say something like, "Writers, yesterday as I was conferring with all of you, I noticed that many of you have tried to elaborate by adding dialogue. And that is definitely one way to elaborate. But we also want to make sure we keep a balance in our writing and use dialogue where it will have the biggest impact and support our meaning. Some of your writing is all talk, and that doesn't work! Today I am going to teach you that you can also elaborate by adding actions, thoughts, and even setting details."

COMMON CORE STATE STANDARDS: W.3.3.a,b,c; W.3.5, W.3.10, W.4.3.b, RL.3.5, SL.3.6, L.3.3.a,b

If your children are overdoing dialogue, and you decide to teach them to balance the kinds of details they add into their drafts, you can illustrate that teaching point with an excerpt from *Come On, Rain!* that has a balance of details, such as the one below.

> I stare out over rooftops,
>
> past chimneys, into the way off distance.
>
> And that's when I see it coming,
>
> clouds rolling in,
>
> gray clouds, bunched and bulging under a purple sky.
>
> A creeper of hope circles 'round my bones.
>
> "Come on, rain!" I whisper.

You can point out that Hesse starts this section with an action. The narrator stares out over rooftops. Then the author tells what the narrator sees and in this way gives some setting details. She sees gray clouds and a purple sky. Then Hesse gives some of the internal story—in other words, she tells the narrator's thoughts and feelings. "A creeper of hope circles 'round my bones" is a way of saying "I feel hopeful." Finally, there is a bit of dialogue as the narrator whispers to herself.

"We can take this idea and apply it to our own writing," you might say to your class, before using your own writing to demonstrate. Start by showing a section of your writing that you prepared ahead of time so that it matches the writing that most of your kids are doing. If dialogue overwhelms many of their stories, mirror that in your demonstration writing. Then show how you choose which kinds of details to add and which to subtract. Because this minilesson is designed to support revision, be sure to model how you would either add carets or numbers or another symbol to show where you add text, and show how you add more pages if you need more space. Show, too, how you cross out.

Before kids leave the carpet and your watchful eye, you'll want to give them a chance to try out this work and give yourself a chance to assess their understanding. You might set them up to try it in their own stories, saying something like, "Now let's help each other find places where you could try balancing out your stories with different kinds of details. Will Partner 1 from each partnership raise a thumb so we know who you are? Partner 1, please read one of your entries. Then Partner 2 (show me which of you is Partner 2), see if there is a place that doesn't feel balanced. Your job is to listen and then point out specific places in the text where the writer could revise for more balance."

Before you send them off, remind writers in your link that they can use this technique in their own writing every day from now on. Add this technique to the anchor chart for the unit, under ways to revise. This is also a perfect time to remind them to reference their narrative checklists and goals. As their own job captains, your children will be making choices about whether to use the minilesson you taught today, or whether other revision is more important. Before your students leave the meeting area, glance over the plans they have made, because this will help guide your conferring. You may want to make a mental note to confer with writers who seem at a loss to make any plans for their revision work.

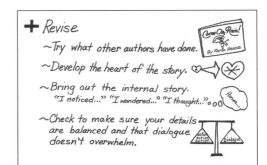

FIG. 15–1

> ## To Write a True Story
>
> - Find story ideas that are focused and important to you and write lots of entries.
> - Make a mental movie of what happened, telling it in small detail, bit by bit.
>   - Detail the actions.
>   - Include the dialogue.
> - Remember your self-assessments of your narrative writing and your goals.
> - Rehearse for your writing by storytelling the story repeatedly.
> - Try different leads for your story (Action? Dialogue?).
> - Write a flash draft, writing fast and furious, eyes on the mental movie.
> - Revise.
>   - Try what other authors have done.
>   - Develop the heart of the story.
> - Bring out the internal story ('I noticed . . . ` 'I wondered . . . ` 'I thought . . . ').

CONFERRING AND SMALL-GROUP WORK

You could draw on the conferring sections in Sessions 9 and 10 of this unit as you plan your small groups and your conferring. You have a few choices about how to formulate your small groups. You could group writers according to where they are in the writing process. Even though you are giving your writers greater independence as they move through the writing process, you will still want to keep an eye on those who are lagging far behind. If you notice a few writers who are still collecting story ideas in their notebooks, for example, you will likely want to convene them to support them in choosing a seed idea and rehearsing for drafting. You could also decide to convene a small group who could use a tune-up session on a strategy you previously taught. In the case of a group like this, especially because they have been taught this strategy before, you will want to keep your demonstration very short so that the bulk of the time is spent with kids writing and you coaching.

MID-WORKSHOP TEACHING

As you confer, be on the lookout for teaching you do that feels applicable to other writers, and use this to plan your mid-workshop teaching. You might want to use this opportunity to remind writers of all the tools they have at their disposal should they run into trouble while steering themselves through the writing process. If you notice that energy is flagging, you might want to call on some of your teaching from earlier in the unit. Remind your writers that they know what to do if they begin to run out of gas, and invite them to set some goals for themselves.

SHARE

You have a few choices about how to structure your share at the end of the session. You could draw on the work of one student and point out the lovely work that he or she did that others could try. Or you could celebrate some of the elaboration moves your writers are trying with a symphony share. Say to your writers, "Look through the work you did today and choose a line or two that you feel very proud of. This could be a line or two that shows a place where you really tried to balance kinds of details. Make a box around that place, and give me a thumbs up when you are ready. I'll be like the conductor in an orchestra. When I point to you, say the lines that you boxed." As you point to each writer, you don't have to give any commentary or feedback. Just "ooh" and "ah" as a way to show your joy over the beauty of the language they are producing.

The previous sessions have been about scaffolding your writers toward greater independence as they move through the writing process. Of course, it is highly likely your writers will be at a range of levels of independence, making the need to differentiate great. This chart addresses a few of the typical issues you might encounter as your writers attempt to revise their stories using all they have learned about structure, elaboration, and general qualities of good narrative writing.

136

"If . . . Then . . ."

If . . .	Then . . .
IF writers are still writing in summaries, not scenes . . .	THEN you might see if they are taking on too large a time frame or too broad a story line. One of the seeming paradoxes of writing is that to elaborate more fully, to really stretch out a moment, it helps tremendously if the moment is smaller (more focused). You might then help the writer stretch out that small moment on a timeline, reliving each scene and then writing to capture the actions, words, and setting.
IF one kind of elaboration, such as dialogue, overwhelms the piece . . .	THEN remind writers that good personal narrative writing has a balance of actions, dialogue, and internal thoughts. It might be helpful to teach writers to test for balance in their own pieces, perhaps using a code that you design together. The letter A could represent action, D for dialogue, T for thoughts, and so on. Then teach them to choose a section that might not be balanced and to label the parts in this section using the code you designed. If the writer notices she has labeled all of the parts in one section with the letter D, for example, it's likely that that part is not really balanced. The writer can think about what other kinds of elaboration might fit there.
IF the parts that tell the internal story are more like summaries that take the writer out of the piece . . .	THEN you might again draw on the show, don't tell, teaching you did during Session 5, focusing on the ways we can *show* the internal thoughts and feelings of a character using descriptive detail, internal thinking, small actions, and dialogue. It will also be helpful to show children how to revisit their planning notebooks, circling and annotating the parts where it's important to show the character's feelings (the key, central moments) and skipping over the parts that are less significant.

Good luck!
Lucy and Marjorie

Commas and Quotation Marks
Punctuating Dialogue

IN THIS SESSION, you'll draw on a mentor text to teach students how writers correctly punctuate dialogue.

GETTING READY

✔ Students' writer's notebooks and writing folders, to be brought to the meeting area

✔ A student's work that illustrates what has been taught so far, especially action details, dialogue, internal thinking, and descriptive details (see Connection)

✔ Lead from *Come On, Rain!* enlarged on chart paper or projected on the document camera (see Teaching)

✔ Chart paper and markers to create a chart, "Look How Hesse Punctuates Quotes" (see Teaching)

✔ An excerpt from a book or your own text that includes dialogue. Practice reading it aloud in a way that highlights where the quotation marks might go (see Active Engagement).

✔ Student work that illustrates how to punctuate direct quotes and how they can keep a story in the moment (see Share)

COMMON CORE STATE STANDARDS: W.3.5, W.3.3b, W.4.3.b,d; RL.3.5, SL.3.6, L.3.2.c,e,f,g; L.3.3.a,b; L3.6, L.4.3.b

TODAY MARKS THE END OF ANOTHER BEND in the road of this unit, and the temporary end of work on a second personal narrative. Neither this piece nor the one students wrote earlier in the unit will be totally done. In the next session, you'll be teaching them that writers look back on their writing, decide which drafts are worth developing, and then throw themselves deeply into the work of revising their best pieces, going from good to great. So it would be easy to conclude that it is premature for students to edit today's writing, looking with great care at the punctuation.

But I have found that if your students edit only just prior to publication at the very end of a unit of study, they will not get the practice they need attending to conventions. So you will find that throughout this series, I encourage you to channel students to use any time they have wrapping up a piece as an occasion for editing—and then to bring the work they do during that editing session into their subsequent first-draft writing. Yes, there will be more work ahead, but still, this piece deserves to be tidied up. And more than that, your students deserve some instruction in mechanics and some encouragement to writing more conventionally as a matter of course.

You will need to decide what the subject of today's minilesson should be. The lesson could easily be revised to support other conventions. I've focused on punctuation and especially on the punctuation required by writing with dialogue simply because this is a challenge for many third-graders and because tackling this now allows children to use what they learn in subsequent writing.

So look over your students' writing and think about what they are able to do and what they are still struggling with. As you do this, guard against the temptation to conclude that no one has ever taught them about periods, capitals, and other forms of punctuation. Chances are good that your students have heard lessons about punctuation marks since first grade!

But, as you may be seeing in their writing, it is not enough for us to simply teach rules for using conventional punctuation marks. We also have to help children apply this knowledge as they write. Sometimes I sense that children believe that because it isn't crucial for their rough drafts and entries to be 100 percent correct, they are free to write for days on end without any end punctuation at all! They sometimes think that it is only prior to publication that they need to reread their drafts and insert periods and capitals—or quotation marks.

You want to demonstrate that as a writer, you are ravenously hungry to learn interesting and wonderful ways other writers use the conventions of written language. This session supports not only the basic punctuation that kids should know, but also the punctuation that is a part of new craft moves that students are just starting to learn.

Of course, there is a grain of truth to these perceptions. It is true that writers focus more on content and craft during early drafts and don't obsess about every last mechanical detail until it's time to publish. But this certainly does not mean children should postpone writing with end punctuation until just prior to publication.

Instead, they need to develop ease and automaticity with end punctuation and quotations. Your observation of your students' writing, then, may serve as a reminder that you need to begin today finding more times throughout the workshop to insert punctuation prompts. "Writers," you might say, "I'm finding that a few of you are so focused on what you are saying that you are forgetting to write with punctuation. Forgetting punctuation reminds me of a time when I drove to work and realized as I pulled into the parking garage in the middle of Manhattan that I'd forgotten my shoes! I bet that anyone I spoke to that day had a hard time listening to me because they probably kept thinking, 'How weird! She's out on the sidewalk in New York City in her stocking feet!' Forgetting your punctuation is like forgetting your shoes. It makes it hard for people to hear what you have to say because your readers, like your friends, keep thinking, 'Something isn't right.' So make sure that after you write a sentence, you punctuate, and when people talk, you punctuate."

Of course, while you are playing Tough Guy Enforcer with bottom-line mechanics and spelling expectations, you also want to demonstrate that as a writer, you are ravenously hungry to learn interesting and wonderful ways other writers use the conventions of written language. This session, then, supports not only the basic punctuation that kids should know, but also the punctuation that is a part of new craft moves that students are just starting to learn. When writers make people speak in their stories, that calls for quotations and other punctuation conventions. In this minilesson, you will draw on a mentor text to teach writers to correctly punctuate dialogue.

Commas and Quotation Marks
Punctuating Dialogue

CONNECTION

Celebrate all that writers have done to write inside the moment with precise details.

"Writers, can I have your eyes and your attention, please? When I gesture toward your table, come find your spot on the rug.

"Your writing is giving me goose bumps! I love that you are trying out different moves that you noticed from studying Karen Hesse. I want to show you the smart work that Lizzie did yesterday. Lizzie thought a lot about how to balance the kinds of details she added to her story. She made sure that one kind of detail didn't overwhelm the piece. Then she elaborated, writing with specifics, adding actions to her story to balance the kinds of details. Listen." (See Figure 16–1.)

> I got into the car with my feet scrunched up so I wouldn't smash the plants.
>
> My mom and I were decorating her classroom for the new school year. There were calendars, posters, plants, and supplies. We carried them in, up the stairs, and into room 205. I set up a magnetic calendar, did a puzzle of the USA, stuck short biographies on the walls, and hung my Mom's tacks up high so she could hang up high things . . .

"Lizzie didn't just say, 'I got in the car' and then stop her sentence, did she? Instead she said more. She said, 'I got in the car *with my feet scrunched up so I wouldn't smash the plants.*' She didn't just say, 'I set up the classroom' and then stop, did she? Instead, she kept going, telling how she set up the classroom.

"Another thing I love—Lizzie told us *exact* details. She could have written, 'I helped my mother unpack *a lot of things.*' If she'd said that, we wouldn't really be able to picture precisely what Lizzie did. Because she instead wrote, 'I set up *a magnetic calendar, did a puzzle of the USA, stuck short biographies on the walls . . . ,*' we can picture how she helped her mother unpack. I'm hoping some of you can learn from Lizzie's smart decision to write with precise and descriptive details, even if it took extending her sentences.

FIG. 16–1 Lizzie's detail-filled entry

"Writers, when you write with such wonderful details and with people's actual words, this makes your writing more beautiful—and more complicated. And complicated writing requires more sophisticated punctuation. And that—the sophisticated punctuation—is the subject of today's minilesson."

❖ Name the teaching point.

"Writers, when you include people talking in your story, you need to capture their exact words and use quotation marks to signal, 'These are the exact words the person said.' It is actually more sophisticated than that. You can study what published writers do to punctuate quotations and try to do those exact same things."

TEACHING

Set up writers to investigate how Karen Hesse captures talk by using quotation marks in purposeful, powerful ways.

"Let's look again at the lead from Karen Hesse's *Come On, Rain!*, and this time, let's look closely at how she uses quotation marks." I revealed a piece of chart paper on which I had copied:

> *"Come on, rain!" I say, squinting into the endless heat.*
>
> *Mamma lifts a listless vine and sighs.*
>
> *"Three weeks and not a drop," she says, sagging over her parched plants.*

"You and I could glance really quickly and just see that Hesse uses quotation marks to surround the speaker's exact words, but let's look more closely and notice other things about how the author punctuates quotes. Will you tell your partner what you notice while I do some of this studying as well? And then look at your piece and see if you have done all of those things or maybe only some of them."

After a minute, I began circling different parts of the punctuation, and as I did, I chronicled what I had heard children noticing. "You are right that both of the quoted parts begin with a capital and end with punctuation. The first part ends in an exclamation point. Andrew took a close look at the second quoted part, where Mamma is talking. Will you each take a look at that? This sentence would usually end with a period, but in this case, it ends with a comma, doesn't it? Hmmm. Why?" I paused to let children think. "I think this shows that Mamma has stopped talking.

"Notice in both cases that the quotation marks have surrounded not just the words, but the end punctuation, too. The punctuation captures not only the talk, but how it was said as well." I revealed a chart, showing these points.

My purpose today is not just to teach how to punctuate dialogue, but to also demonstrate that authors care as much about conventions as craft. Throughout this unit, I use Karen Hesse as my co-teacher, helping me teach each step of the way.

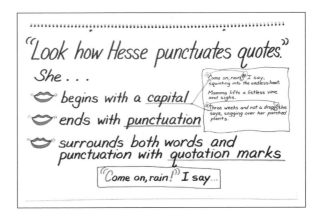

FIG. 16–2 This chart helps reinforce the teaching point.

ACTIVE ENGAGEMENT

Set writers up to practice adding quotations to your demonstration story.

"Let's try this together right now. I am going to tell my story. As I do, I'll get to places where I make people talk or think and I give their actual words. I want you to capture the beginning of those quoted parts by hooking your two fingers on your left hand." I held my two fingers alongside the left side of my mouth. "When I finish those parts, catch my last words with two fingers on your right hand." I held the two fingers of my right hand up to the right side of my mouth.

I read a part of my story aloud, pausing when I read dialogue to help the children capture the quotations with their fingers.

> All the kids were around me, pushing money into my hands.
>
> "Don't forget I want Mars Bars," Phil told me, "As many as you can get."
>
> "I want red licorice," said Amy Jo.
>
> "Okay," I said, looking to see if any teachers were watching. "I'll get everything."

After I finished reading my excerpt, I said, "Writers, that was lovely. You noticed that the parts that had the exact words people said needed quotations. I'm giving an extra thumbs up to Joseph, because I noticed that he was even trying to put in the comma before the quotations. Well done!"

LINK

Invite writers to make plans to revise and edit their stories.

"Writers, I want to remind you to draw on all you know how to do as you edit your drafts. Some of you will finish adding quotation marks to your drafts in about five minutes. But, of course, you aren't the kind of writers who will just say, 'I'm done!' and sit at your seat, staring into space! No way!

"Right now, before you leave the carpet, think about other editing work you can do, other things you can check, and jot a self-assignment to yourself on the top of your page." On the white board I made a box and wrote "self-assignment box." "And if your piece is perfectly edited, there are other things you can do to make it the best it can be. Jot one of those in a self-assignment box as well. Our classroom charts and the narrative writing checklist will help you find ideas, too."

I often use repeated gestures and actions to make what I am teaching more memorable. The more the children actively practice something, the more likely they will be to use it in their own writing when they return to their seats.

I could have just sent the children off and crossed my fingers that editing for punctuation would keep them all busy for a while, but I know all too well that this is hardly ever the case. The link is my opportunity to anticipate possible scenarios and to provide suggestions for other things to do should anyone be "done" with today's work.

Supporting the Use of Conventions and Penmanship

YOU MAY NOTICE as you circulate during conferring that your writers struggle with quotation marks more than you might have anticipated. If so, now is a good time to start emphasizing this convention, because it is a Common Core expectation that by the end of the year third-graders will use commas and quotation marks in dialogue. When the text moves from speaker to speaker without much action in between or when the writer summarizes what someone has said instead of using exact words, inserting quotation marks will be tricky. Be on the lookout for common ways such as these that your writers struggle. You might notice, as you move among the class, coaching children to help each other punctuate the dialogue they've already written, that this seemingly straightforward lesson is not at all straightforward when children try to apply it to their drafts.

I pulled alongside Takeshi, who had sections of text in which one character and then another talked back and forth, interjecting brief comments. His text didn't name the speaker or include any actions, so it was difficult to discern when one voice ended and another began. (See Figure 16–3.)

> One day I was playing on the playground at school then Takuma came and said, what do you want to play. I said I don't know so he said "play by yourself because I'll play kickball." "Okay." "Sure," I said, but in my mind I said to myself I can't believe that he just said that.

(continues)

MID-WORKSHOP TEACHING
Replacing Summarized Conversations with Dialogue

"Writers, can I have your eyes and your attention please? I noticed many places in your drafts where you summarize conversations rather than using the exact words that someone said. I noticed you writing things like, 'My mom told me to get in the car' instead of, '"Get in the car!" yelled my mom.' Do you see what a difference doing it the second way makes? When you summarize conversations, it feels like you're not living inside the memory of that moment anymore. It feels like you are looking back on that moment and writing a report of what happened. Right now, look through your story and see if there are places where you summarized conversations instead of writing the exact words that someone said. Look for phrases that might be clues that you summarized, ones that sound like: 'she told me' or 'she said to me.'"

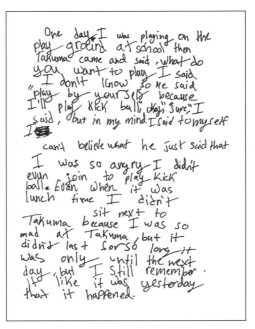

FIG. 16–3 Takeshi's first entry, with beginning attempts to mark the dialogue using quotation marks

As a first step, I showed Takeshi how, in his Little Bill books, Bill Cosby put the dialogue on separate lines to clarify who was speaking. This was also a simple paragraphing strategy for him to use. I left him with the plan that he would start paying closer attention to the dialogue in the books he was reading, as well as in his own writing.

You will also want to look for other ways your students struggle, especially if the struggle affects fluency and stamina. For some children the physical act of writing itself can be a hardship. The penmanship looks like a six-year-old wrote it with capital letters interspersed throughout. Pencil grips are awkward and weak. Posture is poor. If this is the case, it is more important to take care of these issues before worrying about paragraphing and elaboration.

Provide children with additional handwriting practice, either first thing in the morning or as part of homework. Just five minutes of daily letter formation practice can make a huge difference in penmanship. Check how each child holds his pencil, and add special grips that put the fingers in the right place for comfortable writing. Provide alternative tools, such as felt-tip markers or mechanical pencils, depending on how much pressure a child tends to use. Make sure the child's feet are firmly planted on the floor, using taped-up phone books if needed as a foot rest. You might also want to get advice from the school's occupational therapist for additional modifications and materials. For more detailed information, I suggest reading Colleen Cruz's book, *Reaching Struggling Writers* (2008), part of the Workshop Help Desk series.

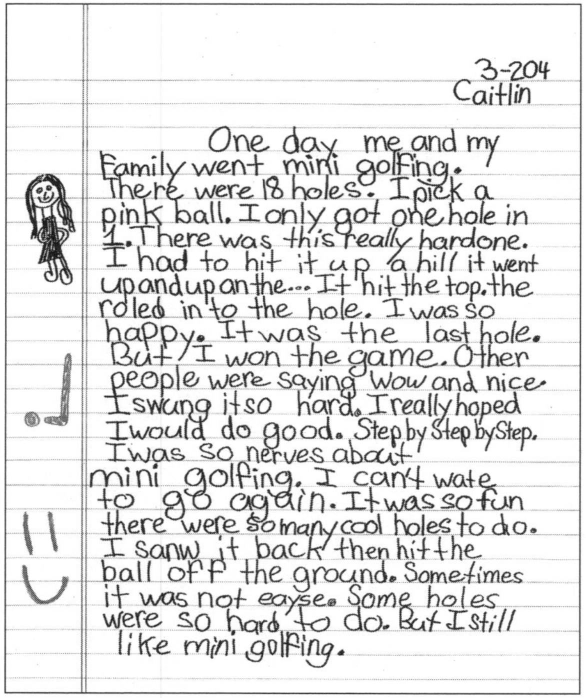

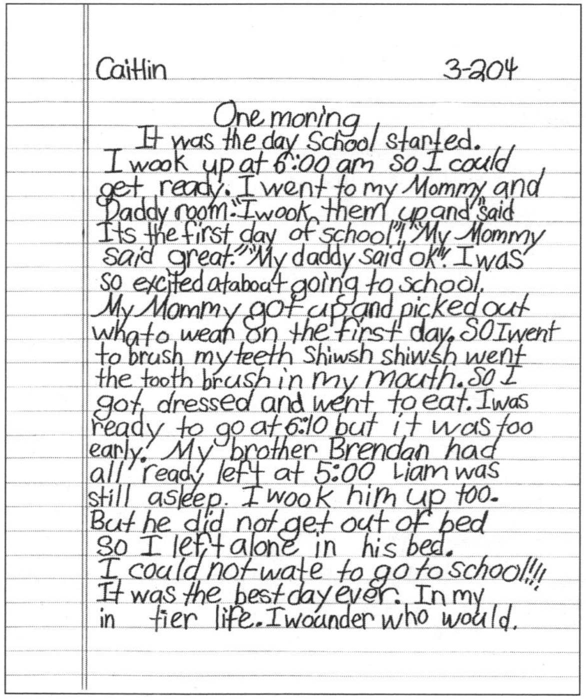

FIG. 16–4   Caitlin's writing

Remembering to Write from Inside the Moment

Convene the class to share one writer's decision making that led to clearer, more powerful writing.

"Writers, I want to share something that Caitlin did. She realized that writers use quotations to show the exact words that someone *said* and so she wrote this" (see Figure 16–5):

> My Dad said, "Hey Caity!" I said, "Yeah!" "Want to go to the carnival?" I said "Sure!" Two minutes later we ran to the car. "Come on let's go Caity!" "Ok!" We got there in like a second. We were walking through the carnival. It was so cool.

"You know what Caitlin did then? She noticed that she shifted out of being in the moment when she wrote, 'It was so cool.' She was *reporting* on what she was thinking instead of being *inside* of it. Then Caitlin thought, 'Instead of just reporting, "It was so cool," how can I write from inside the moment?' So, she went back to that moment and thought, 'What was it like inside that moment? What made me think it was so cool?' And she realized that what made it so cool was everything she saw as soon as she stepped into that carnival. She saw lots of games and rides, like skee ball and a fun house. So she changed her writing to not just say that it was so cool, but to say what she actually saw and then what she thought. In her second version of this moment, Caitlin wrote this." (See Figure 16–6.)

"So, writers, remember that we want to be in the moment, not just report on the moment, and one way to do that is to write with exact details. Write the exact things you said, the exact things you saw, and the exact things you thought. And when it comes to showing your reader the talking and the thinking of the people in your story, don't forget to use punctuation and quotation marks!"

FIG. 16–5   Caitlin's first draft

FIG. 16–6   Caitlin's second draft

Writers Revise in Big, Important Ways

IN THIS SESSION, you'll teach students how revision can bring writing to a new level so that it rings with clarity and purpose.

GETTING READY

✔ Students' current drafts and writing folders, to be brought to the meeting area. Students should sit with their partners.

✔ An oral story or metaphor that shows how revising can change something in big and important ways (see Connection)

✔ Your own story you used from an earlier session, projected on the document camera, to demonstrate revising for redundancy (see Teaching)

✔ Reasons you might be writing your story, to share who and what you are writing about

✔ Questions you want students to consider, on chart paper or white board: "Who are you writing about?" "What are you trying to say?"

✔ On-demand writing from the start of the year available to each child so they can reflect on their growth and progress (see Share)

✔ Narrative Writing Checklist, Grades 3 and 4, easily accessible to each child (see Share)

COMMON CORE STATE STANDARDS: W.3.3.a,b,c; W.3.5, W.3.10, RL.3.1, RFS.3.4, SL.3.1.a,b,c,d; SL.3.6, L.3.2.c, L.3.3.a,b; L.3.1, L.3.6, L.4.6

"MOST WRITERS don't initially say what they want to say," announces Zinsser in *On Writing Well* (1998), "or say it as well as they could. The newly hatched sentence almost always has something wrong with it. It's not clear. It's not logical. It's verbose. It's klunky. It's pretentious. It's boring. It's full of clutter. It's full of clichés. It lacks rhythm. It can be read in several different ways. It doesn't lead out of the previous sentence. It doesn't . . . The point is that clear writing is the result of a lot of tinkering."

It's not easy for children to see this. After all, intense revision is by no means natural to most eight-year-olds. Few other activities in their lives require this kind of hair-splitting reassessment. Children have churned out a quick draft, teased out and story-told the part that is to serve as its "heart," paragraphed and punctuated till the page before them looks visually imposing—more words on a page than they ever wrote in second grade. They're *done*.

But if you want your children to become real writers, it is urgent to teach—and reteach—revision. That such revision won't come easy to most writers makes it all the more urgent to teach it—and then to support young writers as they attempt the brave work that renders many adult writers paralyzed. Deliberating over word choice, making the strategic decision to cut and discard entire parts, rewriting from another angle altogether, sometimes changing the very heart of the story: real revision is soul work, and your young writers can certainly learn this—if only you teach it.

Too often, "revising" has come to be confused with proofreading, adding a comma here and splitting a sentence there. In many classrooms, "revising" means adding more to the story, often in senseless, nondirectional ways that actually weaken the story. In this session, you'll teach how a next draft can truly bring writing to a new level until it rings with clarity and purpose.

Writers Revise in Big, Important Ways

CONNECTION

Set children up to see their writing with new eyes. Point out that writers need to take a step back to ask questions about their writing so they can see it with a fresh perspective.

"Writers, have you ever seen a sculptor at work? It is a fascinating thing to watch. A sculptor is like a writer. First, he takes a bit of clay and throws it onto his work board. The same way a writer throws out words onto a page in a quick first draft.

"Then comes the essential part: shaping the clay till he has a head shape, a nose, ears. Much the same way as you take writing and shape it 'til the story has a heart, a beginning, and ending, 'til there is balance between dialogue and description, actions and feelings.

"But, writers, there is something sculptors do that only the best writers do too. When they've finished sculpting, they step back and look at the completed sculpture with new eyes, sometimes under a different light or from a new angle, and they make big, important revisions. 'Hmm, that nose is way too big for the face,' or 'The ears are not in line with each other,' and they rip apart what might have *looked* finished, and they make it better. They make it perfect.

"The best writers do this too. When they're finished with a piece of writing, they step back from it and ask themselves, 'Is it working? Is it perfect?' Before they send their writing out into the world, they look at it with new eyes and make some final, big decisions about how to make it the best it can be."

❖ Name the teaching point.

"Today I want to teach you that when writers finish a piece of writing, they revise in big, important ways. They try to read their finished work like a stranger might, asking, 'Is this clear? Can I take away a part or add a part to make it *more* clear?' They read it aloud to themselves, checking if it flows."

This is no small task you are asking of your students on this day, but your belief in their ability to try what you are asking will help propel them, and you, forward. Try giving them a bunch of fun revision tools, such as scissors, tape, Post-its, and flaps and let them have a go at it, expecting them to do it like the young third-graders they are.

TEACHING

Demonstrate how reading aloud can help a writer hear whether or not parts sound right, flow smoothly, and are important to the story.

"Writers, here's the latest draft of my story. I'm quite proud of it. I thought, 'That's it. I'm done.' But I know I need to step back from the story and look at it from a stranger's eyes, new eyes. One great way to revise is to read your writing out loud to see if it flows. And let's see what parts can be made better." I began reading, in a loud voice.

> Six or seven kids crowded near me at recess. "Junior Mints, remember," Ginny said, pushing money into my hands.
>
> "Mars Bars, same as always," Phil said. "Get as many as you can."
>
> "A giant-sized box of Dots," Joey called.
>
> "Twizzlers," said Mandy.
>
> I stuffed their dollars into my parka pocket. I didn't have time to write a list because I had to get to the store and back before the teachers realized I was gone.

"Hmm, maybe I've overdone it with the dialogue about candy. I had fun writing and punctuating it, but that doesn't mean I have to keep it if it weakens the piece."

> I raced to the edge of the playground. Then I looked over my shoulder to be sure the recess teacher wasn't watching as I zoomed out of the school yard and down the block to Gates' Deli.
>
> I pushed open the door and the lady at the checkout counter smiled and asked, "Can I help you?"

"Writers, I'm thinking that I didn't show the internal story of what I felt as I raced to the store. I didn't show how scared I was, how guilty I felt, or how desperate I was to do something that would keep the kids liking me. I'm going to put a note here that I could revise this."

Then I scanned the rest of the story, slowing down at the part showing my mother's entrance into the store.

> I spilled my goods onto the counter. Just then the door squeaked open. I glanced up. What? My mom? I froze. "Oh no," I thought. "Oh no!" Blood rushed to my face.

The importance of reading one's writing out loud cannot be overemphasized, as it is the only way to hear the ebb and flow of the words and the tone of the piece. You can also share with your students that this is something most professional writers do and recommend.

Name the specific questions a writer asks to determine what words to keep and what words to cross out.

"I haven't shown my Mom's reaction yet. I expected her to be furious. She has a temper. But what I wasn't prepared for is that she looked hurt. But do I want to say that? Do I want this to be a story of me and my mom or me and my friends?"

"This story started out being about my mom. But it is also about my friends and the risk I took. So who am I writing about? And what am I trying to say?

"Writers, I found three spots where I want to make revisions." Picking up a marker, I marked the portions of my draft I wanted to reconsider. The dialogue at the start, the missing internal story related to my friends, and the question about how to end the story.

> All the kids were around me, pushing money into my hands. "Don't forget I want Mars Bars," Phil
> told me. "As many as you can get."
>
> "I want red licorice," said Amy Jo.
>
> "Junior Mints and Juicy Fruit," said Ginny shoving a dollar my way.
>
> "A giant-sized box of Dots," Joey called.
>
> "Twizzlers for me," said Mandy.

"Writers, I'm going to start by taking out some of the talk up front. It is hard to chop off words that we might have loved when we thought them up. But wherever I can say the same thing in fewer words, I do away with the extra. My reader needs just enough detail to keep the mental movie going. Too much detail distracts."

Debrief. Point out that writers not only get rid of extra words. They also ask, "What am I writing about?"

"Writers, did you note the revisions I have planned? First, I got rid of extra stuff. In writing, less is more, and good revisions almost always need a writer to trim away useless words.

"Then I asked myself a question that every writer must ask when they think they're done. Who or what am I writing about? What am I trying to say? Well, here's the secret: writers don't know the answer to this question when they start out. They might think they're writing about one thing—like my mom—and wind up discovering that this story could be about something else entirely—kids I'm trying impress who'll never accept me. We don't know where our writing will take us. And unless we stand back from a finished draft to ask this tough question, we'll never know. This is the biggest revision we can make—to decide what our story is going to be about and change it so that the reader figures out what we're trying to say about that person or thing."

You, like the kids, are probably gasping at my seemingly ruthless cuts, but if I expect kids to cross out any of their beloved, hard-earned words, then I must do the same, albeit a bit exaggerated.

There is no question but that this is very advanced for third graders. That's okay. Sometimes it helps to show them the horizon even if you know it will be a while until they reach it.

ACTIVE ENGAGEMENT

Set children up to reread their own writing, looking for places that are not clear and parts that may not be necessary to the flow of the story.

"Right now, pick up the draft of the story you are working on and find a part that feels done." I gave them a few seconds to find a part and then I stopped them. "Now read this part like a stranger might, asking, 'Is this clear? Can I take away a part or add a part to make it *more* clear?' Read it aloud to yourselves, checking if it flows."

As the children started reading out loud I voiced over, "Hmm, is there something that is overdone or overused? Are there too many sentences that say the same thing? Who am I writing about? What am I trying to say?

"Partner 2, turn and tell your partner some words you might cross out and why. And Partner 1, listen to see if this makes the writing clearer. Also ask, 'Who are you writing about?' 'What are you trying to say?' I wrote these two questions on the white board to help you remember."

LINK

Remind children that revision is about making the writing clear, and that means that sometimes writers must take parts away that might confuse or tire the reader.

"So, writers, whenever you are revising, keep in mind that revision is not just about adding more. It is also about taking away things that are overused or that don't match your message. Whenever you review, you can step back and ask, 'Is this clear? Can I add or take away a part to make it clearer?' Then you can make the necessary revisions and ask, too, 'what's my story really about?'"

As you walk around, listening in to the partners talk, be on the lookout for any children who seem overly eager to cut out whole swaths of text, or others who seem to think every word is too precious to cut. Both types will need your closer attention.

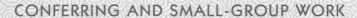

Helping Students Find Meaning in Their Stories

TEACHERS, the work you began today is significant though not always easy. It is no small feat for your new third-grader to pick up his or her piece of writing and deliberately insert significance into it. But resist the urge to walk around the room suggesting to your writers what their piece might be about! If we say to a fumbling new writer, "Might this piece be about your grandfather's death or being afraid of separation from your family?" we're coauthoring and not mentoring. The difference is narrow and all too easy to miss. But unless we teach our writers to find their themes independently, we've just deepened their reliance on us.

"This piece can be about anything you want it to be. You're the writer. You *can't* be wrong," is the first piece of assurance to give a child. Remember, you're *teaching* the *writer*. This is only the first time they're doing this work. Let children come up with what might appear to be sloppy themes or disjointed ideas for what their story is about. But insist on hearing—and seeing—their validations.

"Oh, your story is about the Poconos. What do you want your story to *say* about the Poconos?" "I want to say that it's the best fun time for my family when we go there."

"Right. Where in the story are you showing your family having fun?" "I haven't written that part yet."

"Okay. Here's a tip though: all these before parts—ask yourself, 'Are these parts important to my story, or might I cut them out?' Try to begin *close* to what your story is about, at a part that shows your family having fun *in* the Poconos."

Moves like this can transform not only your teaching, but your relationship with your young writers as you acknowledge what they are trying to say and then show them ways to embed meaning throughout their story by rethinking where and when to start the story, including some key dialogue, and the exact actions that move the reader forward in the story. By giving your young writers such tips, you empower them and help them have a "can-do" attitude as they write.

MID-WORKSHOP TEACHING
Writers Read Their Writing Often and Out Loud

"Writers, can I have your eyes and attention? I am seeing a lot of brave writers today. It is not easy to take away a word or a sentence once it is written down on the page, but I see many of you crossing out some of the first words you wrote. You are acting like professional writers. I want to give you one more tip. Once you have taken away some words and sentences, writers stop and reread their revised writing out loud to make sure it flows and sounds good to the ear. Revisions are meant to make our writing better, so read a part you just revised, listening carefully to how it sounds when you read it out loud."

As I listened in I heard some voices reading loudly, with strong expression, but many were reading timidly word by word, so I stopped them again to give them a more concrete model.

"Writers, can I have your eyes and attention again? I don't think I was clear when I said 'read it out loud,' because while many of you are reading the words out loud, you are not reading them out loud like you would a piece of literature. We revise to make our writing sound like literature. Listen to how Terrance reads his story out loud. He does not just read the words. He reads them as if they are literature found in our library. He reads with expression and fluency. Listen."

Terrance animatedly read a few sentences from his revised draft.

> I walked into my room. I stopped. I screamed. "What are you doing with my computer!" I yelled to my brother.

"So, writers, from now on, remember to read your words out loud in ways that sound like literature. If it doesn't sound like literature, maybe you need to do some more revising."

Reflecting on Growth

Ask students to reflect on their growth as narrative writers.

"This is amazing. You know when there is a house or a person that has a makeover on TV and gets totally transformed, they will sometimes show 'then' and 'now' pictures. We have only been in this writing workshop for a few weeks, but we could already take 'then' and 'now' pictures. Right now, look at the on-demand narrative that you wrote at the start of this year. Then look at our 'Narrative Writing Checklist,' which I have displayed on this chart." The Narrative Writing Checklist is also available on the CD-ROM.

"*Now*, look at the piece of writing you revised today. Compare the two based on our checklist.

"How many of you are writing stories that are much more focused? Have some of you written a lead that shows what's happening and where, and gets readers into the world of the story? You guys, stand and take a bow. How many of you are separating the different parts of your story into paragraphs? Stand up and take bow. Now, the really cool thing is if your Small Moment stories contain lots of details—even the details about what you said and did and what the other person said. If you have details and action and dialogue, give the detailed section of your story some stars and fireworks, right there on your paper."

Celebrate students' growth and ask students to reflect on their goals for the unit.

"Now, here is the most important thing of all. Look back on the goals you wrote long, long ago, and will you and your partner talk about whether you have already been meeting those goals? Turn and talk." Soon I was suggesting we needed to plan a celebration.

Narrative Writing Checklist

	Grade 3	NOT YET	STARTING TO	YES!	Grade 4	NOT YET	STARTING TO	YES!
	Structure				**Structure**			
Overall	I told the story bit by bit.	☐	☐	☐	I wrote the important part of an event bit by bit and took out unimportant parts.	☐	☐	☐
Lead	I wrote a beginning in which I helped readers know who the characters were and what the setting was in my story.	☐	☐	☐	I wrote a beginning in which I showed what was happening and where, getting readers into the world of the story.	☐	☐	☐
Transitions	I told my story in order by using phrases such as *a little later* and *after that.*	☐	☐	☐	I showed how much time went by with words and phrases that mark time such as *just then* and *suddenly* (to show when things happened quickly) or *after a while* and *a little later* (to show when a little time passed).	☐	☐	☐
Ending	I chose the action, talk, or feeling that would make a good ending and worked to write it well.	☐	☐	☐	I wrote an ending that connected to the beginning or the middle of the story. I used action, dialogue, or feeling to bring my story to a close.	☐	☐	☐
Organization	I used paragraphs and skipped lines to separate what happened first from what happened later (and finally) in my story.	☐	☐	☐	I used paragraphs to separate the different parts or times of the story or to show when a new character was speaking.	☐	☐	☐
	Development				**Development**			
Elaboration	I worked to show what happened to (and in) my characters.	☐	☐	☐	I added more to the heart of my story, including not only actions and dialogue but also thought and feelings.	☐	☐	☐

Revising Endings
Learning from Published Writing

ARRATIVE STORIES have a plot and also a resolution. A good story needs a good ending. Many writers I know say that the endings of their stories and poems and essays are their favorite parts. Some even say that they know their endings before they know anything else about their piece! The writer Katherine Anne Porter claimed, "I always write my last line, my last paragraph, my last page, first." Our students may not feel that their endings are their favorite parts, but endings are crucial. Because if leads have to do the work of inviting, even begging, readers to spend time with the story that follows, the endings are what stay in readers' minds the longest. Endings can cause readers to sob, to applaud, even to get up and vow to change themselves or the world. Writers know this, so they spend extra time on the last paragraphs and last sentences of their stories. Long before you teach this lesson, you can convey the power of a good ending to your children during your read-aloud time. Let the pace and intonation of your voice showcase each story's final passages.

As Frank Smith says in his groundbreaking book, *Joining the Literacy Club* (1988), "Children must read like writers in order to learn how to write like writers. There is no other way in which the intricate complexity of a writer's knowledge can be acquired."

While teaching children to draft and revise endings, then, you'll also be teaching children that writers read the works of other authors as insiders, noticing not only the content but also the craftsmanship. You'll teach, also, that writers pull in to write, then pull back to look at what they've written, thinking, "What's good about this?" "What could be better?"

In Session 7, your students learned how to craft powerful leads by studying the opening lines of *Come On, Rain!* by Karen Hesse. In this session, you will help them do the same work with endings, using the same mentor text, modeling how writers try to name specifically what an author has done, and annotating the text so it becomes a teaching tool. Eventually you will want your young writers to extend this type of analysis to that of other authors and to their own writing.

IN THIS SESSION, you'll teach students that writers deliberately craft the endings of their stories, and you'll show students how to learn techniques for improving their own work by studying published writing.

GETTING READY

✔ Students' drafting folders and a pen or pencil, to be brought to the meeting area

✔ A few examples of student leads that used the weather, the time of day, or bit-by-bit actions (see Connection)

✔ Copies of the ending of *Come On, Rain!* or a different ending to put on chart paper or a document camera

✔ Exemplar student work with strong endings (see Share)

COMMON CORE STATE STANDARDS: W.3.3.d, W.3.4, W.3.10, W.3.5, W.4.3.e, RL.3.3, RL.3.4, SL.3.1.a,b,c,d; SL.3.6, L.3.1.e,f, L.3.3.a,b

Revising Endings
Learning from Published Writing

CONNECTION

Remind children of the writing work they have been doing and prepare them for learning something new.

"I love the way you have been writing fast and long on your second discovery drafts. I have something incredibly important to tell you today, now that you've done that! It's a kind of a secret that good writers know but many beginning writers don't know. You will need to listen carefully.

"Remember when we worked really hard to get leads that would capture and hold the attention of a reader? Adam took his lead, 'Last night my dad, Harrison, and I were in the car going to a restaurant.' and turned it into 'One warm evening last spring, Harrison, my dad, and I climbed into our car and zoomed off toward the highway.' What a big difference just putting in a few words about the weather and using strong verbs like *climbed* and *zoomed* made! Adam's little changes set a mood for the story. I get a picture in my mind of a warm night, when you drive in your car with the windows rolled down, the wind blowing in your face—when you feel excited, like anything can happen."

❧ **Name the teaching point.**

"You've all discovered how writers lead into stories, luring the readers to follow them with a special lead. But the secret that many beginning writers don't know is that writers work just as hard—well, maybe even *harder*—on their endings. Today I want to teach you some ways to do that using the ending of one of our mentor texts, *Come On, Rain!* by Karen Hesse."

TEACHING

Demonstrate using a mentor text to learn ways to make endings more powerful. Read the text aloud and explain your thinking.

"We have to be sure that we make something at the end that fits with the idea we're writing about, something that will stay with the reader. Let's look at the ending of *Come On, Rain!* I've projected it using the document camera so we can study Hesse's writing closely and learn ways to make our endings powerful. Watch while I reread and think about what

---

◆ COACHING

At the start of the minilesson, your tone and words need to convey the message, "Listen up. I've been thinking about you all and I have just one crucial tip to share." You may want to scan through lots of minilessons, collecting various ways in which I try to rally children's attention. This connection (and specifically the invitation to hear a secret) is one of my favorites.

If you don't have a way to project a page of Hesse's book, copy it onto chart paper.

Karen Hesse did here to make her ending powerful." I read the following section aloud, marking the things I noticed on the copy of the text.

> I hug Mamma hard, and she hugs me back. The rain has made us new.
>
> As the clouds move off, I trace the drips on Mamma's face.
>
> Everywhere, everyone, everything
>
> is misty limbs, springing back to life.
>
> "We sure did get a soaking, Mamma," I say,
>
> and we head home purely soothed, fresh as dew,
>
> turning toward the first sweet rays of the sun.

"This is such an ending, isn't it? Let's read it again, and this time, I'll think out loud while we read it. Look, the first thing in this ending has Tessie hugging her Mamma hard, and she hugs her back. Karen made it so the girl is doing something, right? But not just doing any old thing; she's not going home, she's hugging her Mamma and her Mamma is hugging her back. I bet the author chose those actions. I'm going to write 'important action' right here to remind me of something I can try in my endings." Then I said, "Will you see if there are other important actions in this ending?" and gave children time to talk. "Point to the precise words," I said, voicing over their partner talk.

ACTIVE ENGAGEMENT

Channel children to reread the text carefully, noticing authorial decisions.

"What else do you notice?" I asked.

Soon children were talking about words characters used. Miles pointed to the line, "We sure did get a good soaking, Mamma" and said, "That's important dialogue, the exact important words people say." Soon we'd also noted the use of colors, the comparisons. As children shared noticings, I annotated the text.

As always, you needn't use the exact text I've chosen. As long as you choose a narrative text with which children are already familiar, one with an ending that is succinct and memorable and has moves in it children can see, then this minilesson will be strong.

Two decades ago Mem Fox, author of Koala Lou, *led a workshop on children's literature at the Teachers College Reading and Writing Project. I was a member of her class. She taught us many things that I'll never forget and one was this: When you read aloud and come to the end of a text, slow . . . your voice . . . down . . . to . . . a . . . stop.*

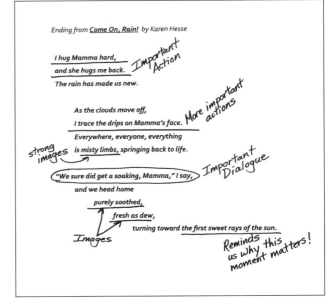

FIG. 18–1 Annotated ending from *Come On, Rain!*

"This very last part—'and we head home purely soothed, fresh as dew, turning toward the first sweet rays of the sun.'—brings our attention back to the relationship between Tessie and her Mamma. It helps us see Tessie's understanding and compassion for her mother. With just a few words, Karen Hesse brings all these powerful emotions together in a way that brings a satisfying end to this story. It's like this story ends with a sigh." I wrote "reminds us why this moment matters" in the margin.

Debrief by naming what you hope children learned.

"Maybe later you can find some other things that Karen did as a writer that make this a powerful ending for you. The things we notice she put in were important actions, important dialogue, images. You can try doing those things yourselves with your endings!"

Remind children that writers work hard on endings.

"Before today, you might have thought that writers write endings in a snap! I used to think that when it came time to end a story, I could just slap, 'And they lived happily ever after' onto my last line. But I think now you understand why some writers say that when they come to the last page of a story, they're halfway home!"

LINK

Get children started, rethinking their endings.

"While we're here in the meeting area, we can't each write an ending for our stories. That would take too much time. But we can begin to plan—to rehearse—for an ending. One way to do this is to reread your draft, asking, 'What is the important message I've conveyed?' So please reread your draft and mark the places in the text that seem to you to be especially important. Your ending will want to somehow relate back to those places."

After a few moments of silence, I said, "Reread your draft again, and this time mark any important actions, words, and images that could maybe be woven into your final scene, your final image." Again I let children work quietly.

Quietly send writers off to think about how they might end their stories.

"Writers, today I'm not going to ask you to tell your partner your thoughts. I don't want to break the spell! Just slip back to your writing space, continue with your draft, and if you are heading toward the end of your story, you can start drafting an ending. Remember that now, if you've reached the final page, you're halfway home!"

You always need to decide whether your teaching aims to nudge children one small step along in their development, or whether it aims to immerse them in a world of literary language. So far, this unit has leaned towards giving simple, doable guidance. Here—just for a patch of time—I break loose and immerse children in the heady world of literary language. There's no question that I'm teaching over their heads here—what else is a sky for?

Of course, you could decide to make a short-term chart titled, "Good Endings." The chart could list important actions, important dialogue, images, and reminders of the whole story.

If you and your class have also been working on a shared text, you could instead ask students in the active engagement to turn to their partners and talk about strong actions, images, or important ideas that could come into the story's ending of that text. Another option is to reread the final page of a beloved novel—say, Charlotte's Web—and to invite children to talk with a partner about ways in which that ending illustrates the characteristics listed on the classroom chart.

Grouping Writers

Y OU'LL PROBABLY WISH you could clone yourself so that you can be at every child's side today. You'll want to get this child back on track, and that one, and this one—so breathe. Realize that the agendas you've laid out for children represent the writing work of the year (or really, of a lifetime), not the work of a week. It's okay that the children who are trying to write focused narratives are still swamped with other problems (perhaps they are including mind-numbing detail, or perhaps they are writing with run-on sentences). It's okay if a large group of children still struggles to fully understand what it means to write a narrative. When we're teaching writing, we're teaching people entirely new habits, a whole new way of living and thinking. That cannot be easy!

But, having said that, yes indeed, you need to work hard today. You will need to group children who currently need the same kind of support. Perhaps five children really need you to remind them about end punctuation. Another four need a push into focusing their narratives. These two write and write and write, but their stories are hard to follow. These three write with detail and now need to learn to be selective in which details they include.

You may want to stand up and announce, "Can I meet with . . . ," and read your list. Once you've convened the group into a huddle, tell them, "I called you over because I've noticed you are ready to learn. . . ." Then tell them, "What I do in this situation is I . . . ," and show them how you expand key paragraphs or how you draft several endings. You need to have examples at their writing level, and you need to highlight the one thing you intend for them to learn how to do. Then say, "So work on that right here, right now." Be specific. Do you want them to reread and correct, to list, to start a new piece or page? Should they work alone or with a partner? Tell them you need

to meet with another group but you'll be back in five minutes to see what they've done. Then call the next group. Don't limit yourself to working with only one group just because you perhaps haven't had a chance to plan a careful lesson for more than that one group. Wing it! Take your cues from the children. Teaching responsibility often leads to our best instruction!

MID-WORKSHOP TEACHING Checking for Sense

"Writers, can I have your eyes and your attention? I've noticed a bunch of you are having a problem that I have too when I'm writing. When I write a true story, I already know how the story goes because I'm the one it happened to! Sometimes I forget that my readers weren't there. I'll say, 'Michelle got lost,' and my reader doesn't know if Michelle is a cat or a child! When I leave out important details, my story doesn't make sense!

"This is what I do to fix that problem: now and then, I read my draft to a person who doesn't know the story. I ask, 'Can I read this to you? Will you stop me if it's confusing?' Sometimes instead of reading to another person, I pretend to be a stranger and I read my draft through the stranger's eyes. As I read, I find places where it's confusing, and then I fix those places.

"Could everyone take a moment right now and read your draft through a stranger's eyes? If you find confusing places, stop and revise. You'll need to do this from time to time from now on."

Trying Endings on for Size

Convene children. Share the work of one child who wrote several possible endings, trying to be sure they referred to important actions, dialogue, and images from the story.

"Writers, can I have your eyes and your attention? I want to remind you that writers know their endings will be the last thing readers encounter, so they usually write several drafts of them. Jill did some smart work today. She reread her narrative about water skiing, deciding she wanted her ending to emphasize the pride she felt in herself afterward because she'd circled half the lake. So she wrote three drafts of endings. She's planning to combine them into one best ending." (See Figure 18–2.)

> "Wow" I thought. That was me. I went around half of the lake. I couldn't wait to rest my legs. I was ready to do it again.
>
> I walked off the boat with a smile on my face and excitement flowing through me. I couldn't wait to talk to my parents and tell them I got half way around the lake.
>
> "Bye" I said, "Thanks." I was so happy that I wanted to jump right back into the lake and do it again! I walked onto the dock and was ready to do it 50 more times.

Jill read aloud the ending she planned to stitch together.

> "Wow," I thought. "That was me. I skied half of the lake." I walked off the boat with a smile on my face and excitement flowing through me. I walked onto the dock and was ready to do it again.

Extract lessons from the one child's work.

"Writers, did you notice that Jill reread her whole narrative, paying attention to what it was she really wants to say in her ending? Then she drafted three versions of an ending. Next, she plans to take the best of all three, but she could have selected one. At the end of today, she'll have produced four lines of text, but that'll be a good day's work."

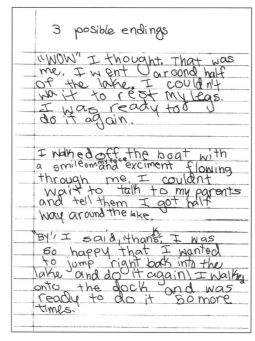

FIG. 18–2   Jill tries out several endings.

Session 19

Using Editing Checklists

WHEN I WAS IN SCHOOL, if there was any instruction about editing at all, it had the tone and purpose of correcting faults. I knew that at some point I'd let go of my writing and it'd come before the teacher, who would scrutinize it, line by line, red-marking each flaw and error. Frankly, I always felt as if it was me, not my writing, that my teacher would scrutinize.

This part of writing made me feel naked and exposed, judged and humiliated. I wasn't alone in these feelings. Mina Shaughnessey, author of *Errors and Expectations* (1979), writes that for many people, "Writing is but a line which creeps across the page, exposing all that the writer does not know. Writing puts us on the line and we don't want to be there."

In this session and in this series, I approach teaching children to write conventionally and to edit their writing in the same way I teach children to do anything writers do: by rallying them to care and demonstrating strategies that are both doable and worth doing.

During this part of the unit, then, encourage students to regard themselves as people with important reasons not only to write well, but also to spell and punctuate well, who are writing for an audience! The editing work you focus on during this first unit of study will depend on the experience of the children you teach and on you, the teacher. You will want to consider how much time you want to spend on editing and how specific you want to be. You also want to remember to celebrate all that your children do know about language, conventions, and writing.

After all, your students are no doubt working with greater independence, and it's very likely that you are able to see marked growth in their writing. More and more, you can teach your writers to be mentors for each other. Celebrate their burgeoning expertise!

Just as children in this unit learned a rudimentary sense of the essentials of narrative writing and were empowered to use that introductory knowledge with independence and confidence, so too, in this session, you'll hand over to children a very rudimentary understanding of how writers edit rough drafts. Watch to be sure that your instruction gives children roots—and wings.

IN THIS SESSION, you'll remind students that writers edit to make their writing exactly how they intend it to be for readers, using checklists to help them.

GETTING READY

✔ Editing checklist that includes the conventions you expect children to know from second grade, along with those you have taught during this first writing unit (see Teaching)

✔ Personalized editing checklists for each child's drafting folder (see Teaching)

✔ Chart-sized version of the editing checklist (see Teaching)

✔ Sample writing that needs editing to make more sense, written on chart paper or projected

✔ Colored pens or pencils for editing in the writing center. Table captains can set these on each table when they set up for the writing workshop.

COMMON CORE STATE STANDARDS: W.3.5, W.3.10, W.3.4, W.4.4, RL.3.1, SL.3.1.a,b,c,d; SL.3.6, L.3.1.b,d,e,i; L.3.2.c,e,f,g; L.4.1.a

Using Editing Checklists

CONNECTION

Create a context for today's lesson by talking about self-help books that fill bookstores and top best-seller lists.

"Writers, I thought about you last night when I stopped at the bookstore. (I only have one book left in the pile beside my bed, so I needed to replenish the pile.) At the bookstore, I noticed a rack of best-seller books, and it was full of what I call self-help books: *How to Become a Millionaire, How to Win Friends and Influence People, How to Start Your Own Company.* I started to realize that it's human nature to want texts in our lives that can act as personalized coaches, whispering bits of advice to us. And I realized that you and I as writers have our own miniature library of self-help texts, and those are our charts.

"Today, I want to give you one more self-help book. It's time for one of my favorite parts of the writing process: editing. And you all deserve to have a self-help text that can act as a personalized coach, whispering bits of advice to you. Just as writers finesse their writing, adding the finishing touches to their drafts, we also finesse our writing, rereading and refining our drafts using editing checklists. The checklists help us give our writing the polish it deserves."

❖ **Name the teaching point.**

"I want to teach you that most writers rely on an editing checklist—either a concrete physical list or a mental one—and each item on the checklist reminds them of a lens they can use to reread and to refine their writing. If we have six items on our checklist, we're apt to reread our draft at least six times, once with each item as our lens."

TEACHING

Tell children they each have a personalized editing checklist. Demonstrate how to read through a draft, using an item on the checklist as a lens.

"You'll see later that I've put an editing checklist inside each of your writing folders, and you'll see that the lists are somewhat personalized so they can each function as a personal coach. But every editing checklist will contain some

◆ COACHING

Did you notice that in this connection, I bypassed the usual process of contextualizing today's session by recalling previous learning? If you did notice this, it suggests you are internalizing the architecture of minilessons. But of course you'll also want to remember that our teaching needs to be shaped to our specific purposes. And today, it didn't seem necessary to go backward before going forward.

shared items, so let's look at one of those shared items. I want to show you how writers use an item or an editing checklist as a lens, rereading the draft through that lens.

"Every writer's editing checklist always says something to the effect of 'Read your writing to be sure it makes sense to strangers.' I'm a lot older than you, and yet, in all these years, that first item has never left my checklist." Referring to a chart-sized editing checklist that contained four items, plus one personal prompt, I read the first item: "Read, asking, 'Will this make sense to a stranger?'"

Editing Checklist

1. Read, asking, "Will this make sense to a stranger?"

2. Check the punctuation.

3. Do your words look correctly spelled to you?

4. Make sure your paragraphs work the way you want them to in your story.

5. Don't forget to check for _____ .

"To check for sense, I pretend I know nothing about the topic or the writer. I pick up the paper and start reading, and as I read, I watch for places where I go, 'Huh?' I mark the places that cause some confusion. Later, I go back and rewrite those places so they're clearer. I also mark places that are for some reason hard to read correctly. Writers have a saying, 'When you falter—alter!' If I stumble as I read something or need to reread to figure out what a part is saying, then I figure the section needs more work.

"Let me show you what I mean by showing you a draft that one of my students from last year wrote." I revealed a copy of a child's story. "Follow along while I read just the start of Esther's story. We'll pretend we're Esther, and we're using the first item on our checklist to prompt us to reread the draft, checking for sense. See if you find yourself going, 'Huh?' We'll want to come back and clarify those confusing places." (See Figure 19–1.)

"Ring, ring!" I ran out of Polish school.

I saw my friend Paulina. "Hi Paulina," I said. "Hi." I ran to her dad's car. I jumped inside.

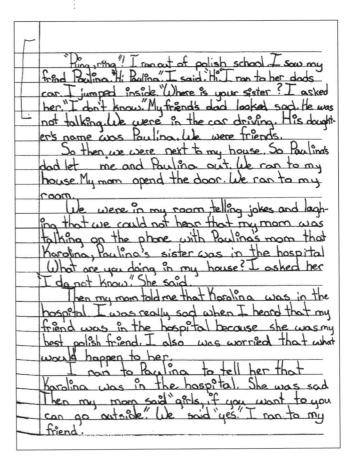

FIG. 19–1 Esther's newly found fluency occasionally comes at the cost of clarity.

"Hmm, I'm a little confused. I understand the words, the vocabulary, in this story, but if I try to make a picture in my mind of what's really happening, I can't do it. Why is she jumping inside her friend's car?"

> "Where is your sister?" I asked her. "I don't know." My friend's dad looked sad.
>
> He was not talking. We were in the car driving. His daughter's name was Paulina.
>
> We were friends.

"Now I'm even more confused, and if I was Esther, I'd want to clarify so no stranger would read this and go, 'Huh?'" Then I said, "Writers, in Esther's case, she'd been trying to do exactly what we taught her, writing her story step by step, but she'd written her piece in such a step-by-step manner that we couldn't understand the big things that were happening. So she went back and clarified."

> "Ring, ring!" The bell rang, telling us we could leave the Saturday Polish school.
>
> So I ran out to the street to find Paulina's dad because he drives me home. I got in the car and noticed Paulina's sister wasn't there. She was always there.

"Writers, did you see that I took the first item on the checklist and acted as if it was a personalized assignment? I read, using that item as a lens, and then I did the work that item led me to do. Then I moved on to the next item on the checklist. On all our lists, this item says, 'Check the punctuation,'" I said, gesturing toward the second item on an enlarged list on chart paper. "So I reread a whole other time, and this time I pay special attention to the road signs that tell us how to read. Sometimes I see that I've left out periods, and my sentence goes on so long I forget what the beginning was. So I repair that. If I have dialogue, I check to make sure I have the punctuation that shows the reader that people are talking and these are their exact words.

"The third item that I put on everyone's checklist is spelling: 'Do your words look correctly spelled to you?'" I said, gesturing to this item on the enlarged chart. "To check my writing for misspellings, I read it very slowly, looking at each word. Does each word look right? If I get to any that I think might be wrong, I circle that word and then go back and check. To check words, I try writing them a few different ways and pick the one that looks right, or I ask someone, look at our word wall, or find them in a dictionary or other book."

Your intonation should suggest this is already confusing.

It was as if, instead of saying, "I picked the flower," Esther had written, "I leaned down. I put my fingers near the flower's stem. I squeezed them. I pulled up . . ." but she hadn't made it clear that she was describing picking the flower! In instances such as this, if you can figure out the intelligence behind students' errors, you can help them enormously. Esther was following my instructions to a T—and going overboard doing so. This happens with nearly every lesson we teach—children often overuse the teaching of the minilesson when they try it for the first few times. Embrace their enthusiasm even as you help them see the teaching in its proper perspective.

Using a different-color pen or pencil, or one with a special flair to it, can be a tool that inspires editing: a fancy editing tool can spark kids to make changes just for the thrill of using it—especially when it comes to adjusting spelling and punctuation.

ACTIVE ENGAGEMENT

Ask children to read through their drafts with their partners, focusing on one item on the editing checklist.

"Writers, right now, with your partner, let's work with the next item on that checklist." I gestured to the chart and read aloud, 'Make sure your paragraphs work the way you want them to in your story.' Partner 2, spread out your draft, and the two of you can read it, checking paragraphs together. If you both find a way the paragraphs could be better for the story, make sure you mark that spot, and maybe make a note in the margin about what needs fixing. Okay, go ahead." The children worked for a bit on that item from their checklist before I interrupted.

"Caitlyn and her partner, Carl, noticed that Caitlyn could make some new paragraphs each time a different person talks in her story, instead of all the dialogue being together in one big paragraph. That is some helpful editing work because it will make it much easier for a reader to understand who is talking."

LINK

Remind children that they can use this strategy forever when they write.

"Writers, I hope you've learned that editing checklists, like self-help books, can function as personalized coaches, giving us a to-do list. Today find the editing checklist in your writing folders, that includes a tip just for you, and use each item as a lens. Reread with that lens, and do the refinements that work prompts you to do. Later today and tomorrow you can start your final draft, and from this day on, always remember that whenever you are going to put your writing into the world, you need to edit it very carefully so that the people reading it will see exactly what you intend for them to see. So when you get started on this important editing work—your last chance to make the writing as perfect as you can get it—you can always use a checklist to help you remember the areas to consider carefully. Someday, you will have used a checklist so often that you won't need it on paper; you can use it right out of your mind!"

At some point, the children will need to assess their writing and decide which editing tasks in particular they need to add to their own editing checklists. The checklist is also a place you can add items you and the child discuss in conferences and strategy lessons. This is another way to help hold the child accountable for all the teaching to date.

Focusing on Tenses and Pronouns

AS PUBLICATION DAY COMES CLOSER, resist the temptation to shoehorn in all the lessons you haven't yet had a chance to teach. For now, you may want to shift toward teaching children that the rhythm of writing changes when we can see a publication date around the next bend. For one thing, writers become readers, rereading their own work and asking, "How will someone else read this?"

Two areas where children can use support in the editing stage are tenses and pronouns. As you confer, pay attention to the tenses they've used in their drafts. Sometimes children misunderstand what we mean by making movies in our minds and recording what we recall, and they write personal narratives exclusively in the present tense, almost as if the story is a caption to a movie, as in John's draft:

Lost Dog

My family, my cousin and I are driving home happily from lunch. As we get out of the car we notice the driveway gate is wide open. I am yelling, "Pepper, Pepper!" I am looking everywhere in my green yard. I can't find my dog.

In general, past tense is the usual tense used for storytelling. There are reasons why a writer might deliberately break stride and write about a past event in present tense, but that is usually a choice made by proficient writers who have a clear reason for placing the narrator in the present. In the story cited above, the writer simply misunderstood the instructions. His piece worked more easily when he was given permission to rewrite it in past tense.

My family, cousin and I drove home from lunch. As we got out of the car, we noticed the driveway gate was open. "Pepper, Pepper," I yelled. I looked everywhere in my yard. I couldn't find my dog.

MID-WORKSHOP TEACHING **Reading with Writing Partners**

"Writers, may I stop you for a moment? You're doing a great job finding places in your own writing that you can make better by editing. Right now, I want to teach you that after you have looked over your own writing carefully and edited it, you can also ask a writing buddy to look it over to see if they find other areas where editing would make the piece stronger. All writers have a friend who helps them edit, or they rely a lot on their editors who help them publish their poems and stories and articles. No one on this whole planet can see every opportunity to make something a little better by herself; they need another pair of eyes!

"Please exchange papers right now and be another pair of eyes for your partners. When more than one person edits a piece of writing, it helps keep all the changes straight if you use different-colored pens. So partners, choose a different color from what the writer used, and put on your best 'editing glasses'!"

If a child struggles to maintain present tense, you may want to help start the draft over again, writing in past tense. The Common Core State Standards expect third-graders to be able to form and use simple verb tenses, such as *I walked, I walk, I will walk*.

Also pay attention to pronouns. You'll see that children often overuse *he* or *she*, and the reader can't keep track of the characters. Tell children that writers are careful to match pronoun references with proper nouns since the pronoun always refers to the person mentioned just before it. You could tell them that one way, then, to edit for clarity is to read while asking, "Is it clear who the character is in every part of my story?"

Becoming Copy Editors

Ask children to show each other what they've done, what they've learned, and what they've resolved to do next.

"Writers, would you gather in the meeting area?" Once the class convened, I said, "Writers, don't you love the days just before a holiday, when everything takes on a special significance and a special urgency? I love the prelude to Valentine's Day as much as I love the day itself. It's fun to make lists of what I need to do, to busy myself with preparations, to anticipate the actual day. I'm telling you this because today is the prelude to another sort of holiday—our first author celebration—and I love the quickening in the air as we ready ourselves. You could say that we are approaching our first deadline, then. For me, however, the word *deadline* is all wrong. When I know I need to hurry and make my writing ready for publication, I feel as if I've been given not a *deadline*, but a *lifeline*.

"Tonight your partner is going to look over the drafts that you've edited today. He or she will function as a copy editor. Every author sends his or her books to a copy editor who reads the manuscript over and makes added corrections.

"Tomorrow won't be a usual writing workshop, because every minute of the day will be reserved for making final copies of our pieces.

"Before you leave your draft with your partner, take a few minutes to savor this special time. Meet with your partner and tell your partner what you did to make your story even better today and what you learned as a writer that you'll carry with you always."

Use a student's piece of writing to further practice editing for spelling mistakes.

If your students need extra practice editing for spelling mistakes, you could use a child's piece of writing as a class text to work on editing together. In the minilesson you might say, "Let's practice together what it's like to edit for spelling. A little girl, Jenna, who lives next door to me asked if I could help edit her writing, so I figured we could all help her." Pass out a copy to each partnership along with editing pencils. "Working with your partner, read this excerpt of Jenna's writing very slowly and carefully, touching each word with your pencil. Ask yourself, 'Does this look right?' If you find a misspelled word you know in a snap, cross it out and write the correctly spelled word above it. Underline any words that don't look right but you're not sure how to spell. Try writing those three different ways at the bottom of the paper and choose the one that looks right to you."

You will probably be uneasy about the idea that publication day is just around the bend. "Shouldn't I send the drafts off to parents who'll type them?" you may ask yourself. It is true that the day is apt to arrive with some children who haven't finished their final draft. I strongly urge you to go forward anyhow. Children need to finish a unit and to celebrate the work they've done right then and there . . . not two weeks later when every loose end is tied up. You can celebrate the end of the unit—whether or not every detail is completely finished. Your real purpose in this celebration is closure on one unit and a drumroll to the next. Your hope, too, is to make writing authentic for children by ensuring that they are writing for readers.

My mission today is to create a sense of occasion around the upcoming author celebration, and to be sure that editing takes on special importance because it is a way of preparing one's work to go out in the world.

I was running fast then I triped over something. I fell in the air. Ahh! I scramed. I was falling off the edge of the street. I was almost going to hit myself on the floor. I put my hands doun so I would not hit myself on the hed so hard.

You could harvest insights by saying, for instance, "Who found some words that were misspelled that you knew in a snap?" Or, "Who found a word that didn't look right but was not sure exactly how the word was spelled?" Point out what they did. "You did a really good job editing this writer's story for spelling. Because you read slowly and carefully, touching each word with your editing pencil, you were able to catch and fix some of the misspelled words." Bring the lesson to a close by saying, "So writers, whenever you want to get your writing ready for readers, for an audience, you need to become an editor by checking your spelling and fixing anything that does not look right or sound right, just like we did here together. This will help your readers be able to read and enjoy your stories easily. And your stories will be ready for our publishing celebration."

End by preparing students for tomorrow's celebration.

"Writers, our first author celebration is just around the bend. Tonight I hope you will help with preparations for that event. You might think this means that I'm hoping you'll bake brownies or mix Kool-Aid, and it's true that I want you to think about ways to make the occasion a special one. But the truth is that when a person writes, when we send our words out into the world, what we long to receive is not a brownie, but a response. One writer said that sometimes authorship feels like tossing rose petals into a well and waiting, hoping to hear a splash.

"Let's be sure that every writer in our community knows that someone has truly heard that writer's work and truly recognized the time and care invested in that story. And who is in a better place to take notice of what a writer has accomplished than the writer's partner?

"At our celebration, it will be your job to introduce your partner to his or her audience. You'll say to the guests who will be at our celebration, 'I want to introduce you to . . . ,' and then you'll say, 'This writer is especially famous for her ability to . . . Notice the way she (or he). . . .' You will need to think tonight about your partner's writing and try to use precise details to exactly name what your writer has done that is especially noteworthy. Keep what you write to yourself, just as you keep Valentines to yourself, until the 'big day' comes."

Session 20

Publishing
A Writing Community Celebrates

THIS FIRST CELEBRATION OF THE YEAR is a momentous occasion for both you and your students! Your students have learned to work productively and independently, to use a repertoire of strategies to generate and develop ideas, and to be able to capture moments on the page, using the conventions of standard English. This day is a celebration of a great accomplishment: your children are published writers!

Today your young writers will feel how their work can affect others; they will share compliments and celebrate each other's work. Some children will be astounded that they've made their classmates laugh; some will be shocked by the attention their words get from the others in the class. Most will be thrilled, as we all are, to feel that they have made something, an artifact that can stay in the world forever. Writing celebrations help our young students regard themselves as authors in a working, thriving community of other authors. In Ralph Peterson's brilliant book, *Life in a Crowded Place* (1992), he explains that celebrations contribute to our sense of belonging by helping us learn to focus on others and their achievements rather than just on our own. The gallery wall of writing you create today is an announcement to the world: "Look! Here we are all authors."

Celebrations need to build in grandeur from the beginning of the year until the end. This first end-of-unit celebration needs to make your writers feel proud and strengthen their motivation for writing while still leaving room for fancier celebrations to come. As children's writing strengthens and deepens, so must the celebrations that honor that work. For now, plan to celebrate children's change into writers rather than celebrating exquisite writing. The truth is, the pieces of writing may yet be far from exquisite. After all, for many writers this may be their first time working through the entire writing process! Don't succumb to the temptation to postpone the celebration until the writing is fantastic or until you've had time to work individually with each child until they've written something impressive. Let the children's finished work stand as examples of their best work to date. This way, the children, and all the grownups watching their development, can see their

IN THIS SESSION, you'll celebrate being a community of flourishing writers and share students' writing with the public.

GETTING READY

✔ A place to display each child's published writing. For example, 9" × 12" sheets of construction paper, one piece for each child, labeled with the child's name.

✔ Several designated areas for sharing, with an author's chair in each area

✔ Invite a class of younger students, perhaps reading buddies, to attend the author celebration.

✔ Stickers for children to decorate and celebrate their published writing

✔ Your baton and party horns from Session 1

✔ Party-like food and drink to toast and celebrate the authors and their accomplishments

COMMON CORE STATE STANDARDS: W.3.4, W.3.5, RL.3.1, RL.3.3, SL.3.1.a,b,c,d; SL.3.6, SL.3.4, L.3.6, L.3.1

growth throughout the year more clearly—something they couldn't see if these first pieces are "propped up." This particular celebration is truly a lovely way to appreciate where children are and encourage their growth as writers from this day forth.

CELEBRATION

Start the school day by building up excitement about the approaching celebration.

When the children lined up on the playground in the morning, ready to come into the classroom for the day, I heightened their excitement. "You all seem bursting with energy this morning," I said. "No wonder—it's our author celebration!" When children convened in the meeting area to review the schedule for the day, I said, "I know for certain what your first question will be: 'When will we have our celebration?' When we started this unit we had a mini-New Year's celebration; today we are going to have a big celebration."

For the celebration, bring the guests into the classroom. As a welcome, describe a reading that you attended at the local bookstore. Explain the structure for today's celebration.

"This is a very special moment," I said once the little children, the class's younger reading buddies, had settled in the meeting area alongside my class. "Today we are gathering to celebrate that Room 203's children are truly becoming writers. Last Saturday, I went to a reading at our local bookstore. Lots and lots of people gathered in a corner of the bookstore, just like we've gathered in a corner of our classroom, and the author's writing partner, a person known as her editor, spoke first. She said, 'I want to introduce you to someone whose writing I know very well.' Then the editor went on to tell us what this writer did so remarkably.

"Afterward, the author read her writing aloud, and we got a chance to ask her questions about her writing life, questions like 'Where did you get the idea for your story?' or 'Who especially helped you to write this story?' or 'What did you learn from writing this?'

"I'm telling you this because today we will celebrate your writing just as they celebrated that famous author's writing. In a few minutes, we will gather in one of our four corners (remember how they gathered in a corner of the bookstore!), and then, in each corner, an author will take her place in the author's chair. (You'll see I have one set up in each corner.) The author's writing partner will sit beside her, and our reading will begin. First, the writing partner will introduce the author. You will read the introductions you wrote at home last night!

"Then, authors, read your stories. When you have finished, please leave a little bit of time for silence. Let there be just a moment when no one speaks and everyone lets the story sink in. Then one of you can ask the writer a writing question—just one, for now."

I know that it is not truly the case that every child in the class is beside herself with excitement over the fact that today is our author celebration, but I'm going to act as though, of course, children feel thrilled at the prospect of sharing their writing. At the start of the year, especially, we are building a culture in our classrooms, and the values of that culture make a very big difference. So I will do everything possible to be sure that this community is one that honors the written word, one that regards author celebrations as one of our most important occasions.

Younger children, not parents, are the audience for this celebration. At the start of the year, your emphasis will have been on helping children cycle through the writing process with independence. In order to be sure that your workshop is a productive one, one where children are able to carry on with independence, you will not have been able to coach and guide every writer about his final piece of writing. Chances are very good that some children will be publishing stories that are laden with problems. At this early stage, it is crucial that you accept that children's best work is worthy of celebration. You will have lots of time to raise the level of that work—for now, some children will publish stories that are still unfocused, underdeveloped, and so forth. For this reason, I suggest you postpone the celebration with the high-stakes audience until a bit later in the year. Meanwhile, this is a wonderful way to induct younger children into the writing culture of your school.

When each member of each group has shared his writing and answered one question, ask everyone to gather in the hallway beside a shrouded bulletin board.

"Writers, the work that you shared deserves to be sent out into the world. At the bookstore, after the reading, the bookstore created a gigantic display of the author's work, and that made me realize we, too, needed a way to display your work. So you'll see," I dramatically pulled the shroud off a beautifully matted bulletin board, "I've created a special display case for your masterpieces!" I paused for the oohing and ahhhing. "Now, when I gesture to you, please say the name of your writing partner, and that writer please come to me for some stickers to decorate your piece. Then you will hang your writing in our display case!"

In this fashion, one child after another was named, approached me for a few stickers, and then hung his writing on the bulletin board.

FIG. 20–1 Miles' final draft

If possible, it would be great to station an adult in each of the four corners, though, of course, the grown-ups can also keep an eye on two corners at once. Your hope is that the author takes his place of honor, and the partner sits beside the author. The partner uses the class's attention-getting signal to ask for everyone's attention and waits (help them do this) until the group is focused and ready to listen. Then one partner begins, saying, "I'm proud to introduce you to my writing partner. I think Miles has a special talent for helping people see!" Then the author reads aloud, and when the listening children hear evidence of what the partner described, the listeners signal with a quiet thumbs up.

You may wonder what, exactly, the work looks like that children are pinning onto the bulletin board. Your first and biggest question is probably this: Is the work totally correct? Although children will have devoted earnest effort to making their writing their best, and you will have had a few editing conferences in which you teach some editing tips in relation to this one piece, there is no way every child in your room (or even most children in your room) will have been able to fully correct their own writing.

Bask in the glory of progress as writers. Remind writers that a whole year for writing stretches ahead of them. Create time for children to compliment each other's writing.

"Writers, I need to tell you that, frankly, I am incredibly excited because I listen to this writing and I think, 'And this is still our first unit!'" I know it will be an amazing thing to see how your writing gets even better. Maybe our last celebration better be at that bookstore, because look out world, here these writers come!

"Before we end our celebration, could we hear from our young guests? What did you notice about these bigger kids' writing? Will you guys turn and talk, and let's hear from our visitors and learn from their observations." We heard from several. "We started by studying other writers and their notebooks, and now others are studying our writing. We really have come full circle.

"Writers and guests, would everyone get yourself something to drink so we can toast our third-grade authors? When we started this unit I acted like the conductor at the symphony, baton in hand, and we blew imaginary horns and clanged imaginary glasses. Today let's celebrate by blowing some real horns and toasting with real glasses." I raised my baton, holding it momentarily in the air before bringing it down. "Here's to the authors of Class 203! Let the party begin!"

Here is Olivia's final draft. (See Figure 20–2.)

The Place: The Finish Line

I held my sled in my hand tight. My heart pumped as me and Alejandra walked over to Balin. The words, "Balin, do you want to race?" wouldn't come out. Finally, they did. "Hey, Balin, do you want to race?" I said. "Sure, why not? On the count of three," was his response.

"I must have sweated buckets as we got our sleds in place. "1," said Balin. My heart pumped. "2," said Balin. I sweated ten buckets. "3," said Balin. I nearly wet my pants.

After three, we were off. It was going very smoothly and we were tied for the lead. Then suddenly me and Alejandra hit a big root and went in the air and landed with a plop, and slowed down. I wondered what we hit but reminded each other we had a race to finish.

So we dug our hands in the cold snow and pushed ourselves forwards. We tried and tried to win. But as we trailed behind Balin we heard him cheering, "I win! I win!" I reminded myself everybody's a winner.

If you are thinking that, for your children, the only way for the work to be absolutely correct is for you to correct it, and even retype it, then you need to know that you are in good company. All of us teach children with needs like that, and frankly, even grown adults rely on copy editors. It goes without saying that although children devote earnest effort to making their writing their best, their texts will not be perfect.

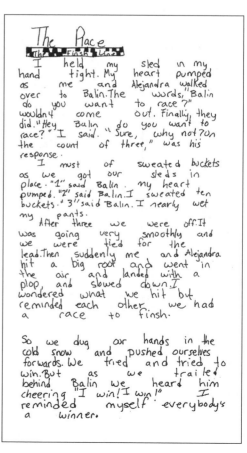

FIG. 20–2   Olivia's final draft

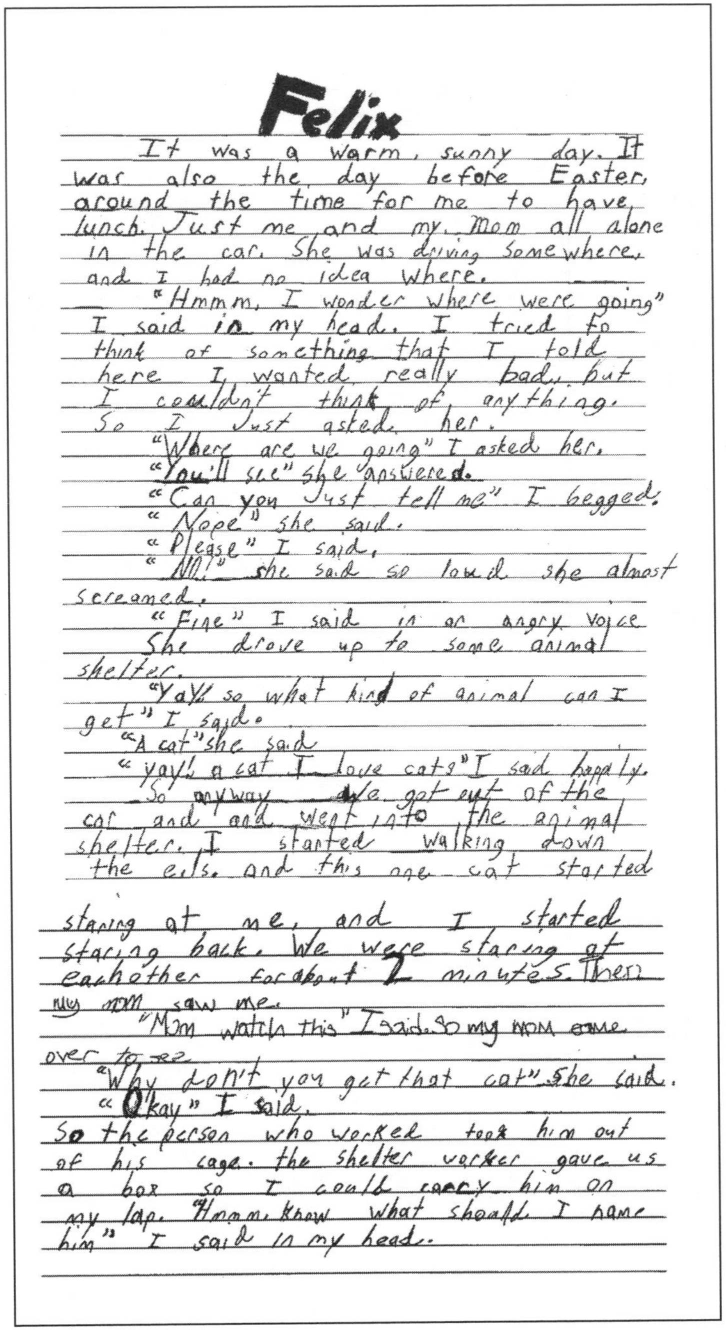

Felix

It was a warm, sunny day. It was also the day before Easter, around the time for me to have lunch. Just me and my mom all alone in the car. She was driving somewhere, and I had no idea where.

"Hmmm, I wonder where we're going" I said in my head. I tried to think of something that I told here I wanted really bad, but I couldn't think of anything. So I just asked her.

"Where are we going" I asked her.

"You'll see" she answered.

"Can you just tell me" I begged.

"Nope" she said.

"Please" I said.

"NO!" she said so loud she almost screamed.

"Fine" I said in an angry voice. She drove up to some animal shelter.

"Yay! so what kind of animal can I get" I said.

"A cat" she said

"yay! a cat I love cats" I said happily. So anyway we got out of the car and and went into the animal shelter. I started walking down the els. and this one cat started

staring at me, and I started staring back. We were staring at eachother for about 2 minutes. Then my mom saw me.

"Mom watch this" I said. So my mom came over to see.

"Why don't you get that cat" she said.

"Okay" I said.

So the person who worked took him out of his cage. the shelter worker gave us a box so I could carry him on my lap. "Hmmm, know what should I name him" I said in my head.

FIG. 20–3   Felix's final draft

Here is Gregory's final draft. (See Figure 20–4.)

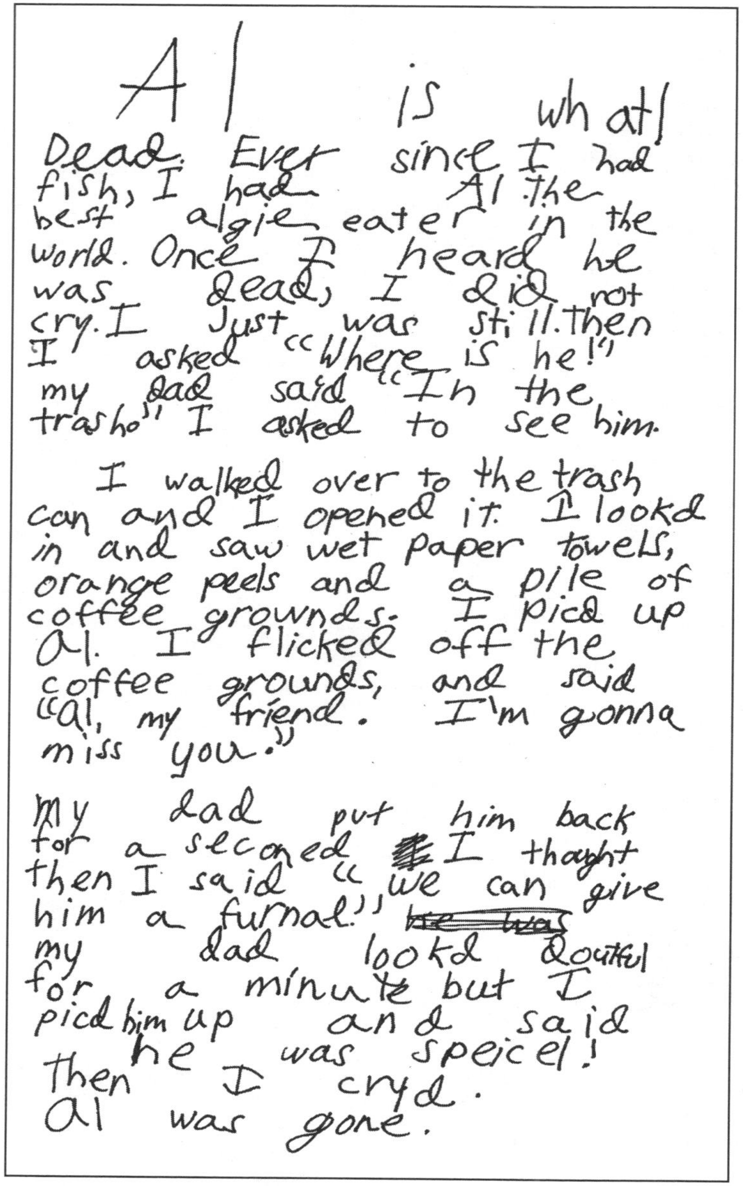

Al is what!

Dead. Ever since I had fish, I had Al the best algie eater in the world. Once I heard he was dead, I did not cry. I Just was still. Then I asked "Where is he!" my dad said "In the trash." I asked to see him.

I walked over to the trash can and I opened it. I lookd in and saw wet paper towels, orange peels and a pile of coffee grownds. I picd up Al. I flicked off the coffee grounds, and said "Al, my friend. I'm gonna miss you."

My dad put him back for a seconed. I thaght then I said "we can give him a furnal." ~~he was~~ my dad lookd doutful for a minute but I picd him up and said he was speicel! Then I cryd. Al was gone.

FIG. 20–4 Gregory's final draft

(More examples of final pieces are available on the CD-ROM.)

You will decide, based on the expectations of your community, whether you need to go through and correct each piece, asking each child to recopy your corrections, or whether you can publish children's best work at this point in the year. I hope you can do the latter. If we are always propping children's work up so that it looks perfect, then how can we keep track of their development over time? How can we hold ourselves responsible for them learning to do significantly more on their own? If your school community has trouble with displays of imperfect work (they no doubt accept this for clay sculpture and portraits, but perhaps do not regard approximation in writing with equal trust), then I recommend moving the display case inside the classroom and perhaps titling it, "See Our Work in Progress" or "Celebrate Rough Drafts and Revisions!"